second edition

anatomy
of
reading

Laura Hackett
Suffolk County Community College

Richard Williamson
College of San Mateo

McGraw-Hill Book Company
New York   St. Louis   San Francisco   Düsseldorf
London   Mexico   Panama   Sydney   Toronto

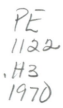

Anatomy of Reading

Library of Congress Catalog Card Number 70-99199

25406

1234567890   HDMM   79876543210

This book was set in Versatile by University Graphics, Inc., printed on permanent paper by Halliday Lithography Corporation, and bound by The Maple Press Company. The designer was Marsha Cohen. The editors were Robert Fry, Cheryl Kupper, and Robert Weber. William P. Weiss supervised the production.

Acknowledgments

Yamabe no Akahito, "I wish I were close," from *One Hundred Poems from the Japanese* by Kenneth Rexroth (trans.). All rights reserved. Reprinted by permission of New Directions Publishing Corporation.

American Cyanamid Company, "Doomsday," advertisement appearing in *The New Yorker,* May 26, 1962, p. 18.

Anthony cartoons reprinted by the kind permission of the artist, Anthony Scott. "Flowers." © New Yorker Magazine, Inc.

Russell Baker, "Observer: Juglipidity and All That," from *The New York Times,* September 2, 1965. Copyright © 1965 by The New York Times Company. Reprinted by permission.

George Barker, "To My Mother," from *Collected Poems* by George Barker. Reprinted by permission of Faber and Faber, Ltd., 1957.

Arna Bontemps, "A Summer Tragedy," from *An Anthology of American Negro Literature* by Arna Bontemps. Copyright © 1944 by Random House, Inc. Reprinted by permission of Harold Ober Associates Inc.

Ray Bradbury, "The Fog Horn," from *The Fog Horn* by Ray Bradbury. Copyright 1952 by Ray Bradbury. Reprinted by permission of Harold Matson Company, Inc.

Preface

Many books do a good job of instructing the student how to write, but very few instruct him how to read: how to approach material, what to look for, what questions to ask. *Anatomy of Reading* proposes to show the student a way to begin. The book is directed to the student who may receive good grades in some courses but has difficulty in understanding what he reads. Although his trouble may stem from lack of interest, we believe it is often due to lack of training in how to approach the printed page.

You will find that the book has been divided into three parts, each of which asks a question. If the student will answer these three basic questions in order, he will have a method which should give him confidence in his ability to understand what he reads. The questions are these: What does the author say? What does the author mean? What do you think of what the author says? By focusing attention on one question at a time, the student is less likely to feel overwhelmed by the demands of analysis and thus is more likely to respond to reading as an active process. Since he will encounter many types of reading as he proceeds through college, we have included a wide range of material: imaginative and factual, contemporary and classic, simple and sophisticated. The book draws upon nursery rhymes, popularized science, and magazine advertisements, as well as upon Shakespeare and sonnets. In general, we have selected material we thought the student would enjoy—for all sorts of reasons.

This second edition is new in a number of ways. We have included more selections. Since our primary concern has been to include selections that students would enjoy, we have eliminated pieces in the original edition that did not elicit strong student response and replaced them with livelier and more provocative selections. We have also added photographs. So much enjoyment is visual these days that the student has to learn to "read" photographs and movies just as he has to learn to read words. And we have included a new section on "Allusion."

We have retained, of course, the various devices that will help the student understand what he reads. Most of these devices are designed to make him examine the text closely; others attempt to make him think about his society and his values. The three main divisions of the text are organized in a rough order of increasing difficulty. Part I, for example, includes a series of informal guidelines or comments designed to orient the student and help him make the transition from passive reading to active analysis. In the last group of selections in Part III, on the other hand, we have omitted all apparatus: the student is on his own. We believe, however, that the questions appended to all the other selections will aid the student in reading more closely, and we believe that they are as important a part of this book as the selections themselves.

We thank all those who permitted us to use their material in this book. We also thank Jamesetta Holliman and Mary Young for their help in assembling the manuscript and James F. Young for reading proof. We especially thank Fred Hackett for his customary brisk assistance.

Laura Hackett
Richard Williamson

Contents

metaphor

allusion

symbol

stereotype

tone

irony

comment

part 3: what do you think of what the author says?

group 1: warfare

group 2: honor

group 3: love

group 4: identity

anatomy
of
reading

1

what does
the author say?

The world is exploding. Constantly we hear of atomic explosions or the population explosion or the knowledge explosion. None is more common and more widespread than the communication explosion. Words bombard us from all directions: radio, television, newspapers, conversation, lectures. Our only defense against this assault is to learn to cope with words and to understand them.

As a college student you are required to understand many words: the spoken ones of your instructors and the written ones of your textbooks. This book is designed to help you learn how to cope with other books—with the whole process of reading. We have divided the book into three parts, each of which asks a question. What does the author say? What does the author mean? What do you think of what the author says? By suggesting ways to answer each question, we hope to show you how you yourself can approach whatever reading you do from now on and understand it.

We are going to go step by step through a process that really cannot be broken down into steps very well. It's a bit like walking: when you walk, you do everything at once without thinking about it, but if we tried to explain just which muscles are involved and exactly how they are used, you would find the explanation somewhat bewildering.

When you read, you also do many things simultaneously. Nevertheless, we are going to point out, one by one, some of the things that make up reading. We shall ask you to focus your attention on one step at a time, not because reading ever consists of just one element, but because by considering each step in turn you can learn to read through a book perceptively with no greater thought of exactly how you do it than you would give to walking along a path.

Part 1 asks "What does the author say?" This question would seem to have obvious answers, but they are not always so obvious as we might like. We shall therefore ask you to concentrate on two things in this part of the book: words themselves and arrangement.

To concentrate on words, you must use the dictionary whenever necessary. Some words may be unfamiliar, but you can guess their meanings quite accurately by studying the sentence in which they appear. For example, in the old proverb "Faint heart never won fair lady," the word *faint* would make no sense if it meant "unemphatic" or "losing consciousness." Although you may want to check its exact meaning, you can guess that in this context "faint" has something to do with lack of courage and boldness in wooing. For other words, however, you must go directly to a dictionary. From time to time we shall ask questions which will require you to consult a dictionary, but you yourself must be ready to look up words whose meanings you do not know.

Now let us move on to a more detailed discussion of arrangement.

Arrangement in Space

When an author writes, he is putting together elements that often must be visualized. What does each one look like? How far away is it? Is it above or below you? Where is it in relation to other objects? And so on. If you can see the arrangement of objects as clearly as the author did when he wrote, you will find it much easier to understand what he is saying.

To help you see these objects clearly, we shall suggest from time to time that you draw a picture. Actually, a diagram will often do. The point is not to produce a work of art but to show your ability to follow the arrangement the author has made of his objects.

From time to time we shall also ask you to make inferences. That is, you will be asked questions to which the selection does not provide direct answers but which can be answered if you read carefully and then use your imagination. For example, Selection 6 describes two office workers who spend their Saturday afternoons window shopping. We ask you to decide what other kinds of entertainment they would enjoy. If you visualize the two girls as they are described in the story, you will be able to make the proper inferences.

As you go through this first section, remember to concentrate on words and arrangement in space, that is, on visualizing what the author says.

1 Little Miss Muffet

Traditional

Little Miss Muffet
Sat on a tuffet,
Eating her curds and whey.
Along came a spider
And sat down beside her
And frightened Miss Muffet away.

UNDERSTANDING THE SELECTION

1. You may wonder what place a nursery rhyme has in a college textbook—after all, "Little Miss Muffet" is so familiar that any child can easily rattle it off. It is precisely because this poem is so familiar, so readily taken for granted, that we include it as our first selection. It presents some prob-

lems you may never have noticed, and thus it demonstrates that you must look sharply at what you read if you are to perceive exactly what the author says.

For instance, what is a *tuffet?* You may find that even your dictionary is not sure, yet to have a clear picture of the poem you need to visualize what Miss Muffet is sitting on.

2. What is *curds and whey?*
3. How old do you think Miss Muffet is? Why do you think so?
4. Is she rich or poor? Why do you think this?
5. Does she live in the city or the country? Again, why do you think so?
6. How big is the spider? Why do you think so?
7. Draw a picture or diagram of the poem.

2   Because River-fog

Fukayabu Kiyowara

Because river-fog
Hiding the mountain-base
Has risen,
The autumn mountain looks as though it hung in the sky.

(Translated by Arthur Waley)

UNDERSTANDING THE SELECTION

1. Fukayabu Kiyowara was a Japanese poet who lived in the Heian period, sometime between 794 and 1192 A.D. He was a Waka poet, one of the thirty-six great poets of his period. As the youngest grandson of Emperor Temmu, he had an official title at the imperial court.
2. What time of day is it in the poem? Why do you think so?
3. Is the mountain bare or covered with trees? Why do you think so?
4. If you were to draw a picture of the poem, where would you place the poet?

3 *Brooklyn Bridge, 1883*

Courtesy of Brooklyn Picture Collection, Brooklyn Public Library.

UNDERSTANDING THE SELECTION

1. We have said that one way to understand what you read is to visualize the elements as a photograph. In the case of actual photographs, the artist already has carefully used space to impress his audience. What makes this photograph of Brooklyn Bridge so effective? In what ways has the photographer used space to make this more than just another amateur photograph of a bridge?

2. To understand a photograph fully, you must "read" it in the same way that you read a story or article; you must ask questions that will help you understand the statement the photographer is making with his work. Some questions you might ask about this phtograph are these: What time of year is it? What time of day is it? What was the occasion for which the picture was taken? What are the men doing on the bridge cables? Are their relative positions important?

3. What effect does this picture have on you? What feelings does it arouse in you? Does it make you think of something other than a bridge with men on it? Do you think the photographer intended to parallel these men with something else?

4. We have said that a reader can draw a picture of a piece of writing that is arranged in space. In the same way, a viewer can see so much in a carefully arranged photograph that he can write a story about it. Look at this photograph carefully, and then write a short story that describes the event pictured.

4 *The Stories behind Words*
Helene and Charlton Laird

1   A liking for words may be—like a taste for olives—an acquired taste, but once it is acquired, it can give you endless fun. A good desk dictionary has 100,000 or more entries, and most of these entries will include an etymology, a history of the origin and growth of the word. And there you'll have the fun. You need meanings and spellings and pronunciations in a dictionary, but the history is usually the most fascinating part, once you have learned to work it out. To have words as a hobby you need little equipment: a good dictionary, an encyclopedia (even a small one), and a sense of curiosity. There are a number of good dictionaries, but *Webster's New World Dictionary of the American Language*, which has Indo-European bases, will be the dictionary referred to here. . . .

2   If you have these, then, an encyclopedia and a dictionary with good etymologies, your only other investment is time. You won't need to spend money to buy more stamps and albums, film or a better camera, new chemicals or test tubes. Your hobby is free. You have your 100,000 words to work with, and you can have fun with them the remainder of your life.

3   You may have to start cultivating words as a hobby just as people start cultivating a taste for olives. They eat one and don't like it. But they have heard olives praised as a delicacy. They know other people like them, and so they try again. When they've tried enough, the salty, tangy taste becomes appealing. If you do the same with words, you'll soon begin to wonder how some unfamiliar word—such as *risible*—came to be, and you'll look it up and enjoy finding out. But surprisingly if you play the game long enough, you'll find that the commonest words can be even more interesting than most of the unfamiliar ones.

4   Suppose some of your father's friends come over, and you hear him greeting them, "Hi, Ralph. Long time no see. . . ." That word *hi* strikes you. Why *hi?* Everybody says it, but what does it mean and how? It is now spelled like *high,* but is it the same? Maybe, just as *good morning* means "I hope you have a good morning," *hi* means "I hope you have a high old time." So you look up *hi* and *high.* (If you do, you will find that this is a bad guess, but you can have as much fun with your bad guesses as you do with your good ones.) Meanwhile your father and his friends are talking business. One of them says, "And take all this cutthroat competition. . . ." *Cutthroat.* Why cutthroat? This one you probably *can* guess correctly—that a cutthroat was a murderer who killed by cutting throats, and that so the word became a modifier meaning "murderous, ruthless, viciously grasping," although you will want to check your dictionary to be sure. And now your father is talking about a "backlog of orders." Why *backlog?* What is a back log anyhow? You can go on having fun this way just listening to people, or thinking of words yourself.

5   Many words you will solve quite easily, but to give you a good start let us try a somewhat longer and harder word. Suppose that in your reading you come across this sentence: "He had no scruples about accepting the money." Perhaps you have a vague idea what *scruples* means, but you want to be certain, and so you turn to a dictionary. *Webster's New World Dictionary of the American Language, College Edition,* which we shall abbreviate WNWD, gives these meanings: "1. a very small quantity or amount; very small part. 2. an ancient Roman weight, $\frac{1}{288}$ of an as ($\frac{1}{24}$ ounce). 3. an apothecaries' weight, equal to $\frac{1}{3}$ dram (20 grains, or $\frac{1}{24}$ ounce)." So far you are getting no help at all—you're not quite sure about *scruple,* but you know that in the sentence you read it does not mean any kind of weight. You read on. "4. a feeling of hesitancy, doubt, or uneasiness arising from difficulty in deciding what is right, proper, expedient, etc.; qualm; misgiving." That's the meaning you're after, but you wonder why the word has all those weight meanings, too. Weight doesn't seem to have much to do with deciding what is right. Now, if you know that many dictionaries give their meanings in historical order, the oldest meaning first and the next oldest meaning next, you can guess that the one you're looking up was late in the history of the word, but you still wonder how *scruple* came to mean "doubt" when it had meant "weight," and there the etymology can help you. The etymology in the WNWD says, "[ME.; OFr. *scrupule;* L. *scrupulus,* small sharp stone, hence small stone used as a weight, small weight; also a sharp stone, as in a man's shoe, uneasiness, difficulty, small trouble, doubt]."

6   Now you have a start. Apparently *scruple* as a difficulty or a doubt comes from this *scrupulus* that was a stone in somebody's shoe. You have probably seen pictures of an ancient Roman wearing sandals, and with sandals on a gravel road you would get stones in your shoes pretty easily. You may even remember that that *street* comes from Latin *strata,* strewn, presumably with gravel. Even if you don't, you would know that there would

be lots of paths and country roads that were not paved. And a small, sharp stone would hurt. If you keep getting stones in your sandals, or even if you think you might, you will be careful and doubtful.

7   Since you want to be sure this is right, you look at some other words near by, and you see *scrupulous,* with the etymology "[< Fr. or L.; Fr. *scrupuleux;* L. *scrupulosus*]." This means that we do not know whether the word came into English directly from Latin, or whether it came into English from French, having first gone from Latin into French. Anyhow, it came directly or indirectly from Latin *scrupulosus.* After you have had a little practice, you will be able to guess that *scrupulosus* is made up of *scrupulus* with its ending *-us* taken off and a new ending *-osus* added to it. There are many such words, and you will soon learn to recognize them, but at first you can make sure by looking up the English ending of the word. For *-ous* you will find "[ME.; OFr. *-ous, -os;* L. *-osus*]," which means that English *-ous* comes from Latin *-osus* through Middle English and Old French. You will also learn from the definition that it is "an adjective-forming suffix," and that it has such meanings as "having, full of, characterized by." So your guess was right. *Scrupulous* means "having scruples," or "being careful," and if you are in doubt, look down to the meanings of *scrupulous.* There it is: "having or showing scruples . . . conscientiously honest . . . careful of details; precise, accurate, and correct."

8   So a stone in a Roman's sandal gave us the word for being scrupulously careful. But what about the meaning of *weight,* where did it come from? If you remember now that a *scrupulus* was a "small sharp stone, hence small stone used as a weight," you will probably guess how a stone came to be a measure of weight. Formerly scales for weighing were all balance scales, and the stone (or usually a number of small stones) was put in a pan on one side of the scales to balance the beans or meat or wheat or whatever was being weighed on the other side of the balance. Thus a small stone became a measure of weight in ancient Rome, $\frac{1}{288}$ of an as, about $\frac{1}{24}$ of an ounce, which would be quite a small stone. Druggists still use this weight, and it is still $\frac{1}{24}$ of an ounce, as definition number three told you.

9   Now that you are started on *weight* words, why not look up some more? You try *weight* itself. You find it came from *wegan* in Old English, since it is marked *AS.,* which means "Anglo-Saxon," or Old English. After that the etymology says, "see *weigh.*" So you turn to *weigh.* There you find, among other things, "AS. *wegan,* to carry, bear; akin to G. *wiegen, wägen,* IE. base *weg̑h-,* to move, draw, etc., seen also in L. *vehere,* to carry, bring (cf. *vehicle*); cf. *wain.*" This means that the word *weigh* comes from an Old English word meaning "to carry" (anything weighed had to be held up in the scales), and that word, like a Latin word and a German word having

about the same meaning all came from a root expression in Indo-European called a base, which was about like *weigh.* This base has an asterisk before it because it has been inferred; no Indo-European exists any more.

10 You can look up *vehicle* and *wain* (and if you do, you will find that *wagon* is also related to *weight*), or you can put that off and look up other weights. If you look up *pound,* you will find "[ME.; AS. *pund;* L. *pondo,* a pound, orig. abl. of *pondus,* a weight (in *libra pondo,* a pound in weight)]." This means that we got the word from Middle English, and since there is no meaning given after ME. the word meant "pound" in Middle English, too. Middle English got it from Old English *pund,* which also meant "pound," because again no definition is given. Old English got it from Latin *pondo,* but when it was first used the Latin word *pondo* did not mean "pound" at all.

11 You can guess that *orig.* is an abbreviation for *originally,* but you may not know that *abl.* is an abbreviation for *ablative,* a form that was used in Latin where we would use phrases beginning with *from, by,* and certain other prepositions. This one is translated for you, "in weight." That is, the idea of "pound" was in the word *libra,* and the idea of "weight" was in the word *pondo.* If you want to be sure, look up *libra,* and you will find that in Latin it meant "pound." Our word *pound,* then, came from the Latin word for "weight," and our abbreviation for a pound comes from the Latin word for a pound weight, *lb.* from *libra.* Many of these words can be found in your encyclopedia, too. For instance, if you look up *libra,* you will find that it was a Latin word for a pair of scales, and from that it became the name of a month in the Latin calendar or zodiac. And now you have gone from weight into time.

12 You can go on looking up weight words, for there are many more. For *ounce* we would find "[ME. *unce, ounce;* OFr. *once;* L. *uncia,* a twelfth, twelfth part of a foot or pound, orig., unit; akin to L. *unus,* one]." You will know, since you are getting to be an old hand now, that our word *ounce* comes from a Middle English word which meant the same thing; that the Middle English word came from an Old French word which also meant "ounce"; that the French got it from Latin *uncia.* But Latin *uncia* meant "a twelfth," originally, any division, and it could be either a twelfth of a pound, our ounce, or a twelfth of a foot—and right there, if you are alert enough, you will look up *inch* to see if it does not come from Latin *uncia,* too. Meanwhile, you will probably recall from your looking up *weight* that in troy weight, used by jewelers, a pound has twelve, not sixteen, ounces.

13 Now you have a whole new series of questions. What is *troy weight,* anyhow, and why *troy?* Surely, not Troy, New York. Maybe the Troy of Homer? Or some other Troy, perhaps named for it? And what about the weights in troy measure, the grains and the pennyweights? When you hunt the stories of words there is always another question, and usually another answer. . . .

UNDERSTANDING THE SELECTION

1. English and most of the other modern Western languages evolved from a common parent language spoken by primitive groups that lived somewhere in Eastern Europe long before writing was invented. Language historians call this elementary parent language Indo-European. As the speakers of this language roved across Europe and Western Asia in search of food, they became separated from other members of the group. They had new experiences. With isolation and new experiences, their language changed into a number of variants which have become today's English and French and German and Bengali and Bulgarian, all of them related to one another.

English is actually a variety of Germanic. It was brought from the European continent by Angle and Saxon invaders in the fifth century A.D. Hence the oldest form of English is called Anglo-Saxon in this selection. As the article suggests, the structure of English in basically Germanic; so are most of our common words, although many English words have come from other sources.

2. Look up the etymologies of *hi, cutthroat,* and *backlog.*

3. What reason do the authors give for the two meanings of the word *scruple:* a "weight" and a "doubt"?

4. In one or two sentences describe the relationship between the words *weight* and *wagon.*

5. Look up the etymologies of the following:

      a. fascinating
      b. hobby
      c. vague
      d. nice
      e. bizarre
      f. treacle

5   *Every Lover*
Robert Burton

Every Lover admires his Mistress, though she be very deformed of her self, ill-favoured, wrinkled, pimpled, pale, red, yellow, tanned, tallow-faced, have a swollen Juggler's platter-face, or a thin, lean, chitty-face, have clouds in her face, be crooked, dry, bald, goggle-ey'd, blear-ey'd, or with staring eyes, she looks like a squis'd [or squeez'd] cat, hold her head still awry, heavy, dull, hollow-eyed, black or yellow about the eyes, or squint-eyed, sparrow-mouthed, Persean hook-nosed, have a sharp Fox nose, a red nose, China flat great nose, snub-nose with wide nostrils, a nose like a promontory, gubber-tushed, rotten teeth, black, uneven, brown teeth, beetle-browed, a Witch's beard, her breath stink all over the room, her nose drop winter and summer, with a Bavarian poke [or pouch] under her chin, a sharp chin, lave eared [or big-eared], with a long crane's neck, which stands awry too, with hanging breasts, her dugs like two double jugs, or else no dugs, in the other extreme, bloody-faln [or chilblain'd] fingers, she have filthy long unpared nails, scabbed hands or wrists, a tanned skin, a rotten carkass, crooked back, she stoops, is lame, splay-footed, as slender in the middle as a Cow in the waist, gouty legs, her ankles hang over her shoes, her feet stink, she breeds lice, a mere changeling, a very monster, an auf [or oaf, or elf], imperfect, her whole complexion savours, an harsh voice, incondite gesture, vile gait, a vast virago, or an ugly Tit, a slug, a fat fustilugs, a truss, a long lean rawbone, a skeleton, a sneaker (suppose, as the poet saith, her unseen beauties somewhat better), and to thy judgement looks like a merd in a lanthorn, whom thou couldest not fancy for a world, but hatest, loathest, and wouldest have spit in her face, or blow thy nose in her bosom, the very antidote of love to another man, a dowdy, a slut, a scold, a nasty, rank, rammy, filthy, beastly quean, dishonest peradventure, obscene, base, beggarly, rude, foolish, untaught, peevish, Irus' daughter, Thersites' sister, Grobian's scholar, if he love her once, he admires her for all this, he takes no notice of any such errors, or imperfections of body or mind.

UNDERSTANDING THE SELECTION

1. This passage is taken from *The Anatomy of Melancholy,* published in 1621 by Robert Burton. Since the English is unfamiliar in some ways to a speaker of modern English, look up some of the words Burton used—*mistress, quean,* and *changeling,* for instance—to learn where they came from, what they once meant, and what they mean now.

2. Which of Burton's words give you the most vivid pictures?

3. Draw or list the different kinds of noses mentioned in the selection.

4. Write one short sentence which has the same meaning as Burton's long sentence.

6   *The Standard of Living*

Dorothy Parker

1   Annabel and Midge came out of the tea room with the arrogant slow gait of the leisured, for their Saturday afternoon stretched ahead of them. They had lunched, as was their wont, on sugar, starches, oils, and butter-fats. Usually they ate sandwiches of spongy new white bread greased with butter and mayonnaise; they ate thick wedges of cake lying wet beneath ice cream and whipped cream and melted chocolate gritty with nuts. As alternates, they ate patties, sweating beads of inferior oil, containing bits of bland meat bogged in pale, stiffening sauce; they ate pastries, limber under rigid icing, filled with an indeterminate yellow sweet stuff, not still solid, not yet liquid, like salve that has been left in the sun. They chose no other sort of food, nor did they consider it. And their skin was like the petals of wood anemones, and their bellies were as flat and their flanks as lean as those of young Indian braves.

2   Annabel and Midge had been best friends almost from the day that Midge had found a job as stenographer with the firm that employed Annabel. By now, Annabel, two years longer in the stenographic department, had worked up to the wages of eighteen dollars and fifty cents a week; Midge was still at sixteen dollars. Each girl lived at home with her family and paid half her salary to its support.

3   The girls sat side by side at their desks, they lunched together every noon, together they set out for home at the end of the day's work. Many of their evenings and most of their Sundays were passed in each other's company. Often they were joined by two young men, but there was no steadiness to any such quartet; the two young men would give place, unlamented, to two other young men, and lament would have been inappropriate, really, since the newcomers were scarcely distinguishable from their predecessors. Invariably the girls spent the fine idle hours of their hot-weather Saturday afternoons together. Constant use had not worn ragged the fabric of their friendship.

4   They looked alike, though the resemblance did not lie in their features. It was in the shape of their bodies, their movements, their style, and their adornments. Annabel and Midge did, and completely, all that young office workers are besought not to do. They painted their lips and their nails, they darkened their lashes and lightened their hair, and scent seemed to shimmer from them. They wore thin, bright dresses, tight over their breasts and high on their legs, and tilted slippers, fancifully strapped. They looked conspicuous and cheap and charming.

5   Now, as they walked across to Fifth Avenue with their skirts swirled by the hot wind, they received audible admiration. Young men grouped lethargically about newsstands awarded them murmurs, exclamations, even—the ultimate tribute—whistles. Annabel and Midge passed without the condescension of hurrying their pace; they held their heads higher and set their feet with exquisite precision, as if they stepped over the necks of peasants.

6   Always the girls went to walk on Fifth Avenue on their free afternoons, for it was the ideal ground for their favorite game. The game could be played anywhere, and, indeed, was, but the great shop windows stimulated the two players to their best form.

7   Annabel had invented the game; or rather she had evolved it from an old one. Basically, it was no more than the ancient sport of what-would-you-do-if-you-had-a-million dollars? But Annabel had drawn a new set of rules for it, had narrowed it, pointed it, made it stricter. Like all games, it was the more absorbing for being more difficult.

8   Annabel's version went like this: You must suppose that somebody dies and leaves you a million dollars, cool. But there is a condition to the bequest. It is stated in the will that you must spend every nickel of the money on yourself.

9   There lay the hazard of the game. If, when playing it, you forgot, and listed among your expenditures the rental of a new apartment for your family, for example, you lost your turn to the other player. It was astonishing how many—and some of them among the experts, too—would forfeit all their innings by such slips.

10   It was essential, of course, that it be played in passionate seriousness. Each purchase must be carefully considered and, if necessary, supported by argument. There was no zest to playing wildly. Once Annabel had introduced the game to Sylvia, another girl who worked in the office. She explained the rules to Sylvia and then offered her the gambit "What would be the first thing you'd do?" Sylvia had not shown the decency of even a second of hesitation. "Well," she said, "the first thing I'd do, I'd go out and hire somebody to shoot Mrs. Gary Cooper, and then . . ." So it is to be seen that she was no fun.

11   But Annabel and Midge were surely born to be comrades, for Midge played the game like a master from the moment she learned it. It was she who added the touches that made the whole thing cozier. According to Midge's innovations, the eccentric who died and left you the money was not anybody you loved, or, for the matter of that, anybody you even knew. It was somebody who had seen you somewhere and had thought, "That girl ought to have lots of nice things. I'm going to leave her a million dol-

lars when I die." And the death was to be neither untimely nor painful. Your benefactor, full of years and comfortably ready to depart, was to slip softly away during sleep and go right to heaven. These embroideries permitted Annabel and Midge to play their game in the luxury of peaceful consciences.

12   Midge played with a seriousness that was not only proper but extreme. The single strain on the girls' friendship had followed an announcement once made by Annabel that the first thing she would buy with her million dollars would be a silver-fox coat. It was as if she had struck Midge across the mouth. When Midge recovered her breath, she cried that she couldn't imagine how Annabel could do such a thing—silver-fox coats were common! Annabel defended her taste with the retort that they were not common, either. Midge then said that they were so. She added that everybody had a silver-fox coat. She went on, with perhaps a slight loss of head, to declare that she herself wouldn't be caught dead in silver fox.

13   For the next few days, though the girls saw each other as constantly, their conversation was careful and infrequent, and they did not once play their game. Then one morning, as soon as Annabel entered the office, she came to Midge and said that she had changed her mind. She would not buy a silver-fox coat with any part of her million dollars. Immediately on receiving the legacy, she would select a coat of mink.

14   Midge smiled and her eyes shone. "I think," she said, "you're doing absolutely the right thing."

15   Now, as they walked along Fifth Avenue, they played the game anew. It was one of those days with which September is repeatedly cursed; hot and glaring, with slivers of dust in the wind. People drooped and shambled, but the girls carried themselves tall and walked a straight line, as befitted young heiresses on their afternoon promenade. There was no longer need for them to start the game at its formal opening. Annabel went direct to the heart of it.

16   "All right," she said. "So you've got this million dollars. So what would be the first thing you'd do?"

17   "Well, the first thing I'd do," Midge said, "I'd get a mink coat." But she said it mechanically, as if she were giving the memorized answer to an expected question.

18   "Yes," Annabel said, "I think you ought to. The terribly dark kind of mink." But she, too, spoke as if by rote. It was too hot; fur, no matter how dark and sleek and supple, was horrid to the thoughts.

19   They stepped along in silence for a while. Then Midge's eye was caught by a shop window. Cool, lovely gleamings were there set off by chaste and elegant darkness.

20   "No," Midge said, "I take it back. I wouldn't get a mink coat the first thing. Know what I'd do? I'd get a string of pearls. Real pearls."

21   Annabel's eyes turned to follow Midge's.

22   "Yes," she said, slowly. "I think that's a kind of a good idea. And it would make sense, too. Because you can wear pearls with anything."

23   Together they went over to the shop window and stood pressed against it. It contained but one object—a double row of great, even pearls clasped by a deep emerald around a little pink velvet throat.

24   "What do you suppose they cost?" Annabel said.

25   "Gee, I don't know," Midge said. "Plenty, I guess."

26   "Like a thousand dollars?" Annabel said.

27   "Oh, I guess like more," Midge said. "On account of the emerald."

28   "Well, like ten thousand dollars?" Annabel said.

29   "Gee, I wouldn't even know," Midge said.

30   The devil nudged Annabel in the ribs. "Dare you to go in and price them," she said.

31   "Like fun!" Midge said.

32   "Dare you," Annabel said.

33   "Why, a store like this wouldn't even be open this afternoon," Midge said.

34   "Yes, it is so, too," Annabel said. "People just came out. And there's a doorman on. Dare you."

35   "Well," Midge said. "But you've got to come too."

36   They tendered thanks, icily, to the doorman for ushering them into the shop. It was cool and quiet, a broad, gracious room with paneled walls and soft carpet. But the girls wore expressions of bitter disdain, as if they stood in a sty.

37   A slim, immaculate clerk came to them and bowed. His neat face showed no astonishment at their appearance.

38   "Good afternoon," he said. He implied that he would never forget it if they would grant him the favor of accepting his soft-spoken greeting.

39   "Good afternoon," Annabel and Midge said together, and in like freezing accents.

40   "Is there something—?" the clerk said.

41   "Oh, we're just looking," Annabel said. It was as if she flung the words down from a dais.

42   The clerk bowed.

43   "My friend and myself merely happened to be passing," Midge said, and stopped, seeming to listen to the phrase. "My friend here and myself," she went on, "merely happened to be wondering how much are those pearls you've got in your window."

44   "Ah, yes," the clerk said. "The double rope. That is two hundred and fifty thousand dollars, Madam."

45   "I see," Midge said.

46   The clerk bowed. "An exceptionally beautiful necklace," he said. "Would you care to look at it?"

47   "No, thank you," Annabel said.

48   "My friend and myself merely happened to be passing," Midge said.

49   They turned to go; to go, from their manner, where the tumbrel awaited them. The clerk sprang ahead and opened the door. He bowed as they swept by him.

50   The girls went on along the Avenue and disdain was still on their faces.

51   "Honestly!" Annabel said. "Can you imagine a thing like that?"

52   "Two hundred and fifty thousand dollars!" Midge said. "That's a quarter of a million dollars right there!"

53   "He's got his nerve!" Annabel said.

54   They walked on. Slowly the disdain went, slowly and completely as if drained from them, and with it went the regal carriage and tread. Their shoulders dropped and they dragged their feet; they bumped against each other, without notice or apology, and caromed away again. They were silent and their eyes were cloudy.

55   Suddenly Midge straightened her back, flung her head high, and spoke, clear and strong.

56   "Listen, Annabel," she said. "Look. Suppose there was this terribly rich person, see? You don't know this person, but this person has seen you somewhere and wants to do something for you. Well, it's a terribly old person, see? And so this person dies, just like going to sleep, and leaves you ten million dollars. Now, what would be the first thing you'd do?"

UNDERSTANDING THE SELECTION

1. In the introduction to this section, we pointed out that reading sometimes requires you to make inferences, to visualize what an author says and then to use your imagination in applying what you have visualized. Some of the following questions require this kind of inferring.

2. Judging from Dorothy Parker's description of the girls in this story, when would you say it was written? What details influenced your answer?

3. Where do Annabel and Midge live? If they lived in your community, in which section of town would they live? Why do you think so?

4. What do they do for entertainment? Do they surf? Do they watch TV? Do they bowl on Friday nights? Sit in pizza parlors? Do they take part in demonstrations of any kind?

5. Are they like other girls? Do they think they are like other girls? How do you know?

6. Are they popular? Attractive? Describe their boyfriends.

7. What strained the girls' friendship for a time? What does this tell you about their personalities?

8. Find pictures in magazines of girls you think look like Annabel and Midge.

Arrangement in Time

A second way to understand what an author says is to follow him in time, to be aware of the sequence of events as the author relates them: ". . . and then . . . and then . . . and then. . . ." Just as you could draw a diagram or a picture of arrangement in space, so you can make a chart of arrangement in time, and we shall ask you to do so.

Time is not always chronological, moving from first to last like the history of the United States. Sometimes it is logical. For example, if you know that all men have two eyes and the Bible says that Adam was a man, you know that Adam had two eyes even though you have never seen him. This kind of reasoning, which is called deductive logic, is possible only because of time. If X is true (all men have two eyes) and Y is true (Adam is a man), Z is true (Adam has two eyes). You must know X and Y, however, before you can know Z. A philosopher who presents a logical argument is arranging his ideas in time just as strictly as is a biographer who writes a life of George Washington from birth to death.

Although the selections which follow contain objects arranged in space which should be visualized, we want you to concentrate on the time arrangement.

7 Haschich Fudge
(which anyone could whip up on a rainy day)
Alice B. Toklas

1   This is the food of Paradise—of Baudelaire's Artificial Paradises: it might provide an entertaining refreshment for a Ladies' Bridge Club or a chapter meeting of the DAR. In Morocco it is thought to be good for warding off the common cold in damp winter weather and is, indeed, more effective if taken with large quantities of hot mint tea. Euphoria and brilliant storms of laughter; ecstatic reveries and extensions of one's personality on several simultaneous planes are to be complacently expected. Almost anything Saint Theresa did, you can do better if you can bear to be ravished by *"un évanouissement reveillé."*

2   Take 1 teaspoon black peppercorns, 1 whole nutmeg, 4 average sticks of cinnamon, 1 teaspoon coriander. These should all be pulverised in a mortar. About a handful each of stoned dates, dried figs, shelled almonds and peanuts: chop these and mix them together. A bunch of *canibus sativa* can be pulverised. This along with the spices should be dusted over the mixed fruit and nuts, kneaded together. About a cup of sugar dissolved

in a big pat of butter. Rolled into a cake and cut into pieces or made into balls about the size of a walnut, it should be eaten with care. Two pieces are quite sufficient.

3   Obtaining the *canibus* may present certain difficulties, but the variety known as *canibus sativa* grows as a common weed, often unrecognised, everywhere in Europe, Asia and parts of Africa; besides being cultivated as a crop for the manufacture of rope. In the Americas, while often discouraged, its cousin, called *canibus indica,* has been observed even in city window boxes. It should be picked and dried as soon as it has gone to seed and while the plant is still green.

UNDERSTANDING THE SELECTION

1. This selection is primarily a recipe, but it also contains remarks by the author. At the end of the first paragraph she uses the French phrase *"un évanouissement reveillé";* translated literally, this means "a swooning revelation," but Miss Toklas means approximately what a hippy means by "a trip." In the final paragraph, *canibus* (more commonly spelled *cannabis*) is the Latin word and scientific name for hemp, the plant which yields hashish and marijuana. (The more common spelling of "haschich" is *hashish* or *hasheesh.*)

2. Which kind of order, space or time, is used in this selection?

3. Who is Baudelaire? What is the DAR?

4. How big is "a big pat of butter"?

5. What did St. Theresa do?

6. What does the author mean by "stoned dates"? What would *you* mean if you used the phrase?

7. Obviously this recipe was not taken from last month's *Ladies' Home Journal.* What are some of the ways by which you can tell?

8   Age of the Solar System

Stuart J. Inglis

1   How old is the solar system? The question is basic to any theory of origins, but how is it to be answered? Age reveals itself in many different ways. The age of a tree is determined by the number of rings in its trunk, that of a horse by its teeth. If there is some analogous sign or evidence in the solar system that will help us determine its age we may expect to find it first at home, on the Earth.

2   To obtain evidence of the Earth's age we must first find some material or object that shows signs of change over a long period of time. Then to determine this period, three factors must be considered:

1. The material's present condition.
2. Its assumed condition when formed.
3. Its rate of change.

3   Rain water, for instance, is nearly pure (that is, fresh); the oceans are salty; and the Great Salt Lake and Dead Sea are even saltier. The rain falls on the land and carries salts from it into the ocean. The ocean's water evaporates, leaving the salt behind, to form clouds that cause rain to wash again down the mountain slopes and deposit more salt into the oceans. The cycle goes on; how long has it been doing so?

4   The ocean's present condition is one of water with dissolved salts. It is reasonable to assume that its condition when formed was one of fresh water, as fresh as river water. Its rate of change from a fresh to a saline condition may be deduced from the amount of salt carried into the oceans each year by the present rivers. If we divide the number of tons of salt in the oceans at the present time by the number of tons deposited each year, we obtain the length of time this process has been going on. From this calculation it has been estimated that the oceans are about 300 million years old.

5   But the geologists warn us to be careful because the Earth that we now see is *not* typical of its past history. There are many more rugged mountains now than in former geological epochs. This means that the rivers erode the Earth's surface more rapidly and thus carry more salt than usual into the oceans. Consequently we postulated too rapid a rate of salt cumulation and 300 million years turns out to be too short a time interval. When we take into consideration the slower rates of cumulation before the present era, we arrive at an age for the oceans that is closer to a few billion years.

6   This method, approximate though it may be, does enable us to be certain of one thing: the oceans are not infinitely old; they did begin sometime. If salt had been deposited in them for an infinite length of time they would have become completely saturated and could have held no more salt, for they are finite in size and therefore the amount of salt required to saturate them is also finite. If the oceans had become saturated with salt any additional salt would have settled to the bottom. If this had happened we would have to investigate the amount of sediment on the ocean floors to arrive at an estimate of the length of time that sedimentation has been going on.

7   The age of the oceans, however, need not be the same as the age of the Earth. Indeed, we expect that they would be younger, for the assumption has been made (and not without good reason) that the surface of the Earth was originally molten and much too hot for any water to collect or even for any rain to fall. We must look for some other change that will give us a clue to the age of the Earth itself.

8   One branch of physics (nuclear physics) concerns itself partly with radioactivity. A radioactive element is one whose atoms are unstable and therefore break up or *decay* into other atoms. It has been found that the rate of radioactive decay is constant and quite independent of any pressure or temperature that man has imposed on any radioactive substance. Some of these elements appear naturally in the rocks of the Earth, and the fact that they decay at a known rate gives us a clue to the age of the rocks.

9   Uranium 238 (the 238 is the atomic mass of this particular kind of uranium) is one of these natural radioactive elements. It decays into another radioactive element, thorium 234, which decays into yet another radioactive element, protactinium 234, and so on through a number of radioactive elements until lead 206 is reached. Lead 206 is stable and does not decay into any other element. Furthermore it is a solid and thus accumulates in the rock that contains the uranium 238 just as salt accumulates in the oceans.

10   The rate of decay of a radioactive element is generally measured by the *half-life* of that element. The half-life of any radioactive element is the time it takes for half of the original atoms to decay. For example, the half-life of the uranium 238-lead 206 process is 4.5 billion years, which means that no matter how many atoms of uranium 238 we start with, in 4.5 billion years half as many atoms of lead 206 will have been formed.

11   To find the age of a particular rock we first determine its present condition by measuring the amount of lead and uranium in it. We can simplify this example by assuming that the rock contained no lead when it was formed; therefore all the lead it now contains comes from the radioactive decay of uranium. We can then obtain the age of the rock, that is, the length of time since it solidified, by applying the known rate at which lead has been formed through the decay of uranium.

12   This sounds very easy. Unfortunately, however, we were not justified in assuming that the rock started without lead; if there was uranium in the primordial rock there may certainly have been some lead. In fact we are confronted with the initial problem of determining the amount of primordial lead.

13   Harrison Brown, of the California Institute of Technology, has attacked this problem by recognizing and investigating the fact that certain sections of meteorites contain no radioactive elements. By measuring the amount of lead in these sections he deduced the amount of primordial lead in the meteorites studied. From this and other measurements he estimated the age of the *meteorites* he studied to be 4.5 billion years. Other scientists have used different methods and determined the age of some terrestrial rocks to be 3.4 billion years, although not all rocks are of the same age.

Since the terrestrial rocks that have been studied have different ages we cannot be sure that the oldest one has yet been [found]. On the other hand, all the meteorites studied are of more nearly the same age, as well as being older than any rock yet found on the Earth. The age of the solar system is therefore generally taken as 4.5 billion years.

UNDERSTANDING THE SELECTION

1. Many college texts, unlike this one, are full of facts and dates and figures that you must understand, absorb, and memorize. One way to understand writing that includes many facts is to arrange them in some kind of order. Arrange in chronological order the steps which are used to discover the age of oceans, of rocks, and of meteorites.

2. This article, though written largely in standard English, contains some terms used primarily by scientists. If you are unsure of the meanings of the following terms, look them up in a dictionary or a geology textbook: *saline, deduced, geological epochs, postulated, cumulation, radioactive decay, primordial rock, terrestrial rock.*

3. What is the age of the oceans? Of terrestrial rocks? Of meteorites?

4. Why did Inglis discuss oceans first, then terrestrial rocks, and then meteorites?

5. In paragraph 2, Inglis lists three factors to be considered in determining the age of the earth. Why does he put them in the order shown?

9   *Doomsday*

Anonymous

1   **Thursday, November 13, 2026. Remember this date . . . It's Doomsday.** This Doomsday is nothing to scoff at. It is not the work of crackpots. It is a carefully considered estimate published in *Science* magazine by three serious scientists.

2   These men have been studying the rate at which people have been giving birth to people since 5000 B.C. Then they calculated ahead and concluded that on November 13, 2026 the planet earth will contain 50 billion people (current total: less than three billion). And that, unless our world's production of food is stepped up immeasurably, these people will almost certainly starve.

3   If our heaping dinner tables make Doomsday seem absurd; if our highly publicized crop surpluses make the Starvation Age seem remote, ponder this:

4   If those 50 billion future citizens were invited to share our plenty, they could eat their way through America's gigantic stored surpluses *in less than one day.*

5   That's the population explosion you've heard about.

6   Cyanamid has heard about it, too. That's one reason why several hundred Cyanamid scientists and technicians are at work in a new Agricultural Research Center—a rolling, 640-acre laboratory-farm near Princeton, New Jersey.

7   There, they work, read, talk and sometimes stare out at the countryside. They consider, as the autos roll by, that New Jersey now has 800 persons per square mile (and so, incidentally, has Japan). And that in 2026 it will have *10,000* per square mile (and so, incidentally, will Japan). All of which makes them search a little harder for ways to match that population explosion with a food explosion.

8   These scientists know that agricultural science must hurry. It must replace two ears of corn with four, four chickens with eight, eight hogs with sixteen. Then they must do it again. And again.

9   The people of Princeton are confident that they can do it. Already they are discovering which nutrients produce the biggest, healthiest livestock. They are growing plants in man-made, man-controlled temperatures ranging from arctic to jungle; in humidities ranging from desert to New York in August.

10   They're discovering better ways to cope with insects, too. Right now, insects and disease eat or destroy *30*% of all the food we plant. With fifty billion mouths to feed, we really won't be able to afford that kind of freeloading much longer.

11   Much progress has already been made. Cyanamid's AUREOMYCIN® chlortetracycline has enabled a farmer to bring a plump, tender broiler to market in *6* weeks instead of 12.

12   And much progress is being made today. A new insecticide called CYGON® dimethoate is stopping our old friend *musca domestica,* the common house fly, in his tracks. Fly-free cows, science knows, will grow fatter and give more milk.

13   Cyanamid subscribes to the often-ignored axiom: Look after the future in the present. That's one reason for the new multimillion dollar Princeton Agricultural Center.

14   Another reason is that agricultural research is sound, profitable business. Good ideas that have reached their time usually are.

15   This is the story of one research effort by one Cyanamid division. Eleven other divisions operate in the United States and eighty-seven foreign countries. Working together they create an atmosphere charged with diversity, alertness, and progress.

UNDERSTANDING THE SELECTION

1. This advertisement is an example of an "if . . . then" arrangement. What are the "ifs" that cause scientists to say, ". . . then Doomsday"?
2. What are the "ifs" that cause Cyanamid to develop insecticides?
3. What reasons are given for agricultural research? How is saying "That's one reason for . . ." an arrangement in time?
4. If we want to avoid the Starvation Age, then we need agricultural research, says the American Cyanamid Company. Why does the company mention only one alternative to the Starvation Age? Write a brief paper suggesting other alternatives. Use an "if . . . then" arrangement.

10   Po' Boy

Traditional

My mammy's in the cold, cold ground;
My daddy went away;
My sister married a gamblin' man;
And now I've gone astray.
I sit here in the prison;   5
I do the best I can;
But I get to thinkin' of the woman I love;
She ran away with another man.

Chorus: She ran away with another man, po' boy,
          She ran away with another man.   10
          I get to thinkin' of the woman I love;
          She ran away with another man.

Away out on the prairie,
I stopped that Katy train;
I took the mail from the baggage car;   15
And walked away in the rain.
They got the bloodhounds on me,
And chased me up a tree;
And then they said, "Come down, my boy,
And go to the penitentiaree."   20

Chorus: She ran away with another man, po' boy, etc.

"Oh, mister judge, oh, mister judge,
What are you going to do to me?"
"If the jury finds you guilty, my boy,
I'm going to send you the penitentiaree."   *25*
They took me to the railroad station;
A train came rolling by;
I looked in the window, saw the woman I love;
Hung down my head and cried.

Chorus: Hung down my head in shame, po' boy,   *30*
        Hung down my head and cried;
        I looked in the window, saw the woman I love,
        Hung down my head and cried, po' boy!

UNDERSTANDING THE SELECTION

1. Familiar as you are today with the techniques of motion pictures and television, you all are used to the flashback, in which the time sequence of a story is interrupted for a view of the past. Although writers have employed this device for a long time, it complicates your understanding of the events described. The writer uses the flashback, however, not to confuse you but to focus your attention on important moments. To understand a selection like "Po' Boy" that involves time shifts, you must trace the order in which the events occurred.

Incidentally, in line 14 of this folk song, Po' Boy says that he stopped the "Katy train." He is referring to the Missouri-Kansas-Texas line, commonly known as "K.T." or "Katy."

2. List the events which Po' Boy mentions in the order given them in the song.

3. List every event which Po' Boy mentions in as strict a *chronological* order as you can. What happened just before and just after Po' Boy's girl ran away with another man?

11 The Musgrave Ritual

Sir Arthur Conan Doyle

1   An anomaly which often struck me in the character of my friend Sherlock Holmes was that, although in his methods of thought he was the neatest and most methodical of mankind, and although also he affected a certain quiet primness of dress, he was none the less in his personal habits one of the most untidy men that ever drove a fellow-lodger to distraction. Not that I am in the least conventional in that respect myself. The rough-and-tumble work in Afghanistan, coming on the top of natural Bohemianism of disposition, has made me rather more lax than befits a medical man. But with me there is a limit, and when I find a man who keeps his cigars in the coal-scuttle, his tobacco in the toe end of a Persian slipper, and his unanswered correspondence transfixed by a jack-knife into the very centre of his wooden mantelpiece, then I begin to give myself virtuous airs. I have always held, too, that pistol practice should be distinctly an open-air pastime; and when Holmes, in one of his queer humours, would sit in an armchair with his hair-trigger and a hundred Boxer cartridges and proceed to adorn the opposite wall with a patriotic V.R. done in bullet-pocks, I felt strongly that neither the atmosphere nor the appearance of our room was improved by it.

2   Our chambers were always full of chemicals and of criminal relics which had a way of wandering into unlikely positions, and of turning up in the butter-dish or in even less desirable places. But his papers were my great crux. He had a horror of destroying documents, especially those which were connected with his past cases, and yet it was only once in every year or two that he would muster energy to docket and arrange them; for, as I have mentioned somewhere in these incoherent memoirs, the outbursts of passionate energy when he performed the remarkable feats with which his name is associated were followed by reactions of lethargy during which he would lie about with his violin and his books, hardly moving save from the sofa to the table. Thus month after month his papers accumulated until every corner of the room was stacked with bundles of manuscript which were on no account to be burned, and which could not be put away save by their owner. One winter's night, as we sat together by the fire, I ventured to suggest to him that, as he had finished pasting extracts into his commonplace book, he might employ the next two hours in making our room a little more habitable. He could not deny the justice of my request, so with a rather rueful face he went off to his bedroom, from which he returned presently pulling a large tin box behind him. This he placed in the middle of the floor, and, squatting down upon a stool in front of it, he threw back the lid. I could see that it was already a third full of bundles of paper tied up with red tape into separate packages.

3   "There are cases enough here, Watson," said he, looking at me with mischievous eyes. "I think that if you knew all that I had in this box you would ask me to pull some out instead of putting others in."

4   "These are the records of your early work, then?" I asked. "I have often wished that I had notes of those cases."

5   "Yes, my boy, these were all done prematurely before my biographer had come to glorify me." He lifted bundle after bundle in a tender,

caressing sort of way. "They are not all successes, Watson," said he. "But there are some pretty little problems among them. Here's the record of the Tarleton murders, and the case of Vamberry, the wine merchant, and the adventure of the old Russian woman, and the singular affair of the aluminum crutch, as well as a full account of Ricoletti of the club-foot, and his abominable wife. And here—ah, now, this really is something a little *recherché*."

6 He dived his arm down to the bottom of the chest and brought up a small wooden box with a sliding lid such as children's toys are kept in. From within he produced a crumpled piece of paper, an old-fashioned brass key, a peg of wood with a ball of string attached to it, and three rusty old discs of metal.

7 "Well, my boy, what do you make of this lot?" he asked, smiling at my expression.

8 "It is a curious collection."

9 "Very curious, and the story that hangs round it will strike you as being more curious still."

10 "These relics have a history, then?"

11 "So much so that they *are* history."

12 "What do you mean by that?"

13 Sherlock Holmes picked them up one by one and laid them along the edge of the table. Then he reseated himself in his chair and looked them over with a gleam of satisfaction in his eyes.

14 "These," said he, "are all that I have left to remind me of the adventure of the Musgrave Ritual."

15 I had heard him mention the case more the once, though I had never been able to gather the details. "I should be so glad," said I, "if you would give me an account of it."

16 "And leave the litter as it is?" he cried mischievously. "Your tidiness won't bear much strain, after all, Watson. But I should be glad that you should add this case to your annals, for there are points in it which make it quite unique in the criminal records of this or, I believe, of any other country. A collection of my trifling achievements would certainly be incomplete which contained no account of this very singular business.

17 "You may remember how the affair of the *Gloria Scott*, and my conversation with the unhappy man whose fate I told you of, first turned my attention in the direction of the profession which has become my life's work. You see me now when my name has become known far and wide, and when I am generally recognized both by the public and by the official force as being a final court of appeal in doubtful cases. Even when you knew me first, at the time of the affair which you have commemorated in 'A Study in Scarlet,' I had already established a considerable, though not a very lucrative, connection. You can hardly realize, then, how difficult I found it

at first, and how long I had to wait before I succeeded in making any headway.

18   "When I first came up to London I had rooms in Montague Street, just round the corner from the British Museum, and there I waited, filling in my too abundant leisure time by studying all those branches of science which might make me more efficient. Now and again cases came in my way, principally through the introduction of old fellow-students, for during my last years at the university there was a good deal of talk there about myself and my methods. The third of these cases was that of the Musgrave Ritual, and it is to the interest which was aroused by that singular chain of events, and the large issues which proved to be at stake, that I trace my first stride towards the position which I now hold.

19   "Reginald Musgrave had been in the same college as myself, and I had some slight acquaintance with him. He was not generally popular among the undergraduates, though it always seemed to me that what was set down as pride was really an attempt to cover extreme natural diffidence. In appearance he was a man of an exceedingly aristocratic type, thin, high-nosed, and large-eyed, with languid and yet courtly manners. He was indeed a scion of one of the very oldest families in the kingdom, though his branch was a cadet one which had separated from the northern Musgraves some time in the sixteenth century and had established itself in western Sussex, where the Manor House of Hurlstone is perhaps the oldest inhabited building in the county. Something of his birth-place seemed to cling to the man, and I never looked at his pale, keen face or the poise of his head without associating him with gray archways and mullioned windows and all the venerable wreckage of a feudal keep. Once or twice we drifted into talk, and I can remember that more than once he expressed a keen interest in my methods of observation and inference.

20   "For four years I had seen nothing of him until one morning he walked into my room in Montague Street. He had changed little, was dressed like a young man of fashion—he was always a bit of a dandy—and preserved the same quiet, suave manner which had formerly distinguished him.

21   "'How has all gone with you, Musgrave?' I asked after we had cordially shaken hands.

22   "'You probably heard of my poor father's death,' said he; 'he was carried off about two years ago. Since then I have of course had the Hurlstone estate to manage, and as I am member for my district as well, my life has been a busy one. But I understand, Holmes, that you are turning to practical ends those powers with which you used to amaze us?'

23   "'Yes,' said I, 'I have taken to living by my wits.'

24   "'I am delighted to hear it, for your advice at present would be exceedingly valuable to me. We have had some very strange doings at Hurl-

stone, and the police have been able to throw no light upon the matter. It is really the most extraordinary and inexplicable business.'

25   "You can imagine with what eagerness I listened to him, Watson, for the very chance for which I had been panting during all those months of inaction seemed to have come within my reach. In my inmost heart I believed that I could succeed where others failed, and now I had the opportunity to test myself.

26   "'Pray let me have the details,' I cried.

27   "Reginald Musgrave sat down opposite to me and lit the cigarette which I had pushed towards him.

28   "'You must know,' said he, 'that though I am a bachelor, I have to keep up a considerable staff of servants at Hurlstone, for it is a rambling old place and takes a good deal of looking after. I preserve, too, and in the pheasant months I usually have a house-party, so that it would not do to be short-handed. Altogether there are eight maids, the cook, the butler, two footmen, and a boy. The garden and the stables of course have a separate staff.

29   "'Of these servants the one who had been longest in our service was Brunton, the butler. He was a young schoolmaster out of place when he was first taken up by my father, but he was a man of great energy and character, and he soon became quite invaluable in the household. He was a well-grown, handsome man, with a splendid forehead, and though he has been with us for twenty years he cannot be more than forty now. With his personal advantages and his extraordinary gifts—for he can speak several languages and play nearly every musical instrument—it is wonderful that he should have been satisfied so long in such a position, but I suppose that he was comfortable and lacked energy to make any change. The butler of Hurlstone is always a thing that is remembered by all who visit us.

30   "'But this paragon has one fault. He is a bit of a Don Juan, and you can imagine that for a man like him it is not a very difficult part to play in a quiet country district. When he was married it was all right, but since he has been a widower we have had no end of trouble with him. A few months ago we were in hopes that he was about to settle down again, for he became engaged to Rachel Howells, our second housemaid; but he has thrown her over since then and taken up with Janet Tregellis, the daughter of the head game-keeper. Rachel—who is a very good girl, but of an excitable Welsh temperament—had a sharp touch of brain-fever and goes about the house now—or did until yesterday—like a black-eyed shadow of her former self. That was our first drama at Hurlstone; but a second one came to drive it from our minds, and it was prefaced by the disgrace and dismissal of butler Brunton.

31   "'This was how it came about. I have said that the man was intelligent, and this very intelligence has caused his ruin, for it seems to have led to an insatiable curiosity about things which did not in the least concern him. I had no idea of the lengths to which this would carry him until the merest accident opened my eyes to it.

32   "'I have said that the house is a rambling one. One day last week— on Thursday night, to be more exact—I found that I could not sleep, having foolishly taken a cup of strong *café noir* after my dinner. After struggling against it until two in the morning, I felt it was quite hopeless, so I rose and lit the candle with the intention of continuing a novel which I was reading. The book, however, had been left in the billiard-room, so I pulled on my dressing-gown and started off to get it.

33   "'In order to reach the billiard-room I had to descend a flight of stairs and then to cross the head of a passage which led to the library and the gun-room. You can imagine my surprise when, as I looked down this corridor, I saw a glimmer of light coming from the open door of the library. I had myself extinguished the lamp and closed the door before coming to bed. Naturally my first thought was of burglars. The corridors at Hurlstone have their walls largely decorated with trophies of old weapons. From one of these I picked a battle-axe, and then, leaving my candle behind me, I crept on tiptoe down the passage and peeped in at the open door.

34   "'Brunton, the butler, was in the library. He was sitting, fully dressed, in an easy-chair, with a slip of paper which looked like a map upon his knee, and his forehead sunk forward upon his hand in deep thought. I stood dumb with astonishment, watching him from the darkness. A small taper on the edge of the table shed a feeble light which sufficed to show me that he was fully dressed. Suddenly, as I looked, he rose from his chair, and, walking over to a bureau at the side, he unlocked it and drew out one of the drawers. From this he took a paper, and, returning to his seat, he flattened it out beside the taper on the edge of the table and began to study it with minute attention. My indignation at this calm examination of our family documents overcame me so far that I took a step forward, and Brunton, looking up, saw me standing in the doorway. He sprang to his feet, his face turned livid with fear, and he thrust into his breast the chart-like paper which he had been originally studying.

35   "'"So!" said I. "This is how you repay the trust which we have reposed in you. You will leave my service to-morrow."

36   "'He bowed with the look of a man who is utterly crushed and slunk past me without a word. The taper was still on the table, and by its light I glanced to see what the paper was which Brunton had taken from the bureau. To my surprise it was nothing of any importance at all, but simply a copy of the questions and answers in the singular old observance called the Musgrave Ritual. It is a sort of ceremony peculiar to our family, which

each Musgrave for centuries past has gone through on his coming of age—
a thing of private interest, and perhaps of some little importance to the ar-
chaeologist, like our own blazonings and charges, but of no practical use
whatever.'

37   "'"We had better come back to the paper afterwards," said I.

38   "'"If you think it really necessary," he answered with some hesitation. To continue my statement, however: I relocked the bureau, using
the key which Brunton had left, and I had turned to go when I was surprised
to find that the butler had returned, and was standing before me.

39   "'"Mr. Musgrave, sir," he cried in a voice which was hoarse with
emotion, "I can't bear disgrace, sir. I've always been proud above my station in life, and disgrace would kill me. My blood will be on your head, sir—
it will, indeed—if you drive me to despair. If you cannot keep me after what
has passed, then for God's sake let me give you notice and leave in a month,
as if of my own free will. I could stand that, Mr. Musgrave, but not to be
cast out before all the folk that I know so well."

40   "'"You don't deserve much consideration, Brunton," I answered.
"Your conduct has been most infamous. However, as you have been a long
time in the family, I have no wish to bring public disgrace upon you. A month,
however, is too long. Take yourself away in a week, and give what reason
you like for going."

41   "'"Only a week, sir?" he cried in a despairing voice. "A fortnight—say
at least a fortnight!"

42   "'"A week," I repeated,"and you may consider yourself to have been
very leniently dealt with."

43   "'He crept away, his face sunk upon his breast, like a broken man,
while I put out the light and returned to my room.

44   "'For two days after this Brunton was most assiduous in his attention to his duties. I made no allusion to what had passed and waited with
some curiosity to see how he would cover his disgrace. On the third morning, however, he did not appear, as was his custom, after breakfast to receive my instructions for the day. As I left the dining-room I happened to
meet Rachel Howells, the maid. I have told you that she had only recently
recovered from an illness and was looking so wretchedly pale and wan that
I remonstrated with her for being at work.

45   "'"You should be in bed," I said. "Come back to your duties when
you are stronger."

46   "'She looked at me with so strange an expression that I began to
suspect that her brain was affected.

47   "'"I am strong enough, Mr. Musgrave," said she.

48   "'"We will see what the doctor says," I answered. "You must stop
work now, and when you go downstairs just say that I wish to see Brunton."

49   "'"The butler is gone," said she.

50   "'"Gone! Gone where?"

51   "'"He is gone. No one has seen him. He is not in his room. Oh, yes, he is gone, he is gone!" She fell back against the wall with shriek after shriek of laughter, while I, horrified at this sudden hysterical attack, rushed to the bell to summon help. The girl was taken to her room, still screaming and sobbing, while I made inquiries about Brunton. There was no doubt about it that he had disappeared. His bed had not been slept in, he had been seen by no one since he had retired to his room the night before, and yet it was difficult to see how he could have left the house, as both windows and doors were found to be fastened in the morning. His clothes, his watch, and even his money were in his room, but the black suit which he usually wore was missing. His slippers, too, were gone, but his boots were left behind. Where then could butler Brunton have gone in the night, and what could have become of him now?

52   "'Of course we searched the house from cellar to garret, but there was no trace of him. It is, as I have said, a labyrinth of an old house, especially the original wing, which is now practically uninhabited; but we ransacked every room and cellar without discovering the least sign of the missing man. It was incredible to me that he could have gone away leaving all his property behind him, and yet where could he be? I called in the local police, but without success. Rain had fallen on the night before, and we examined the lawn and the paths all round the house, but in vain. Matters were in this state, when a new development quite drew our attention away from the original mystery.

53   "'For two days Rachel Howells had been so ill, sometimes delirious, sometimes hysterical, that a nurse had been employed to sit up with her at night. On the third night after Brunton's disappearance, the nurse, finding her patient sleeping nicely, had dropped into a nap in the armchair, when she woke in the early morning to find the bed empty, the window open, and no signs of the invalid. I was instantly aroused, and, with the two footmen, started off at once in search of the missing girl. It was not difficult to tell the direction which she had taken, for, starting from under her window, we could follow her foot-marks easily across the lawn to the edge of the mere, where they vanished close to the gravel path which leads out of the grounds. The lake there is eight feet deep, and you can imagine our feelings when we saw that the trail of the poor demented girl came to an end at the edge of it.

54   "'Of course, we had the drags at once and set to work to recover the remains, but no trace of the body could we find. On the other hand, we brought to the surface an object of a most unexpected kind. It was a linen bag which contained within it a mass of old rusted and discoloured metal and several dull-coloured pieces of pebble or glass. This strange find

was all that we could get from the mere, and, although we made every
possible search and inquiry yesterday, we know nothing of the fate either
of Rachel Howells or of Richard Brunton. The county police are at their
wit's end, and I have come up to you as a last resource.'

55   "You can imagine, Watson, with what eagerness I listened to this
extraordinary sequence of events, and endeavoured to piece them together,
and to devise some common thread upon which they might all hang. The
butler was gone. The maid was gone. The maid had loved the butler, but
had afterwards had cause to hate him. She was of Welsh blood, fiery and
passionate. She had been terribly excited immediately after his disappearance. She had flung into the lake a bag containing some curious contents.
These were all factors which had to be taken into consideration, and yet
none of them got quite to the heart of the matter. What was the starting-
point of this chain of events? There lay the end of this tangled line.

56   "'I must see that paper, Musgrave,' said I, 'which this butler of yours
thought it worth his while to consult, even at the risk of the loss of his place.'

57   "'It is rather an absurd business, this ritual of ours,' he answered.
'But it has at least the saving grace of antiquity to excuse it. I have a copy
of the questions and answers here if you care to run your eye over them.'

58   "He handed me the very paper which I have here, Watson, and this
is the strange catechism to which each Musgrave had to submit when he
came to man's estate. I will read you the questions and answers as they
stand.

59   "'Whose was it?'
60   "'His who is gone.'
61   "'Who shall have it?'
62   "'He who will come.'
63   "'Where was the sun?'
64   "'Over the oak.'
65   "'Where was the shadow?'
66   "'Under the elm.'
67   "'How was it stepped?'
68   "'North by ten and by ten, east by five and by five, south by two and
by two, west by one and by one, and so under.'
69   "'What shall we give for it?'
70   "'All that is ours.'
71   "'Why should we give it?'
72   "'For the sake of the trust.'

73   "'The original has no date, but is in the spelling of the middle of the
seventeenth century,' remarked Musgrave. 'I am afraid, however, that it
can be of little help to you in solving this mystery.'

74   "'At least,' said I, 'it gives us another mystery, and one which is even

more interesting than the first. It may be that the solution of the one may prove to be the solution of the other. You will excuse me, Musgrave, if I say that your butler appears to me to have been a very clever man, and to have had a clearer insight than ten generations of his masters.'

75   "'I hardly follow you,' said Musgrave. 'The paper seems to me to be of no practical importance.'

76   "'But to me it seems immensely practical, and I fancy that Brunton took the same view. He had probably seen it before that night on which you caught him.'

77   "'It is very possible. We took no pains to hide it.'

78   "'He simply wished, I should imagine, to refresh his memory upon that last occasion. He had, as I understand, some sort of map or chart which he was comparing with the manuscript, and which he thrust into his pocket when you appeared.'

79   "'That is true. But what could he have to do with this old family custom of ours, and what does this rigmarole mean?'

80   "'I don't think that we should have much difficulty in determining that,' said I; 'with your permission we will take the first train down to Sussex and go a little more deeply into the matter upon the spot.'

81   "The same afternoon saw us both at Hurlstone. Possibly you have seen pictures and read descriptions of the famous old building, so I will confine my account of it to saying that it is built in the shape of an L, the long arm being the more modern portion, and the shorter the ancient nucleus from which the other has developed. Over the low, heavy-lintelled door, in the centre of this old part, is chiselled the date, 1607, but experts are agreed that the beams and stonework are really much older than this. The enormously thick walls and tiny windows of this part had in the last century driven the family into building the new wing, and the old one was used now as a storehouse and a cellar, when it was used at all. A splendid park with fine old timber surrounds the house, and the lake, to which my client had referred, lay close to the avenue, about two hundred yards from the building.

82   "I was already firmly convinced, Watson, that there were not three separate mysteries here, but one only, and that if I could read the Musgrave Ritual aright I should hold in my hand the clue which would lead me to the truth concerning both the butler Brunton and the maid Howells. To that then I turned all my energies. Why should this servant be so anxious to master this old formula? Evidently because he saw something in it which had escaped all those generations of country squires, and from which he expected some personal advantage. What was it then, and how had it affected his fate?

83   "It was perfectly obvious to me, on reading the Ritual, that the mea-

surements must refer to some spot to which the rest of the document alluded, and that if we could find that spot we should be in a fair way towards
finding what the secret was which the old Musgraves had thought it necessary to embalm in so curious a fashion. There were two guides given
us to start with, an oak and an elm. As to the oak there could be no question at all. Right in front of the house, upon the left-hand side of the drive,
there stood a patriarch among oaks, one of the most magnificent trees that
I have ever seen.

84   "'That was there when your ritual was drawn up,' said I as we drove
past it.

85   "'It was there at the Norman Conquest in all probability,' he answered.
'It has a girth of twenty-three feet.'

86   "Here was one of my fixed points secured.

87   "'Have you any old elms?' I asked.

88   "'There used to be a very old one over yonder, but it was struck by
lightning ten years ago, and we cut down the stump.'

89   "'You can see where it used to be?'

90   "'Oh, yes.'

91   "'There are no other elms?'

92   "'No old ones, but plenty of beeches.'

93   "'I should like to see where it grew.'

94   "We had driven up in a dog-cart, and my client led me away at once,
without our entering the house, to the scar on the lawn where the elm had
stood. It was nearly midway between the oak and the house. My investigation seemed to be progressing.

95   "'I suppose it is impossible to find out how high the elm was?' I asked.

96   "'I can give you it at once. It was sixty-four feet.'

97   "'How do you come to know it?' I asked in surprise.

98   "'When my old tutor used to give me an exercise in trigonometry,
it always took the shape of measuring heights. When I was a lad I worked
out every tree and building in the estate.'

99   "This was an unexpected piece of luck. My data were coming more
quickly than I could have reasonably hoped.

100   "'Tell me,' I asked, 'did your butler ever ask you such a question?'

101   "Reginald Musgrave looked at me in astonishment. 'Now that you
call it to my mind,' he answered, 'Brunton *did* ask me about the height of
the tree some months ago in connection with some little argument with
the groom.'

102   "This was excellent news, Watson, for it showed me that I was on
the right road. I looked up at the sun. It was low in the heavens, and I calculated that in less than an hour it would lie just above the topmost branches
of the old oak. One condition mentioned in the Ritual would then be fulfilled.

And the shadow of the elm must mean the farther end of the shadow, otherwise the trunk would have been chosen as the guide. I had, then, to find where the far end of the shadow would fall when the sun was just clear of the oak."

103   "That must have been difficult, Holmes, when the elm was no longer there."

104   "Well, at least I knew that if Brunton could do it, I could also. Besides, there was no real difficulty. I went with Musgrave to his study and whittled myself this peg, to which I tied this long string with a knot at each yard. Then I took two lengths of a fishing-rod, which came to just six feet, and I went back with my client to where the elm had been. The sun was just grazing the top of the oak. I fastened the rod on end, marked out the direction of the shadow, and measured it. It was nine feet in length.

105   "Of course the calculation now was a simple one. If a rod of six feet threw a shadow of nine, a tree of sixty-four feet would throw one of ninety-six, and the line of the one would of course be the line of the other. I measured out the distance, which brought me almost to the wall of the house, and I thrust a peg into the spot. You can imagine my exultation, Watson, when within two inches of my peg I saw a conical depression in the ground. I knew that it was the mark made by Brunton in his measurements, and that I was still upon his trail.

106   "From this starting-point I proceeded to step, having first taken the cardinal points by my pocket-compass. Ten steps with each foot took me along parallel with the wall of the house, and again I marked my spot with a peg. Then I carefully paced off five to the east and two to the south. It brought me to the very threshold of the old door. Two steps to the west meant now that I was to go two paces down the stone-flagged passage, and this was the place indicated by the Ritual.

107   "Never have I felt such a cold chill of disappointment, Watson. For a moment it seemed to me that there must be some radical mistake in my calculations. The setting sun shone full upon the passage floor, and I could see that the old, foot-worn gray stones with which it was paved were firmly cemented together, and had certainly not been moved for many a long year. Brunton had not been at work here. I tapped upon the floor, but it sounded the same all over, and there was no sign of any crack or crevice. But, fortunately, Musgrave, who had begun to appreciate the meaning of my proceedings, and who was now as excited as myself, took out his manuscript to check my calculations.

108   "'And under,' he cried. 'You have omitted the "and under."'

109   "I had thought that it meant that we were to dig, but now, of course, I saw at once that I was wrong. 'There is a cellar under this then?' I cried.

110   "'Yes, and as old as the house. Down here, through this door.'

111 "We went down a winding stone stair, and my companion, striking a match, lit a large lantern which stood on a barrel in the corner. In an instant it was obvious that we had at last come upon the true place, and that we had not been the only people to visit the spot recently.

112 "It had been used for the storage of wood, but the billets, which had evidently been littered over the floor, were now piled at the sides, so as to leave a clear space in the middle. In this space lay a large and heavy flagstone with a rusted iron ring in the centre to which a thick shepherd's-check muffler was attached.

113 "'By Jove!' cried my client. 'That's Brunton's muffler. I have seen it on him and could swear to it. What has the villain been doing here?'

114 "At my suggestion a couple of the county police were summoned to be present, and I then endeavoured to raise the stone by pulling on the cravat. I could only move it slightly, and it was with the aid of one of the constables that I succeeded at last in carrying it to one side. A black hole yawned beneath into which we all peered, while Musgrave, kneeling at the side, pushed down the lantern.

115 "A small chamber about seven feet deep and four feet square lay open to us. At one side of this was a squat, brass-bound wooden box, the lid of which was hinged upward, with this curious old-fashioned key projecting from the lock. It was furred outside by a thick layer of dust, and damp and worms had eaten through the wood, so that a crop of livid fungi was growing on the inside of it. Several discs of metal, old coins apparently, such as I hold here, were scattered over the bottom of the box, but it contained nothing else.

116 "At the moment, however, we had no thought for the old chest, for our eyes were riveted upon that which crouched beside it. It was the figure of a man, clad in a suit of black, who squatted down upon his hams with his forehead sunk upon the edge of the box and his two arms thrown out on each side of it. The attitude had drawn all the stagnant blood to the face, and no man could have recognized that distorted liver-coloured countenance; but his height, his dress, and his hair were all sufficient to show my client, when we had drawn the body up, that it was indeed his missing butler. He had been dead some days, but there was no wound or bruise upon his person to show how he had met his dreadful end. When his body had been carried from the cellar we found ourselves still confronted with a problem which was almost as formidable as that with which we had started.

117 "I confess that so far, Watson, I had been disappointed in my investigation. I had reckoned upon solving the matter when once I had found the place referred to in the Ritual; but now I was there, and was apparently as far as ever from knowing what it was which the family had concealed with such elaborate precautions. It is true that I had thrown a light upon the fate of Brunton, but now I had to ascertain how that fate had come upon him, and what part had been played in the matter by the woman who had disappeared. I sat down upon a keg in the corner and thought the whole matter carefully over.

118 "You know my methods in such cases, Watson. I put myself in the man's place, and, having first gauged his intelligence, I try to imagine how I should myself have proceeded under the same circumstances. In this case the matter was simplified by Brunton's intelligence being quite first-rate, so that it was unnecessary to make any allowance for the personal equation, as the astronomers have dubbed it. He knew that something valuable was concealed. He had spotted the place. He found that the stone which covered it was just too heavy for a man to move unaided. What would he do next? He could not get help from outside, even if he had someone whom he could trust, without the unbarring of doors and considerable risk of detection. It was better, if he could, to have his helpmate inside the house. But whom could he ask? This girl had been devoted to him. A man always finds it hard to realize that he may have finally lost a woman's love, however badly he may have treated her. He would try by a few attentions to make his peace with the girl Howells, and then would engage her as his accomplice. Together they would come at night to the cellar, and their united force would suffice to raise the stone. So far I could follow their actions as if I had actually seen them.

119 "But for two of them, and one a woman, it must have been heavy work, the raising of that stone. A burly Sussex policeman and I had found it no light job. What would they do to assist them? Probably what I should have done myself. I rose and examined carefully the different billets of wood which were scattered round the floor. Almost at once I came upon what I expected. One piece, about three feet in length, had a very marked indentation at one end, while several were flattened at the sides as if they had been compressed by some considerable weight. Evidently, as they had dragged the stone up, they had thrust the chunks of wood into the chink until at last when the opening was large enough to crawl through, they would hold it open by a billet placed lengthwise, which might very well become indented at the lower end, since the whole weight of the stone would press it down on to the edge of this other slab. So far I was still on safe ground.

120 "And now how was I to proceed to reconstruct this midnight drama? Clearly, only one could fit into the hole, and that one was Brunton. The girl must have waited above. Brunton then unlocked the box, handed up the contents presumably—since they were not to be found—and then—and then what happened?

121 "What smouldering fire of vengeance had suddenly sprung into flame in this passionate Celtic woman's soul when she saw the man who had wronged her—wronged her, perhaps, far more than we suspected—in her power? Was it a chance that the wood had slipped and that the stone had shut Brunton into what had become his sepulchre? Had she only been guilty of silence as to his fate? Or had some sudden blow from her hand dashed the support away and sent the slab crashing down into its place? Be that as it might, I seemed to see that woman's figure still clutching at her treasure trove and flying wildly up the winding stair, with her ears ringing perhaps with the muffled screams from behind her and with the drumming of frenzied hands against the slab of stone which was choking her faithless lover's life out.

122   "Here was the secret of her blanched face, her shaken nerves, her peals of hysterical laughter on the next morning. But what had been in the box? What had she done with that? Of course, it must have been the old metal and pebbles which my client had dragged from the mere. She had thrown them in there at the first opportunity to remove the last trace of her crime.

123   "For twenty minutes I had sat motionless, thinking the matter out. Musgrave still stood with a very pale face, swinging his lantern and peering down into the hole.

124   "'These are coins of Charles the First,' said he, holding out the few which had been in the box; 'you see we were right in fixing our date for the Ritual.'

125   "'We may find something else of Charles the First,' I cried, as the probable meaning of the first two questions of the Ritual broke suddenly upon me. 'Let me see the contents of the bag which you fished from the mere.'

126   "We ascended to his study, and he laid the debris before me. I could understand his regarding it as of small importance when I looked at it, for the metal was almost black and the stones lustreless and dull. I rubbed one of them on my sleeve, however, and it glowed afterwards like a spark in the dark hollow of my hand. The metal work was in the form of a double ring, but it had been bent and twisted out of its original shape.

127   "'You must bear in mind,' said I, 'that the royal party made head in England even after the death of the king, and that when they at last fled they probably left many of their most precious possessions buried behind them, with the intention of returning for them in more peaceful times.'

128   "'My ancestor, Sir Ralph Musgrave, was a prominent cavalier and the right-hand man of Charles the Second in his wanderings,' said my friend.

129   "'Ah, indeed!' I answered. 'Well now, I think that really should give us the last link that we wanted. I must congratulate you on coming into the possession, though in rather a tragic manner, of a relic which is of great intrinsic value, but of even greater importance as a historical curiosity.'

130   "'What is it, then?' he gasped in astonishment.

131   "'It is nothing less than the ancient crown of the kings of England.'

132   "'The crown!'

133   "'Precisely. Consider what the Ritual says. How does it run? "Who [whose] was it?" "His who is gone." That was after the execution of Charles. Then, "Who shall have it?" "He who will come." That was Charles the Second, whose advent was already foreseen. There can, I think, be no doubt that this battered and shapeless diadem once encircled the brows of the royal Stuarts.'

134   "'And how came it in the pond?'

135   "'Ah, that is a question that will take some time to answer.' And with that I sketched out to him the whole long chain of surmise and of proof which I had constructed. The twilight had closed in and the moon was shining brightly in the sky before my narrative was finished.

136   "'And how was it then that Charles did not get his crown when he returned?' asked Musgrave, pushing back the relic into its linen bag.

137   "'Ah, there you lay your finger upon the one point which we shall probably never be able to clear up. It is likely that the Musgrave who held the secret died in the interval, and by some oversight left this guide to his descendant without explaining the meaning of it. From that day to this it has been handed down from father to son, until at last it came within reach of a man who tore its secret out of it and lost his life in the venture.'

138   "And that's the story of the Musgrave Ritual, Watson. They have the crown down at Hurlstone—though they had some legal bother and a considerable sum to pay before they were allowed to retain it. I am sure that if you mentioned my name they would be happy to show it to you. Of the woman nothing was ever heard, and the probability is that she got away out of England and carried herself and the memory of her crime to some land beyond the seas."

UNDERSTANDING THE SELECTION

1. Because it was written in the nineteenth century, this story contains references and language that may be unfamiliar to you. In paragraph 1, for example, Watson observes that Holmes shot the initials "V.R." in the wall of their room with his pistol. The V.R., called "patriotic" by Watson, is Holmes' tribute to the reigning Queen of Great Britain, Victoria Regina.

While you may have difficulty in understanding the references in this tale, coping with the unfamiliar language should not be so great a problem. Each of us has, in effect, three vocabularies: a relatively small one that we use for speaking, a larger one that we use when we write, and a reading vocabulary, which includes words that we never use either in speech or in writing but understand when we encounter them in context. Here are a couple of

passages that contain words which you probably never use in these particular senses when you speak or write yet understood when you read the
story. Take another look at them. What do you think the italicized words
mean as you see them in context? Check your tentative definitions in a
dictionary.

> Something of his birth-place seemed to cling to the man, and I never looked
> at his pale, *keen* face or the *poise* of his head without associating him with
> gray archways and mullioned windows and all the *venerable wreckage* of a
> *feudal keep* (paragraph 19).

> . . . if we could find that spot we should be in a *fair way* towards finding
> what the secret was which the old Musgraves had thought it necessary to
> *embalm* in so *curious* a *fashion* (paragraph 83).

2. Can you draw a version of the map leading to the old vault?

3. Arrange in the order of their age the following things: *(a)* the parchment
on which the Musgrave Ritual is written, *(b)* the old wing of Hurlstone, *(c)*
the oak, *(d)* the new wing of Hurlstone, *(e)* the crown. Why is it desirable
for you to know the relative ages of these things?

4. Arrange in the order of their occurrence the following events: *(a)*
Holmes' first acquaintance with Dr. Watson, *(b)* his first acquaintance with
Musgrave, *(c)* the case of *A Study in Scarlet,* *(d)* Brunton's rejection of
Rachel, *(e)* Brunton's solution of the meaning of the ritual. How important
is it for you to know the sequence of these events?

What do you think Holmes' attitude would be toward space travel,
supermarkets, tract houses, boxing, and patriotism? What support can you
find for your opinion?

Arrangement in Space and Time

The next six selections comprise a photograph, two poems, two short stories, and an example of nonfiction. Two of the selections are fantasy: they deal with impossible creatures, a Pobble and a monster. The nonfiction is full of places and dates and facts. Nevertheless, your approach to all six pieces requires the same steps. Visualize the arrangement in space; follow the arrangement in time.

Much of the difficulty some students experience in reading stems from the notion that you approach a poem in a way completely different from that in which you approach an essay or a story. We believe, however, that if you note arrangement carefully in whatever kind of material you are reading, you will have a useful device to help determine what the author says.

12 Ring-around-a-rosy

Eva and Louis Millette

Photograph by Eva and Louis Millette.

UNDERSTANDING THE SELECTION

1. Photographs are necessarily arranged in space. How does this one also suggest time?

2. Suppose the picture were arranged only in space, as most photographs are. What would be gained by such an alteration? What would be lost?

3. When and where do you think the picture was taken? Do you need to know these things? Would knowing them influence your reaction to the photograph?

4. Would this photograph be as effective if the children were playing hide-and-seek? London Bridge? Tag? Explain.

5. Why is the little girl in the upper right-hand corner not playing with the others?

6. Does the picture tell a story?

13   *North Beach Alba*

Gary Snyder

Waking half-drunk in a strange pad
making it out to the cool gray
      san francisco dawn—
white gulls over white houses,
      fog down the bay,
tamalpais a fresh green hill in the new sun,
driving across the bridge in a beat old car
      to work.

UNDERSTANDING THE SELECTION

1. North Beach is a section of San Francisco that was originally settled by Italian immigrants, most of whom were fishermen. Even today Italian is the "official" language of North Beach, and the neighborhood newspaper is published in it. North Beach was also the haunt of the hippies before they moved to the Haight-Ashbury. It is comparable in many ways to New York's Greenwich Village.

Tamalpais (tam-ul-pie-us) is a mountain north of San Francisco and across the bay from it.

2. *Alba* means "dawn" in Italian and comes from *albus*, which means "white" in Latin. Why do you think this change in meaning occurred?

3. In "The Stories behind Words" (Selection 4) you read something about words that derive from a common root. One root for "white" is *alba-* or *albu-*. Look up the following words in your dictionary and determine which ones have this root: *alb, albacore, albatross, albino, albumin.*

4. What words in this poem show arrangement in space?

5. What words show arrangement in time?
6. Compare the words describing the writer and his life with those describing nature. Are the words similar or different?

14 Over There—Darkness

William O'Farrell

1   Everything that Miss Fox owned was of the finest quality. She was a middle-aged woman with delicate features and soft, graying hair who lived alone in self-contained elegance. She dressed beautifully, spending a great deal of thought and money on her clothes. Her only companion was a dog named Vanessa, a pedigreed black poodle who, unlike her mistress, was a little overweight.

2   Miss Fox was as graceful and slim as she had ever been. She had a sizeable income from a trust fund and her own lovely furniture in a four-room apartment. The apartment was in a huge, well managed building which was located, incongruously, in a rowdy neighborhood of the Chelsea district in New York.

3   She was hardly aware of the neighborhood. She had signed a long term lease during the housing shortage, and the management had considerably insulated her from any outside crudeness from the day she had moved in. There was a supermarket on the ground floor of the building. There was also a rental library, a beauty salon and an excellent restaurant. Theoretically, she could have remained inside the apartment house indefinitely, and in effect that is what she did. But twice a day she walked the poodle along West Twenty-third Street. Six times a week, her favorite elevator boy took the dog for longer walks at night.

4   Once, in the spring of 1943, a captain in the Quartermaster Corps had asked Miss Fox to marry him. He had given her the ring of her selection, and two weeks later entered a hospital in Virginia. The captain had died there of a kidney complaint, and she had not seen him again before his death. Wartime travel was difficult and Miss Fox preferred to remember him as he had been, unwasted by illness. She had telegraphed flowers, relying on her florist to send something suitable. He was a member of the American Florists Association and had good taste.

5   The ring was exquisite, a diamond solitaire surrounded by emeralds, and Miss Fox still wore it. Her ring, her dog and Eddie McMahon—the last in a different way and on a lower level—were the only things capable of stirring in her more than casual interest. All three were beautiful and Eddie McMahon was very useful, too.

6   Eddie was the nighttime dog walker. He was young—not tall, but well proportioned—and he had long-lashed blue eyes and wavy brown hair that turned black under the dim lights of the elevator. He wore a neat navy blue uniform with a gold stripe down the trousers and had good manners. As men go, he was nice.

7   She paid him five dollars a week. That was above the going rate for dog walking, but she did not begrudge the extra money. The arrangement might have continued for as long as he kept his job and she stayed on in the apartment, if she had not made one small mistake.

8   That happened just before Christmas, and at the time she did not recognize it as a mistake. As in past years, she handed the doorman an envelope containing money to be divided among the other employees and himself, but in a separate envelope on which Eddie's name was written she put a twenty-dollar bill. It seemed to her that from that time on his attitude sharply changed.

9   He was as respectful as ever, but in early January, he asked for his five dollars before it was due. The same thing happened in March and, although she gave him the money on both occasions, Miss Fox was disturbed. She lived within her income and expected other people to be as provident as herself. Then, about the middle of April, he appeared unexpectedly at her apartment on his day off.

10   There was a knock on the door. She opened it and Eddie came in without being asked. Such a thing was unprecedented. It was necessary occasionally to admit a repair man or an employee of the gas company, but their visits were always preceded by a call on the house telephone and Miss Fox kept the door open while they were inside. Eddie closed the door. He also leaned against it, breathing heavily.

11   "Climbed the stairs," he explained. "Fourteen flights. Not supposed to hang around the building my day off."

12   It was the first time she had seen him out of uniform. His suit was clean, but badly cut. It changed his whole appearance. He seemed older and heavier—a stranger, and an unprepossessing one.

13   "Then what are you doing here?" she asked.

14   "Miss Fox,"—his breathing was a little easier—"I have to talk to you. Just for a minute, please?"

15   He was almost pleading, and Miss Fox felt distaste. She walked through the small foyer into the living room.

16   "Come in," she said. Then, hearing his footsteps following her too closely, on impulse she called, "Vanessa!"

17   The poodle lay in its basket in a corner. It looked at her and immediately went to sleep again. Miss Fox walked to the windows overlooking the avenue, and stood there with her back turned to the room.

18   "Yes, Eddie?" She had always been proud of her gentle voice. It was a relief to hear it now, in perfect control.

19   Eddie took two more forward steps. When next he spoke, she judged that he was standing beside the coffee table on which she had just placed a cup of tea. The tea was getting cold and that annoyed her. She liked it steaming hot.

20   "Miss Fox, will you let me take fifty dollars? I need it bad. I'll pay you back. It'll take three, four weeks, but today I have to send this money order . . ."

21   His voice dwindled into silence. Miss Fox stood quietly, unshocked by the preposterous request. She felt, rather, an odd sense of satisfaction, as though having known that something like this was bound to come, she was glad to have it in the clear at last.

22   "You say this money is important to you?"

23   "Yes, ma'am. Very important."

24   "Why come to me?" she asked.

25   "Because I've already tried everywhere else. My watch is in hock. The union gave me a loan, but that's all gone. You couldn't unscrew an advance from the management here with a Stillson wrench. And because"— he hesitated—"because you're kind."

26   She turned. "Sit down, Eddie." She waited until he was sitting stiffly on the couch. "Why is it necessary to send a money order in such a rush? To whom?"

27   "To my girl." He saw her lips tighten and added quickly, "She's in this sanitarium. The state pays half the expenses, see, and I promised to pay the other half. I done it so far, too, but now there's this extra—"

28   "You're engaged?"

29   "I guess you could call it that," he said.

30   But there had been a pause before he spoke and obviously the idea was new to him. New and strange. Miss Fox glanced at the ring on her left hand. Her own romance had not been conducted in so casual a manner. There had been the short, but proper courtship, the proposal, the betrothal kiss. Marriage would have been the next orderly step if tragedy had not intervened.

31   She sighed and shook her head. "I can't lend you fifty dollars, Eddie. Don't you earn a good salary?"

32   "Seventy a week," he said morosely, "but not take-home pay."

33   "No matter how little you actually take home, it's merely a question of planning, Eddie. I live on a fixed income and every cent is budgeted. Fifty dollars?" she shrugged. "I couldn't possibly spare an amount as large as that."

34   Eddie was no longer listening. His eyes were fixed on something behind her back. She looked over her shoulder and saw her white gloves and alligator bag.

35   They were lying on the living room table. Miss Fox grew hot, then cold—which was ridiculous, because there was no earthly way for Eddie to have learned that she had cashed a fairly large check only a few hours before.

36   "I'm sorry," she said firmly. "It's impossible."

37   His eyes had left the table. They were focused on her ring. For a moment he was silent. Then he rose.

38   "Yes, ma'am. My fault for asking. Excuse me, please." He went out and closed the door.

39   A vague unrest covered the remainder of her day. She couldn't read. The laundry was delivered at four o'clock, and after she had put it away there was nothing more to do until six. At two minutes before the hour she turned on the television.

40   The program was a good one, but this evening nothing could have held her interest. The memory of Eddie's bland presumption kept creeping back into her mind. She snapped off the television and poured a glass of sherry. It was infuriating to think that, because he was vulgarly good-looking and a few years younger than herself, the boy had actually believed that he could take her in.

41   She drank her sherry, went into the bedroom. When she came back, she had changed her dress and was wearing a light spring coat. A bright scarf was tied around her head. It was a fetching ensemble and made her look ten years younger, but she hardly glanced at the mirror as she picked up her bag, pulled on her gloves. She went downstairs to dinner a full three quarters of an hour earlier than she usually did. She had an excellent dinner, which she did not enjoy, and was back in her apartment before eight o'clock.

42   At a quarter to ten, when the dog whimpered to go out, Miss Fox attached a leash of shocking pink to the poodle's matching collar and once more pulled on her gloves, picked up her alligator bag.

43   The weather was freakishly warm for April, so warm that the doorman had propped open the front doors of the apartment house. It had rained earlier, and the street lamps were reflected from the still-wet pavement like little moons put there to guide her feet. There was an exhilarating quality about the night. It called for adventure and Miss Fox responded to it. She walked west instead of, as she usually did, in the direction of the well lighted avenue toward the east.

44   On her right, as she strolled along, were the amber windows of her own apartment house. These extended west for a hundred yards. The building ended there and was succeeded by a long row of brownstone fronts—

respectable once, but fallen now into almost sinister disrepair. The demarcating line was like a frontier between light and darkness, and she determined to go only as far as the end of the building and then turn back.

45   Reaching the predetermined spot, she pulled gently at Vanessa's leash. But the poodle had scented something beyond the dark frontier and strained forward. After a token struggle, Miss Fox let the dog have her way.

46   "Oh, very well," she said aloud, "but only as far as the next tree, dear."

47   They never reached the tree. Halfway there, a rough arm encircled Miss Fox's throat. She was bent over backwards and a hand was clasped across her mouth. Blood pounded in her ears as above her she saw, for just an instant, a man's shadowed face. She tried to scream and couldn't, and the last thing she heard was Vanessa's frantic yelp. Then the black world tilted up on end and slid away. When she regained consciousness, she was lying on the sidewalk, the doorman from the apartment house was kneeling beside her, the glove had been stripped from her left hand, and her diamond and emerald ring was gone.

48   So was her alligator bag containing a hundred and eighty dollars, but as she explained to Detective Sergeant Kirby in her apartment a half hour later, the money wasn't important. What she wanted, what she demanded in fact, was the immediate return of her ring.

49   Sergeant Kirby assured her that everything possible would be done. "We don't have a lot to work on, though. You say you wouldn't know the man if you saw him again."

50   Miss Fox thoughtfully fingered the bandage around her throat. The policeman was trying to be helpful, but he was going about it in such a plodding way. The fact that she had glimpsed her assailant only for an instant and in deep shadow meant very little. He had brutally manhandled her. She would be able to pick him out of any crowd.

51   "I did say that," she admitted, "but now I'm beginning to remember how he looked."

52   "Description?"

53   "He had dark hair and—let me think—he was strong, but not especially tall . . ."

54   "Clothes?"

55   "I didn't notice. His sleeve was of some coarse material."

56   "Did he say anything?"

57   "No. I heard nothing, but the dog. Now that I think of it," Miss Fox said, "it's odd that she didn't bark until after the attack."

58   "I've thought of that." Kirby got up from his chair. "Another point is that the mugger only tore the glove off your left hand. It's almost as though he knew about the ring."

59   Eddie! The abrupt revelation caused Miss Fox no surprise. It was only logical. That afternoon he had tried to borrow fifty dollars. Refused, he had stared at her ring—as now it came to her quite clearly—with unconcealed cupidity. There could be no doubt about it. Eddie was the thief.

60   But she said nothing. If, employing their own means, the police found and arrested him, that was their business. Her business was to get the ring back. That, she believed, she knew how to do.

61   Sergeant Kirby was leaving and she rose to say good-bye. "Thank you so much. I may expect to hear from you?"

62   "Probably very soon. If it isn't soon it may be never. That's how these things work." He rubbed Vanessa's ears. "You can thank your dog for spreading the alarm, Miss Fox."

63   "Yes. Good night, Sergeant."

64   She went to bed, but could not fall asleep. After a tortured half-hour, she had to take a capsule. It worked, but just as she was dozing off, she was aroused by the ringing of the telephone.

65   "Hope I didn't wake you," Sergeant Kirby said. "We've picked up a man who may have done the job. Can you come down?"

66   Miss Fox was half-doped and thoroughly exasperated. There was no reason why this unpleasant business of identification could not have been postponed until the morning. "At this hour? Come down where?"

67   He gave her the station house address. "It's only one o'clock."

68   "Does he have my ring?"

69   "Not on him. But if you make a positive I.D., I'll get it back."

70   "Very well. As soon as I can find a taxi, I'll be there."

71   The station house was only a few blocks away. The taxi rounded a corner and pulled up at the curb. Miss Fox saw a dreary looking building with a green light beside its wide front door. "Here you are, lady," the taxi driver said.

72   Then she was in a functionally furnished room and Sergeant Kirby was telling her that the suspect had been arrested in a Tenth Avenue bar. "Within a block of where it happened and only twenty minutes later. He was half-drunk and flashing a wad of bills he can't account for. Bad record, too. Looks like we wound this up in record time."

73   "If you have," Miss Fox said, "no one will be happier than I, Sergeant Kirby."

74   But she was disappointed. The man shoved through the doorway by a uniformed policeman was not Eddie. He was Eddie's height and had dark hair, but there was no resemblance otherwise. His hands were filthy. It was unthinkable that she had been touched by such grimy hands.

75   "No." She shook her head. "It is not he."

76   "You're sure?" Kirby sounded disappointed.

77   "Quite sure," she said, avoiding the man's eyes.

78   His eyes were insolent. He wore a flashy suit, black shirt and yellow tie, but Miss Fox paid no attention to his clothes. She was too agitated by his dirty hands and bullying stare.

79   "Well, thanks for coming," Kirby said. "Be seeing you."

80   Miss Fox went home and slept until ten the following morning. Eddie's shift on the elevator started at noon. She took the dog out at eleven and told the doorman that she wanted to see Eddie as soon as he came in. He knocked on her door a few minutes before twelve.

81   She opened it. "Come in."

82   "Say, Miss Fox, I heard about what happened!"

83   "Come in, Eddie, and sit down," she said.

84   His expression, as he obeyed, was one of puzzled innocence. It was a pity, she thought, that so handsome a face should conceal a mind so devious. She stood erectly, steeling herself to a distasteful task.

85   "So you've heard."

86   "Yes, ma'am. I always said this neighborhood ain't safe."

87   "You know I was robbed of some money and my ring?"

88   "That's what they say."

89   "Very well. Now listen carefully. I want to be quite sure you understand. I don't care about the money, but I want my ring. Its description has been circulated. Trying to sell it would be dangerous."

90   "That's right. It's plenty hot."

91   "So it might as well be returned to me. Particularly if I promise to forget the hundred and eighty dollars that I've lost, and say no more about the matter. Don't you agree?"

92   Eddie appeared to be thinking deeply. "Well, I don't know. This guy that mugged you—there is a couple of things he could do. He could break the ring up, get rid of the stones that way. Or he could wait until the heat's off and sell it somewheres out of town."

93   "He would still be taking a risk. I have a better idea. I'm prepared to pay five hundred dollars for its return. Five hundred dollars, Eddie, and no questions asked."

94   He got up slowly. "I sure hope you get it back. Excuse me—I got to go to work." He walked toward the door, but stopped before he reached the foyer. "Look, Miss Fox, don't count too much on that plan of yours. What would you do—advertise? Chances are the guy would never see your ad, and if he did he'd be dumb to stick his neck out."

95   "You don't think I'll get my ring back?" There was an edge to Miss Fox's normally soft voice.

96   "No, ma'am. Not that way, I don't."

97   "You may go, Eddie," Miss Fox said.

98   The doorman announced Sergeant Kirby an hour later. He entered briskly and came directly to business.

99   "You have an arrangement with an elevator boy named McMahon to walk your dog. Yesterday was his day off, but he was seen leaving your apartment about two in the afternoon. Is that correct?"

100   Miss Fox walked to the window and stood with her back turned, as she had done the day before. "Why do you ask?"

101   "Routine. McMahon has a good record and he's a steady worker. On the other hand, he needs money. Why did he come here?"

102   She did not move. Her voice was cool and impersonal as she replied. "You seem to have ferreted out almost everything. You might as well know the rest. He wanted me to lend him fifty dollars."

103   "Did you do it?"

104   "Of course not."

105   There was a silence. Then Kirby asked quietly, "Was it McMahon?"

106   She turned and looked directly into the detective's eyes. "I had hoped it wouldn't come to this. I gave him his chance. I even offered him money to return the ring. He refused."

107   "You positively identify him?"

108   Unconsciously, she had already passed her own personal line of demarcation between light and darkness. "Yes, it was Eddie," Miss Fox said.

109   She did not look at Eddie during the trial. She kept her eyes averted as she testified. It was a short trial. He had no alibi. They brought him in and tried him, and sent him to prison for three years.

110   Or maybe it was for one year with the other two suspended. Miss Fox wasn't sure. She had her own problems now that Eddie was no longer on the elevator. She had to find someone else to walk Vanessa, and the other boys had suddenly become very busy. They seemed curiously indifferent as to whether or not they made extra money every week.

111   Eventually she was forced to hire a professional. He was unsatisfactory. The third night he called, Miss Fox smelled liquor on his breath. From then on she took the dog out every night herself.

112   At first she shunned the sidewalk west of the apartment house. She never even approached it until, in the heat of summer, the streets became more crowded and consequently safe. Then she found that her dread of the dark frontier had lessened greatly. Fear was now no more than a rather pleasurable titillation of her senses. She sometimes permitted Vanessa to pull her right up to the line, and she would stand within inches of it peering into unexplored darkness.

113 Summer passed and was succeeded by the fall, and in all that time she had no news of her ring. Sergeant Kirby told her that Eddie still insisted he was innocent, but of course Eddie would do that. She telephoned Kirby several times and he was always courteous, until one day in November two policemen came to her apartment and brusquely told her that the sergeant wanted to see her at the station house.

114 She was indignant. "Why doesn't he come here?"

115 "Couldn't tell you, lady. Just said he wanted to talk to you."

116 Miss Fox graciously agreed to go.

117 Kirby met her in the bare room she had been in once before. He looked grim. "We've found your ring," he said.

118 She displayed none of the emotion she was feeling. "I knew that sooner or later Eddie would tell the truth."

119 "McMahon never had it." The grimness in the detective's face was reflected in his voice. "Remember the man you didn't identify? We got him on another charge and the ring was in his room. He confessed."

120 Something was wrong. Something was so drastically wrong that Miss Fox couldn't absorb it immediately. "But I saw him! I saw Eddie!"

121 "Did you?"

122 "Well, I thought I did. I was so sure!"

123 "You certainly succeeded in giving that impression. As a result, I look like a fool and an innocent man's in jail."

124 Miss Fox said angrily, "I may have made a mistake, but it was an honest one. I believe it's the duty of the police to check these things. Could it have been that you were so anxious to arrest someone that you didn't care whether or not he was guilty?"

125 Kirby shrugged, looking past her at a blank space on the wall.

126 "If you have nothing further to say, give me my ring."

127 He wouldn't do it. He showed it to her, and there was no question about it being hers, and he said it would be returned in due time. Meanwhile, it was evidence and must be held. He wouldn't even tell her when Eddie would be released.

128 "I don't know," he said. "Why should you care?"

129 Miss Fox did care. She foresaw a period of strain when and if Eddie returned to his old job, and she wanted to avoid that by finding another apartment first. She disliked friction of any kind, and so she bought a box of expensive cigars and sent them to Sergeant Kirby. After that she was able to dismiss the detective from her mind.

130 During the weeks that followed she inspected a number of apartments, but none of them met her fastidious standards. She flinched from the ordeal of moving anyway, and at last was forced to the realization that she was better off where she was. Having accepted this, she made a generous gesture. She spoke personally to the manager of the apartment house and was surprised to learn that her request had been anticipated. He had already written Eddie, offering to take him back.

131   "But it's thoughtful of you, Miss Fox," he said. "I must say I'm relieved."

132   She left his office satisfied he would tell Eddie what she'd done. Eddie would be grateful. What might have been a tense situation had been eased.

133   Eddie came back to work the week before Christmas. One morning she buckled on Vanessa's leash and pushed the elevator bell. With a minimum of delay the elevator door slid open, and there he was. Everything was as it had been, including his respectful smile.

134   "Good morning, Miss Fox."

135   "Eddie!" she said. "I can't tell you how happy I am."

136   He took her down to the lobby. By the time she had walked the dog, riding up in the elevator again, she had recovered from her surprise. "Hold the car a moment," she said, stepping out on the fourteenth floor. "There's something I must say to you."

137   He held the door open, waiting. She turned in the softly lighted corridor to study him. He had changed. His smile was fixed and meaningless, and there was a glassy quality in his eyes.

138   Never mind. It was in her power to change that, and she would. "I want you to know that it wasn't easy for me to testify against you, Eddie. I only told the court what I believed to be the truth."

139   "Sure, Miss Fox."

140   "It was a terrible experience for both of us. I think the best thing we can do is to forget it and start afresh."

141   "Yes, ma'am."

142   "Good," she said. "Vanessa will be waiting when you finish work tonight." She started down the corridor.

143   He stopped her. "Miss Fox, I won't be walking your dog any more."

144   She turned, incredulous and a little piqued. "You want more money, I suppose?"

145   "It isn't that," he said. "It's just that I can get along now on my pay. I don't have any extra expenses now."

146   "How about your fiancee?"

147   "She died," he said.

148   The elevator door slid shut. Miss Fox was alone.

149   She let herself into the apartment, sat down and thought about it rationally. Everything had worked out for the best. The girl had been ill. Eddie would have found her an intolerable burden. He would get over her death. She had gone through the same natural sequence of suffering and recuperation when the captain died. She told herself these things, but still remained unsatisfied, sensing that somewhere there was something she had overlooked. At two o'clock she put on her coat again, walked to an elevator at the far end of the building and went down to her bank.

150   When she returned, she told the doorman that she wanted to see Eddie during his coffee break. He came to her apartment at four o'clock. Miss Fox did not invite him to come in.

151   "I've been thinking about you," she said. "I want to help you—well, to rehabilitate yourself. As I once told you, I was prepared to pay five hundred dollars for my ring. I had the money set aside, and I can think of no better use for it than to give it to you." She handed him an envelope. "Shall we call it a Christmas present, Eddie? Five one-hundred dollar bills."

152   There was a long moment while he stood holding the white envelope, looking at the floor. Then he put the envelope in his pocket. "Thank you very much, Miss Fox," he said.

153   Miss Fox was greatly relieved as she shut the door. It was a pity that Eddie had not accepted the five hundred dollars when she'd offered it to him eight months before. It would have been so simple. He could have taken the money and returned her ring—

154   But Eddie had not stolen the ring, she suddenly remembered. She shrugged. Anyway, it was finished now. She drank a cup of steaming tea and had a nice, long nap.

155   When she went out with the dog at ten that night, Eddie had already gone off duty. It was snowing, and she had always enjoyed the first snowfall of the season. Vanessa pulled to the right and Miss Fox humored her by walking west, mildly exhilarated by the drifting flakes.

156   She came to the end of the lighted apartment house and stood, as she had often stood before, on the very edge of darkness. A few yards ahead was the spot where the man had thrown her down. She smiled nervously, telling herself that she was glad now it had happened. It was rather thrilling to look back from her present security to a danger safely passed.

157   "Let's go home, dear," she told Vanessa, and turned back.

158   A man blocked her way. He had come up behind her silently. Miss Fox gasped. Then her shrill scream echoed down the street.

159   He raised his arm. His open palm found and covered her face. He pushed. Miss Fox staggered backward, tripped and fell. She had time to scream once more before he stopped the noise at its source. The last thing she heard was the far-off yelping of her dog.

160   This time when the doorman found her, he was too late. She lay on her back, snowflakes falling in her open eyes. Between her rapidly stiffening fingers were five one-hundred dollar bills.

1. "The Musgrave Ritual," an early detective story, hinged on the ability of Sherlock Holmes to solve a mystery. Today the writers of detective stories pay as close attention to the personalities of their characters as to the exploits of their detectives. Such a writer is William O'Farrell.

2. Assume that you are a newspaperman reporting the murder of Miss Fox. *(a)* List in chronological order all the known events of the case that you might use in your story. *(b)* Prepare a map to accompany the story, showing the apartment building, the position of the doorman, the site where the body was found, and any other details that will illustrate the murder scene for your readers.

3. Draw a picture or find one in a newspaper that shows what you think the man who stole Miss Fox's ring looks like. Draw a picture or find one that shows what Eddie looks like.

4. Imagine that you are the attorney *defending* Eddie for the murder of Miss Fox. What arguments would you present to the jury?

5. What would Miss Fox's attitude be toward the following? How do you know?

      a. world events
      b. romantic poetry
      c. dog licenses
      d. children
      e. your birthday

15 *Bigfoot*

Ivan T. Sanderson

1   In August of 1958—on the morning of the 27th to be precise—a very sane and sober citizen by the name of Mr. Jerald Crew, of Salyer township, Humboldt County, northwest California, an active member of the Baptist Church, a teetotaler, and a man with a reputation in his community that can only be described as heroic in face of certain almost unique personal tragedy, went to his work with heavy-duty equipment at the head of this new lumber access road being pushed into uninhabited and only roughly surveyed territory near the borders of Humboldt and Del Norte Counties. This huge block of territory is crossed kitty-corner from the south at Willow Creek to the northeast by a winding blacktop road, and from east to west by only four other roads of lower grade. Logging trails and some "jeep-roads" now finger into it from these roads and from the main arteries that enclose it to north, west, south, and east, but these are of very limited extent and are hardly used at all. "Jerry" Crew's crawler-tractor had been left overnight at the head of the new road, about 20 miles north of its digression from the narrow blacktop that runs north through the Hoopa [as it is on maps] Amerindian Reservation from Willow Creek to a place with the delightful name of Happy Camp up near the Oregon border.

2   Jerry was an older member of a crew bulldozing this new road into virtually unexplored territory for one Mr. Ray Wallace, subcontractor to Messrs. Block and Company who had, in turn, contracted with the National Parks Service to carry out the work. He is a local man. His fellow workers were for the most part also local men and included a nephew, James Crew, a very level-headed young chap, others whom I shall mention by name in a minute, and two experienced loggers of Hǔppa Indian origin. The crew had considerable heavy equipment at the scene of operations and had started work in late May as soon as what little snow there is in this area had melted and the much more deadly mud had firmed up. The road had been under construction for two seasons already. The country is mountainous; though this is the understatement of the year, being to most intents and everywhere almost vertical so that you can only go up on all fours or down on your bottom. Unless you make an exaggerated and exhausting climb you cannot see more than about four square miles of the country because you are always on the side of something going either straight up or almost straight down and unless a tree has fallen or been cut out, you can't see *anything* because bare rock is confined to the uppermost summits of the peaks and ridges. The road crawls laboriously up the face of the western wall that encloses a stream known as Bluff Creek. It is still unsurfaced and when I visited it in 1959 was ankle-deep in ultrafine dust that surpasses anything the deserts of Arizona can produce at their damnedest. All along this mountainous trail there are the stumps of vast trees cut and hauled out, and great slides of friable shales, gray, brown, blue, or even green that have been sliced out of the sheer valley side. The great dozers and crawlers clank and roar in the hot summer sunlight as they gnaw their relentless way into this timeless land. The great trees seem to recoil a little from their mechanical jangling and screeching, but day by day these bright yellow and red monsters munch away ever deeper into one of the last of America's real wildernesses.

3   Those employed on this work lived during the work-week in camp near this road-head. They had trailers or tents or prefabricated houses and some of them had their families with them and stayed there all week. Others with families resident in nearby communities normally went home on Friday night and returned on the following Monday morning. The younger

fellows usually did likewise, for the drive to Willow Creek took only about 2 hours for those who knew the road. Jerry Crew's practice was to return to his family over the week end, leaving his màchine parked at the scene of current operations. He had been on this job for 3 months that year before the eventful morning which blew up the storm that literally rocked Humboldt County, California and made the pages of the world press but which then sort of folded in upon itself and was heard of no more for a year.

4   What Jerry Crew discovered when he went to start up his "cat" was that somebody had inspected it rather thoroughly during the previous night, as could be plainly seen by a series of footprints that formed a track to, all around, and then away from the machine. Such tracks would not have aroused his curiosity under normal circumstances because there were three dozen men at the road-head and the newly scraped roadbed was covered with soft mud areas alternating with patches of loose shale. What did startle him was that these footprints were of a shoeless or naked foot of distinctly human shape and proportions but by actual measurement just 17 inches long!

5   Of these, Jerry Crew took an extremely dim view. He had heard tell of similar tracks having been seen by another road gang working 8 miles north of a place called Korbel on the Mad River earlier that year and his nephew, Jim Crew, had also mentioned having come across something similar in this area. Being a pragmatic family man he felt, he told me, some considerable annoyance that some "outsider" should try to pull such a silly stunt on him. He at first stressed an outsider because, although his fellow workers liked a harmless joke as much as any man, he knew they were far too tired to go clomping around in the dark after the sort of working day they put in on that job, making silly footprints around the equipment. Then, he tells me, he got to thinking about this outsider and wondered just how he had got there without passing the camps farther down the road and being spotted, and how he had gotten out again, or where he had gone over these precipitous mountains clothed in tangled undergrowth. He followed the tracks up. And that is where he got his second shock.

6   Going backward he found that they came almost straight down an incline of about 75 degrees on to the road ahead of the parked "cat," then proceeded down the road on one side, circled the machine, and then went on down the road toward the camp. Before getting there, however, they cut across the road and went straight down an even steeper incline and continued into the forest with measured stride varying only when an obstacle had to be stepped over or the bank was so steep purchase could be obtained by digging in the heels. The stride was enormous and proved on measurement to be from 46 to 60 inches and to average about 50 inches or almost twice that of his own. Jerald Crew was not only mystified; he was

considerably peeved. He went to fetch some of his colleagues. Then he received his third shock that morning.

7   The majority of them, stout fellows and good friends that they were, refused to even go and look at this preposterous phenomenon that he told them he had found and he had a hard time persuading any of them that even the tracks were there. Eventually, some of the men, who had in any case to go that way to their work, agreed to go along with him and take a look. Then they got their shocks and, Jerry told me, some of them "looked at me real queer." But there were others who reacted differently, and it then transpired that all of them had either seen something similar there-abouts or elsewhere, or had heard of them from friends and acquaintances whom they regarded as totally reliable. The only Amerinds present said nothing at that time. Then they all went back to work.

8   Nothing further happened for almost a month, then once again these monstrous Bigfeet appeared again overnight around the equipment and farther down the road toward the valley, notably around a spring. About that time, Mr. Ray Wallace, the contractor, returned from a business trip. He had heard rumors on his way in that either his men were pulling some kind of stunt up in the hills or that some "outsider" was pulling one on them. He paid little attention to these reports but he was, he told me, somewhat apprehensive because the job was a tough one, skilled and reliable work-ers were not plentiful, and the location was not conducive to the staying power of anyone. When he reached the camp and heard the details of the Bigfeet he was more than just skeptical. He was downright angry. More-over, all he encountered was more talk which he at that time suspected was some sort of prank but just possibly one prompted by more than mere high spirits or boredom.

9   The matter was until then and for a further 3 weeks a purely local affair known only to the men working on the road, and their immediate families for they did not care to speak about it to casual acquaintances or even friends. Then in the middle of September a Mrs. Jess Bemis, wife of one of the men working on the road and one of the skeptics among the crew, wrote a letter to the leading local newspaper, the *Humboldt Times* of Eureka, which said in part "A rumor started among the men, at once, of the existence of a Wild Man. We regarded it as a joke. It was only yes-terday that my husband became convinced that the existence of such a person (?) is a fact. Have you heard of this wild man?" Mr. Andrew Gen-zoli of that paper told me that he regarded this letter with a thoroughly jaun-diced eye but that the longer he saw it about his desk the brighter grew the clear blue light of his built-in news-sense, until he could restrain him-self no longer and ran the letter in a daily column that he writes.

10   There was little response where he had expected a near storm of

derision; instead a trickle of tentatively confirmatory correspondence began to come in from the Willow Creek area. This was continuing sub rosa when, on October 2, the maker of the tracks appeared again on his apparently rather regular round leaving tracks for 3 nights in succession and then vanishing again for about 5 days. This time Jerry Crew had prepared for his advent with a supply of plaster of Paris and made a series of casts of both right and left feet early one morning. Two days later he took a couple of days off to drive to Eureka on personal business and carried the casts along with him to show to a friend. While there somebody mentioned to Andrew Genzoli that a man was in town who had made casts of the prints and he was persuaded to go and fetch Jerry. Andrew Genzoli is an old newshand but of the new school; he can sense a good story as fast as any man but he is properly averse to too good a story. When he met Jerry Crew and saw his trophies he realized he had some real live news, not just a "story," on his hands, and he ran a front-pager on it with photographs the next day. Then the balloon went up.

11   The wire services picked it up and almost every paper in the country printed it while cables of inquiry flooded in from abroad. The first I heard of it was a cable from a friend in London: he seemed to be slightly hysterical. I get a lot of esoteric cables during the year about sea monsters, two-headed calves, reincarnated Indian girls, and so forth, the majority of which I am constrained to do something about because the world is, after all, a large place and we don't know much about a lot of it as yet, but this one I frankly refused to accept mostly because I rather naturally assumed that the location as given (California) must be a complete error or a misquote. I wracked my brains for any place name in Eurasia or Africa that might have nine letters, begin with "K" and end in "ia." The best we could come up with was Corinthia but this was even more unlikely. Then somebody suggested Carpathia, the country of Dracula and other humanoid unpleasantnesses, and we actually spent 6 dollars on a follow-up. There are few people interested enough in such abstruse matters as to spend that sum in pursuit of truth but I fancy there were many on the morning of October 6, 1958 who doubted what they read in their morning papers just as fervently as I did this cable.

12   The point I want to make is that this whole bit did sound quite absurd even to us, who became immune to such shocks years ago. It is all very well for abominable creatures to be pounding over snow-covered passes in Nepal and Tibet; after all giant pandas and yaks, and an antelope with a nose like Jimmy Durante, and other unlikely things come from thereabouts; and it is even conceivable that there might be little hairy men in the vast forests of Mozambique in view of the almost equally unlikely more or less hairless pygmies of the eastern Congo which are there for all tourists to see, but a wild man with a 17-inch foot and a 50-inch stride tromping around California was then a little too much to ask even us to stomach, especially as we had not yet got the news-stories. The amazing thing in this case was that the world press took it seriously enough even to carry it as a news-item. *13* Not so the rest of humanity. One and all, apart from a few ardent mystics and professional crackpots, and including even the citizens of Humboldt County itself rose up in one concerted howl of righteous indignation. Everybody connected with the business, and notably poor Mr. Genzoli, was immediately almost smothered in brickbats. In the meantime, however, a number of other things had happened. Most notable among these was the reappearance of "Bigfoot" as he was called one night before Ray Wallace returned to his operations. Now it so happened that a brother of the contractor, Wilbur Wallace, was working on this job and he, besides seeing the foot-tracks many times, witnessed three other annoying and to him most startling occurrences, which he had reported to his brother. I will repeat these roughly in his own words which appeared to me not only straightforward but most convincing.

14 First, it was reported to him by one of his men that a nearly full 55-gallon drum of diesel fuel which had been left standing beside the road was missing and that Bigfoot tracks led down the road from a steep bank to this spot where it had stood, then crossed the road, continued on down the hill and finally went over the lower bank and away into the bush. Wilbur Wallace went to inspect and found the tracks exactly as the men had stated. He also found the oil drum at the bottom of a steep bank about 175 feet from the road. It had rolled down this bank and had apparently been thrown from the top. What is more, it had been lifted from its original resting place and apparently carried to this point, for there were no marks in the soft mud of its having been either rolled or dragged all that distance. Second, a length of 18-inch galvanized steel culvert disappeared from a dump overnight and was found at the bottom of another bank some distance away. Third, he reported a wheel with tire for a "carry-all" earth-mover, weighing over 700 pounds, had likewise been in part lifted and in part rolled a quarter of a mile down the road and hurled into a deep ravine. Ray Wallace, however, still remained skeptical even after hearing this from his own brother. However, on his first morning at the location he stopped for a drink at a spring on the way down the hill and stepped right into a mass of the big prints in the soft mud around the outflow. Then, I gather from him, though he is a man with a wonderfully good humor, he got "good and mad." There was for him no longer any question about the existence of these monstrous human-like tracks but there remained the question as to who was perpetrating them, and why. Ray Wallace is a hard-boiled and pragmatic man and he was already experiencing trouble keeping men on the job. Hand-picked as they were not a few had just *had* to leave for one apparently good reason or another. Only later did he learn that almost all of them did so not because they were scared by the Bigfoot, but either because their wives were or because of the ribbing they had to take when they went back to civilization, even for the evening to nearby Willow Creek.

15   Ray Wallace said he at first thought somebody was deliberately trying to wreck his contract and he was not alone. However, the local representative of the *Humboldt Times*, Mrs. Elizabeth (Betty) Allen, set about to investigate the possibility on her own, and discovered beyond a doubt that neither good nor bad publicity, nor any kind of "scare" actually made any difference to Mr. Wallace's contract. First he was a subcontractor; second he was more than up to schedule; third there was no time set on the job; and fourth, it was basically contracted by Messrs. Block and Company with the Forest Service on a performance, not a time, basis. Ray Wallace got so angry he brought in a man named Ray Kerr, who had read of the matter in the press and asked for a job in order to be able to spend his spare time trying to track the culprit. Kerr brought with him a friend by the name of Bob Breazele, who had hunted professionally in Mexico, owned four good dogs, and a British-made gun of enormous caliber which considerably impressed the locals. Kerr, an experienced equipment operator, did a full daily job: Breazele did not take a job but hunted.

16   Tracks were seen and followed by them. Then one night in late October, these two were driving down the new road after dark and state that they came upon a gigantic humanoid or human-shaped creature, covered with 6-inch brown fur, squatting by the road. They said it sprang up in their headlights and crossed the road in two strides to vanish into the undergrowth. They went after it with a flashlight but the underbrush was too thick to see anything. They measured the road and found it to be exactly 20 feet wide from the place where the creature had squatted to the little ditch where it had landed after those two strides. Spurred by this encounter they redoubled their hunting forays but their dogs disappeared a few days later when they were following Bigfoot's tracks some distance from the roadhead. They were never seen again though a story was told—but later denied by its teller—that their skins and bones were found spattered about some trees. Though this story was denied, there is as much reason to believe that this was done to obviate ridicule as to clear a conscience.

UNDERSTANDING THE SELECTION

1. We have all read newspaper accounts of mysterious phenomena: ghosts, sea monsters, abominable snowmen. Usually we dismiss these stories as either the delusions of crackpots or sensational attempts by pub-

lishers to increase newspaper circulation. Anyway, ghosts seem to materi-
alize mostly in Lancashire, not Louisiana; unidentified flying objects seem
to be seen by couples returning from parties, not by sober meteorologists.
The Abominable Snowman was glimpsed only in the snowy wastes of Nepal
—or was until Ivan Sanderson, a reputable and well-known scientist, not a
newspaperman, gave credence to reports of the existence of Bigfoot in a
section of our most populous state. Then, early in 1968, two men returned
from the northern California wilderness with motion pictures of Bigfoot
(whom they called "The Adorable Snowwoman"). The controversy flared
anew, with scientists trying to evaluate the authenticity of the photographs.
Still photos of Bigfoot were printed—along with both sides of the argument—in *Argosy* magazine, February 1968, and *National Wildlife* magazine,
April - May 1968.

We have included this selection because we believe that a reader must
weigh and evaluate the evidence presented by a writer, however unlikely
the report may seem on first reading.

2. When and where did the events in this selection occur?

3. Is this selection arranged according to time or space or both?

4. What three shocks did Jerry Crew get?

5. What three bits of evidence did Wilbur Wallace find?

6. How much time elapsed between Jerry Crew's shocks and the disappearance of the dogs?

7. Exactly what evidence is presented to prove the existence of Bigfoot?
Do you believe Bigfoot exists? What evidence can you present to sustain
your belief?

8. Can you believe what people say? Why or why not? Can you believe
what newspapers print? Why or why not? Can you believe what scientists
like Sanderson put in books? Why or why not?

16   The Pobble Who Has No Toes

Edward Lear

The Pobble who has no toes
  Had once as many as we;
When they said, "Some day you may lose them all;"
  He replied, "Fish fiddle de-dee!"
And His Aunt Jobiska make him drink   5
Lavender-water tinged with pink;
For she said, "The World in general knows
There's nothing so good for a Pobble's toes!"

The Pobble who has no toes
  Swam across the Bristol Channel: *10*
But before he set out he wrapped his nose
  In a piece of scarlet flannel.
For his Aunt Jobiska said, "No harm
Can come to his toes if his nose is warm;
And it's perfectly known that a Pobble's toes   *15*
Are safe—provided he minds his nose."

The Pobble swam fast and well,
  And when boats or ships came near him,
He tinkledy-binkledy-winkled a bell
  So that all the world could hear him.   *20*
And all the Sailors and Admirals cried,
When they saw him nearing the further side,—
"He has gone to fish, for his Aunt Jobiska's
Runcible Cat with crimson whiskers!"

But before he touched the shore,—   *25*
  The shore of the Bristol Channel,
A sea-green Porpoise carried away
  His wrapper of scarlet flannel.
And when he came to observe his feet,
Formerly garnished with toes so neat,   *30*
His face at once became forlorn
On perceiving that all his toes were gone!

And nobody ever knew,
  From that dark day to the present,
Whoso had taken the Pobble's toes,   *35*
  In a manner so far from pleasant.
Whether the shrimps or crawfish gray,
Or crafty Mermaids stole them away,
Nobody knew; and nobody knows
How the Pobble was robbed of his twice five toes!   *40*

The Pobble who has no toes
  Was placed in a friendly Bark,
And they rowed him back, and carried him up
  To his Aunt Jobiska's Park.
And she made him a feast, at his earnest wish,   *45*
Of eggs and buttercups fried with fish;
And she said, "It's a fact the whole world knows,
That Pobbles are happier without their toes."

1. "The Pobble Who Has No Toes" is nonsense. It has a Pobble, whatever that is. And it has a runcible cat, whatever that is. And it has Aunt Jobiska, but everyone knows what an Aunt Jobiska is, although your Aunt Jobiska may be named Mary or Ellen or Sarah. Nevertheless, nonsense says something just as effectively as sense does. In this case, we have an epic tale of a hero who sets out to perform a feat of great difficulty and danger. He is a hero like Sir Lancelot, Davy Crockett, Frodo, and John Glenn.
2. How old is the Pobble? Is he muscular or flabby? Does he like animals? Do people like him? Does he eat nutritious food?
3. Draw a picture of the Pobble.
4. Why did the Pobble try to swim the Bristol Channel? Where is the Bristol Channel?
5. Who took the Pobble's toes? Did he know when they were taken? Was the loss of his toes painful?
6. Does the word *runcible* (line 24) refer to the cat's shape? Color? Size? Personality? Habits? Do all runcible cats have crimson whiskers?
7. Draw a picture of a runcible cat.

17 The Fog Horn

Ray Bradbury

1   Out there in the cold water, far from land, we waited every night for the coming of the fog, and it came, and we oiled the brass machinery and lit the fog light up in the stone tower. Feeling like two birds in the gray sky, McDunn and I sent the light touching out, red, then white, then red again, to eye the lonely ships. And if they did not see our light, then there was always our Voice, the great deep cry of our Fog Horn shuddering through the rags of mist to startle the gulls away like decks of scattered cards and make the waves turn high and foam.

2   "It's a lonely life, but you're used to it now, aren't you?" asked McDunn.

3   "Yes," I said. "You're a good talker, thank the Lord."

4   "Well, it's your turn on land tomorrow," he said, smiling, "to dance the ladies and drink gin."

5   "What do you think, McDunn, when I leave you out here alone?"

6   "On the mysteries of the sea." McDunn lit his pipe. It was a quarter past seven of a cold November evening, the heat on, the light switch-

ing its tail in two hundred directions, the Fog Horn bumbling in the high throat of the tower. There wasn't a town for a hundred miles down the coast, just a road which came lonely through dead country to the sea, with few cars on it, a stretch of two miles of cold water out to our rock, and rare few ships.

7   "The mysteries of the sea," said McDunn thoughtfully. "You know, the ocean's the biggest damned snowflake ever? It rolls and swells a thousand shapes and colors, no two alike. Strange. One night, years ago, I was here alone, when all of the fish of the sea surfaced out there. Something made them swim in and lie in the bay, sort of trembling and staring up at the tower light going red, white, red, white across them so I could see their funny eyes. I turned cold. They were like a big peacock's tail, moving out there until midnight. Then, without so much as a sound, they slipped away, the million of them was gone. I kind of think maybe, in some sort of way, they came all those miles to worship. Strange. But think how the tower must look to them, standing seventy feet above the water, the God-light flashing out from it, and the tower declaring itself with a monster voice. They never came back, those fish, but don't you think for a while they thought they were in the Presence?"

8   I shivered. I looked out at the long gray lawn of the sea stretching away into nothing and nowhere.

9   "Oh, the sea's full." McDunn puffed his pipe nervously, blinking. He had been nervous all day and hadn't said why. "For all our engines and so-called submarines, it'll be ten thousand centuries before we set foot on the real bottom of the sunken lands, in the fairy kingdoms there, and know *real* terror. Think of it, it's still the year 300,000 Before Christ down under there. While we've paraded around with trumpets, lopping off each other's countries and heads, they have been living beneath the sea twelve miles deep and cold in a time as old as the beard of a comet."

10   "Yes, it's an old world."

11   "Come on. I got something special I been saving up to tell you."

12   We ascended the eighty steps, talking and taking our time. At the top, McDunn switched off the room lights so there'd be no reflection in the plate glass. The great eye of the light was humming, turning easily in its oiled socket. The Fog Horn was blowing steadily, once every fifteen seconds.

13   "Sounds like an animal, don't it?" McDunn nodded to himself. "A big lonely animal crying in the night. Sitting here on the edge of ten billion years calling out to the Deeps, I'm here, I'm here, I'm here. And the Deeps do answer, yes, they do. You been here now for three months, Johnny, so I better prepare you. About this time of year," he said, studying the murk and fog, "something comes to visit the lighthouse."

14   "The swarms of fish like you said?"

15   "No, this is something else. I've put off telling you because you might think I'm daft. But tonight's the latest I can put it off, for if my calendar's marked right from last year, tonight's the night it comes. I won't go into detail, you'll have to see it yourself. Just sit down there. If you want, tomorrow you can pack your duffel and take the motorboat in to land and get your car parked there at the dinghy pier on the cape and drive on back to some little inland town and keep your lights burning nights, I won't question or blame you. It's happened three years now, and this is the only time anyone's been here with me to verify it. You wait and watch."

16   Half an hour passed with only a few whispers between us. When we grew tired waiting, McDunn began describing some of his ideas to me. He had some theories about the Fog Horn itself.

17   "One day many years ago a man walked along and stood in the sound of the ocean on a cold sunless shore and said, 'We need a voice to call across the water, to warn ships; I'll make one. I'll make a voice like all of time and all of the fog that ever was; I'll make a voice that is like an empty bed beside you all night long, and like an empty house when you open the door, and like trees in autumn with no leaves. A sound like the birds flying south, crying, and a sound like November wind and the sea on the hard, cold shore. I'll make a sound that's so alone that no one can miss it, that whoever hears it will weep in their souls, and hearths will seem warmer, and being inside will seem better to all who hear it in the distant towns. I'll make me a sound and an apparatus and they'll call it a Fog Horn and whoever hears it will know the sadness of eternity and the briefness of life.'"

18   The Fog Horn blew.

19   "I made up that story," said McDunn quietly, "to try to explain why this thing keeps coming back to the lighthouse every year. The Fog Horn calls it, I think, and it comes. . . ."

20   "But—" I said.

21   "Sssst!" said McDunn. "There!" He nodded out to the Deeps.

22   Something was swimming toward the lighthouse tower.

23   It was a cold night, as I have said; the high tower was cold, the light coming and going, and the Fog Horn calling and calling through the raveling mist. You couldn't see far and you couldn't see plain, but there was the deep sea moving on its way about the night earth, flat and quiet, the color of gray mud, and here were the two of us alone in the high tower, and there, far out at first, was a ripple, followed by a wave, a rising, a bubble, a bit of froth. And then, from the surface of the cold sea came a head, a large head, dark-colored, with immense eyes, and then a neck. And then—not a body—but more neck and more! The head rose a full forty feet above the water on a slender and beautiful dark neck. Only then did the body, like a little island of black coral and shells and crayfish, drip up from the subterranean. There was a flicker of tail. In all, from head to tip of tail, I estimated the monster at ninety or a hundred feet.

24   I don't know what I said. I said something.

25   "Steady, boy, steady," whispered McDunn.

26   "It's impossible!" I said.

27   "No, Johnny, *we're* impossible. *It's* like it always was ten million years ago. *It* hasn't changed. It's *us* and the land that've changed, become impossible. *Us!*"

28   It swam slowly and with a great dark majesty out in the icy waters, far away. The fog came and went about it, momentarily erasing its shape. One of the monster eyes caught and held and flashed back our immense light, red, white, red, white, like a disk held high and sending a message in primeval code. It was as silent as the fog through which it swam.

29   "It's a dinosaur of some sort!" I crouched down, holding to the stair rail.

30   "Yes, one of the tribe."

31   "But they died out!"

32   "No, only hid away in the Deeps. Deep, deep down in the deepest Deeps. Isn't *that* a word now, Johnny, a real word, it says so much: the Deeps. There's all the coldness and darkness and deepness in the world in a word like that."

33   "What'll we do?"

34   "Do? We got our job, we can't leave. Besides, we're safer here than in any boat trying to get to land. That thing's as big as a destroyer and almost as swift."

35   "But here, why does it come *here?*"

36   The next moment I had my answer.

37   The Fog Horn blew.

38   And the monster answered.

39   A cry came across a million years of water and mist. A cry so anguished and alone that it shuddered in my head and my body. The monster cried out at the tower. The Fog Horn blew. The monster roared again. The Fog Horn blew. The monster opened its great toothed mouth and the sound that came from it was the sound of the Fog Horn itself. Lonely and vast and far away. The sound of isolation, a viewless sea, a cold night, apartness. That was the sound.

40   "Now," whispered McDunn, "do you know why it comes here?"

41   I nodded.

42   "All year long, Johnny, that poor monster there lying far out, a thou-

sand miles at sea, and twenty miles deep maybe, biding its time, perhaps it's a million years old, this one creature. Think of it, waiting a million years; could *you* wait that long? Maybe it's the last of its kind. I sort of think that's true. Anyway, here come men on land and build this lighthouse, five years ago. And set up their Fog Horn and sound it and sound it out toward the place where you bury yourself in sleep and sea memories of a world where there were thousands like yourself, but now you're alone, all alone in a world not made for you, a world where you have to hide.

43   "But the sound of the Fog Horn comes and goes, comes and goes, and you stir from the muddy bottom of the Deeps, and your eyes open like the lenses of two-foot cameras and you move, slow, slow, for you have the ocean sea on your shoulders, heavy. But that Fog Horn comes through a thousand miles of water, faint and familiar, and the furnace in your belly stokes up, and you begin to rise, slow, slow. You feed yourself on great slakes of cod and minnow, on rivers of jellyfish, and you rise slow through the autumn months, through September when the fogs started, through October with more fog and the horn still calling you on, and then, late in November, after pressurizing yourself day by day, a few feet higher every hour, you are near the surface and still alive. You've got to go slow; if you surfaced all at once you'd explode. So it takes you all of three months to surface, and then a number of days to swim through the cold waters to the lighthouse. And there you are, out there, in the night, Johnny, the biggest damn monster in creation. And here's the lighthouse calling to you, with a long neck like your neck sticking way up out of the water, and a body like your body, and, most important of all, a voice like your voice. Do you understand now, Johnny, do you understand?"

44   The Fog Horn blew.

45   The monster answered.

46   I saw it all, I knew it all—the million years of waiting alone, for someone to come back who never came back. The million years of isolation at the bottom of the sea, the insanity of time there, while the skies cleared of reptile-birds, the swamps dried on the continental lands, the sloths and saber-tooths had their day and sank in tar pits, and men ran like white ants upon the hills.

47   The Fog Horn blew.

48   "Last year," said McDunn, "that creature swam round and round, round and round, all night. Not coming too near, puzzled, I'd say. Afraid, maybe. And a bit angry after coming all this way. But the next day, unexpectedly, the fog lifted, the sun came out fresh, the sky was as blue as a painting. And the monster swam off away from the heat and the silence

and didn't come back. I suppose it's been brooding on it for a year now, thinking it over from every which way."

49   The monster was only a hundred yards off now, it and the Fog Horn crying at each other. As the lights hit them, the monster's eyes were fire and ice, fire and ice.

50   "That's life for you," said McDunn. "Someone always waiting for someone who never comes home. Always someone loving some thing more than that thing loves them. And after a while you want to destroy whatever that thing is, so it can't hurt you no more."

51   The monster was rushing at the lighthouse.

52   The Fog Horn blew.

53   "Let's see what happens," said McDunn.

54   He switched the Fog Horn off.

55   The ensuing minute of silence was so intense that we could hear our hearts pounding in the glassed area of the tower, could hear the slow greased turn of the light.

56   The monster stopped and froze. Its great lantern eyes blinked. Its mouth gaped. It gave a sort of rumble, like a volcano. It twitched its head this way and that, as if to seek the sounds now dwindled off into the fog. It peered at the lighthouse. It rumbled again. Then its eyes caught fire. It reared up, threshed the water, and rushed at the tower, its eyes filled with angry torment.

57   "McDunn!" I cried. "Switch on the horn!"

58   McDunn fumbled with the switch. But even as he flicked it on, the monster was rearing up. I had a glimpse of its gigantic paws, fishskin glittering in webs between the finger-like projections, clawing at the tower. The huge eye on the right side of its anguished head glittered before me like a caldron into which I might drop, screaming. The tower shook. The Fog Horn cried; the monster cried. It seized the tower and gnashed at the glass, which shattered in upon us.

59   McDunn seized my arm. "Downstairs!"

60   The tower rocked, trembled, and started to give. The Fog Horn and the monster roared. We stumbled and half fell down the stairs. "Quick!"

61   We reached the bottom as the tower buckled down toward us. We ducked under the stairs into the small stone cellar. There were a thousand concussions as the rocks rained down; the Fog Horn stopped abruptly. The monster crashed upon the tower. The tower fell. We knelt together, McDunn and I, holding tight, while our world exploded.

62   Then it was over, and there was nothing but darkness and the wash of the sea on the raw stones.

63   That and the other sound.

64   "Listen," said McDunn quietly. "Listen."

65   We waited a moment. And then I began to hear it. First a great vac-uumed sucking of air, and then the lament, the bewilderment, the lone-liness of the great monster, folded over and upon us, above us, so that the sickening reek of its body filled the air, a stone's thickness away from our cellar. The monster gasped and cried. The tower was gone. The light was gone. The thing that had called to it across a million years was gone. And the monster was opening its mouth and sending out great sounds. The sounds of a Fog Horn, again and again. And ships far at sea, not finding the light, not seeing anything, but passing and hearing late that night, must've thought: There it is, the lonely sound, the Lonesome Bay horn. All's well. We've rounded the cape.

66   And so it went for the rest of that night.

67   The sun was hot and yellow the next afternoon when the rescuers came out to dig us from our stoned-under cellar.

68   "It fell apart, is all," said Mr. McDunn gravely. "We had a few bad knocks from the waves and it just crumbled." He pinched my arm.

69   There was nothing to see. The ocean was calm, the sky blue. The only thing was a great algaic stink from the green matter that covered the fallen tower stones and the shore rocks. Flies buzzed about. The ocean washed empty on the shore.

70   The next year they built a new lighthouse, but by that time I had a job in the little town and a wife and a good small warm house that glowed yellow on autumn nights, the doors locked, the chimney puffing smoke. As for McDunn, he was master of the new lighthouse, built to his own speci-fications, out of steel-reinforced concrete. "Just in case," he said.

71   The new lighthouse was ready in November. I drove down alone one evening late and parked my car and looked across the gray waters and listened to the new horn sounding, once, twice, three, four times a minute far out there, by itself.

72   The monster?

73   It never came back.

74   "It's gone away," said McDunn. "It's gone back to the Deeps. It's learned you can't love anything too much in this world. It's gone into the deepest Deeps to wait another million years. Ah, the poor thing! Waiting out there, and waiting out there, while man comes and goes on this piti-ful little planet. Waiting and waiting."

75   I sat in my car, listening. I couldn't see the lighthouse or the light

standing out in Lonesome Bay. I could only hear the Horn, the Horn, the Horn. It sounded like the monster calling.

76   I sat there wishing there was something I could say.

UNDERSTANDING THE SELECTION

1. Many persons who consider themselves realists see no value in fantasy, in flights into the impossible. "There's a difference between fiction and fantasy," they say. "Fiction describes imaginary worlds which *could* be real. Fantasy is just lies." They forget that many of the West's greatest writers have seen fantasy as an ingenious way to make a point—Shakespeare in *The Tempest*, for instance, or Nathaniel Hawthorne or Edgar Allan Poe. Ray Bradbury, the author of this selection, would probably be outraged by the suggestion that "The Fog Horn" has nothing to do with the real world.

2. Which is more important in this story, space or time?

3. Bigfoot, the Pobble, and the monster all are grotesque. Which one looks the most nearly human? Which one acts in the most nearly human fashion?

4. What does the author say about the nature of love?

5. What do you think will happen to the monster now that it has destroyed the lighthouse?

part

2

what does
the author mean?

"He words me, girls, he words me," said Cleopatra to her attendants. Her world had just exploded. Antony, the Roman general who was her lover, had killed himself in shame. Egypt, the country she ruled, had been conquered by Octavius Caesar. And Caesar himself had just left her, saying as he went, "We remain your friend." She knew what he had *said,* but what did he *mean?* Was he promising her freedom or did he intend to kill her or—worst of all—take her prisoner to Rome and drag her behind his chariot through the streets?

Knowing what someone says does not lead to complete understanding; you must also be able to answer the question "What does he mean?"

The first selection you read in this book was "Little Miss Muffet." Here is a variation on that poem which makes you wonder about the meaning of the original.

Little Miss Muffet: Variation IV

Philip Murray

Little Miss Muffet
(It was about three-fifteen when we first missed her)
Sat on a tuffet
(We had been warned that she was not to be trusted)
Eating her curds and whey
(If only we had given her more to eat)
Along came a spider
(She had been complaining recently about the food)
Who sat down beside her
(She was too friendly for her own good)
And frightened Miss Muffet away
(We really don't know what happened next,
Though we found the half-eaten curds and whey
Beside the empty tuffet at five after five
And the grass nearby was still bent towards the lake
As if something had been dragged through it like a rake;
In the middle of the pond, there was a giant insect hovering;
I ran for my camera, but I was too late.
The others had not seen anything, they said;
Would they have admitted it, if they had?)

In order to interpret a work as Philip Murray has, you must know something about writing effects and techniques. These tools of the author's trade have their special names, but you do not need to know the entire vocabulary of literature. We shall discuss only eight of the three or four hundred terms that can be used. These eight we have selected for their usefulness; however we do not mean to imply that other terms are not useful, but only that these seem to us the most necessary.

We shall explain each term separately and try to show you how to use the principle it represents in determining meaning. Remember, however, that to answer the question "What does the author mean?" you must first—and always—have a clear idea of what the author says.

Connotation

One way to understand the meaning behind what words say is to under-stand *connotation:* the emotional and sensory effect of words. All words have *denotation:* their dictionary definition or core meaning on which speak-ers of English generally agree. In addition, many words have *connotation:* the cluster of feelings they call up. It is quite possible, then, for two words to denote the same thing but to have different connotations: *brothers* and *siblings, cabin* and *shack, mug* and *cup.* It is also possible for two people to assign different connotations to the same word.

Before you try to examine connotations in a selection to deter-mine how they affect its meaning, discuss the connotations of the follow-ing sets of words:

1. *Christmas* and *Xmas*
2. *Fourth of July* and *Independence Day*
3. *women* and *ladies*
4. *blood red* and *fire-engine red*
5. *serpent* and *snake*
6. *thin, slender,* and *skinny*
7. *unhappy, sad, blue,* and *down*
8. *nude* and *naked*
9. *ignorant, stupid,* and *dumb*
10. *policeman, cop, copper, fuzz,* and *pig*

18   *Once Upon a Red*

Anonymous

There was a girl whose complexion was Snow White, whose hair made ravens despair. She lived in a forest of tall buildings and television aerials and yearned for a knight on a white super-charger to carry her away. One day she came upon a shop with a swinging sign that said: "Magic Spoken Here," and she entered. The shop was crammed from Chock to Bursting with pills, potions, spells and wishing wells. But on the counter, gleaming brighter than a gold tinderbox, was a slim gold cylinder. It was longer than a match and smaller than a magic wand. In it was a color that was redder than poppy, riper than persimmon, richer than rubies and righter than rain! The girl said, "Does this mean the end of my search?" And the proprietress twinkled and said, "No, this is the way to begin your story. It starts, you see, Once Upon A Red. . . . "

(continued at your favorite cosmetic counter.)

1. At what point did you realize that the passage is an advertisement? What product is being advertised? Would the advertisement persuade you to buy the product?
2. Why did the writer of this advertisement choose so many fairy-tale connotations? Why should these connotations appeal to consumers?
3. What connotations other than fairy-tale are included? Are the clusters of feelings they call up consistent or inconsistent with the fairy-tale ones?

19   *Juglipidity and All That*

Russell Baker

1   The English language is suffering from a word shortage. This is because society changes so rapidly nowadays that word makers cannot produce new words fast enough to keep up with all the new things that are happening.

2   The Volkswagen, for example, has been with us for . . . years, but there is still not a good noun to describe the peculiar state of mind which the Volkswagen induces in its driver. Lacking such a word, other motorists have no effective way of dealing with the Volkswagen driver as he weaves in and out of heavy traffic feeling dangerously like a broken-field runner on an asphalt gridiron.

3   All you can do when you catch one of these people at a red light is lean out the window and say, "You're suffering from lethal delusions of mobility," or something equally cumbersome. By the time you have uttered this mouthful, he will have squirted between a moving van and a motorcycle and be blithely out of earshot.

4   The word we need is, obviously, "miniphoria," a descriptive compound suggesting the odd euphoria that comes over people hunched in miniature machines. "Miniphoria" helps make life tolerable for other motorists who must contend with Volkswagen drivers. When you catch one at the red light, you simply lean out the window and roar, "You stupid miniphoriac!" and the world instantly becomes familiar and satisfying again.

5   Another modern condition for which there is no adequate word is the appearance of women walking down the street in stretch pants. Everybody is familiar with this modern spectacle, but at present dozens of imprecise words are needed to describe it. Words like "rippling," "quivering," "bulging," "ballooning," etc.

6   What we need is a single noun that succinctly sums up the condition. Such a word might be "juglipidity." With "juglipidity," the spectacle no longer throws us off stride and leaves us speechless. When we see one of these poor creatures in public, we have only to say, "that poor woman's juglipidity is acute," and the situation is satisfactorily dismissed.

7   Another modern phenomenon for which there is no word is the crime of robbery by machine. In the typical mechanized robbery, the victim puts fifteen cents into a soda-pop vending machine. The machine seizes the money, drops it into a metal loot box and refuses to come across with the soda pop.

8   The victim normally is baffled. If we were robbed by a man with a gun, he would know his rights. He would go to the police, report the commission of a felony and, after the bandit had been tracked down, testify in court to put the rascal behind bars.

9   Against a felonious machine he is frustrated and baffled. What is the word for this offense that has been committed against him? What are the victim's rights after he has futilely punched the coin-returner lever a few times? Is it permissible to kick the machine? Should it be turned over to the police?

10   If there were a familiar word for this all too familiar modern crime, the victim could act with reason. The word we need is "slottery," a noun meaning "robbery by a coin-vending machine."

11   Give crime its proper name and man can deal with it. When the machine grabs his fifteen cents, the victim, no longer faced with an indefinable situation, will cry, "So slottery's your game, eh?" He will then feel perfectly justified in attacking the thief with a jack handle, recovering his money from the loot box and stuffing the machine's slots with chewing gum.

12   With the crime defined, Congress would quickly decree stiff punishment for companies that allowed "slottery" to take place on their property and criminal machines would soon be replaced by decent law-abiders.

13   There are thousands of similar new phenomena which make modern life doubly frustrating only because we lack words to help us deal with them.

14   We need a new word to describe the peculiar quality of courage involved in trying to enter a turnpike during rush-hour traffic, and another to describe the irresistible compulsion to answer a ringing telephone no matter how inconvenient the time or circumstances.

15   We need a new noun meaning "the act of getting expelled from college to demonstrate one's personal maturity"; a new adjective to describe the taste of frozen hamburger patties, and a new verb meaning "to go to foreign movies and pretend to understand the dialogue by criticizing the subtitles as inadequate."

16   In this strange new world where miniphoriacs abound, where juglipidity is rampant in the streets and where the machines are getting away
with slottery, one of the worst miseries is that we don't even have the words
to explain it all.

UNDERSTANDING THE SELECTION

1. What inferences can you draw about the driver who shouts, "You're
suffering from lethal delusions of mobility" (paragraph 3)? What kind of
person is he? What kind of car does he drive? How old is he? What does he
do for a living? Describe him as fully as you can. Why do you think of him
as you do?

2. What inferences can you draw about the driver who "squirts" his car
between a moving van and a motorcycle? Describe him fully: his clothes,
his occupation, his habits.

3. In paragraphs 14 and 15, Russell Baker lists some phenomena for
which he feels we need new words. Create those words. What influenced
you when you coined them? Why does your word for "the taste of frozen
hamburger patties" differ from the word one of your classmates created
for that taste?

4. Think of some experience you have had, some object you have seen,
or some phenomenon you have witnessed for which you felt there was no
adequate word. Create a word to describe it, making that word as connotative—that is, rich in emotional and sensory effect—as you can. Try the
word on your classmates to see if it arouses in them the same feelings you
hoped to convey.

20   *August*
Elinor Wylie

Why should this Negro insolently stride
Down the red noonday on such noiseless feet?
Piled in his barrow, tawnier than wheat,
Lie heaps of smoldering daisies, somber-eyed,
Their copper petals shriveled up with pride,   *5*
Hot with a superfluity of heat,
Like a great brazier borne along the street
By captive leopards, black and burning-pied.

Are there no water-lilies, smooth as cream,
With long stems dripping crystal? Are there none   *10*
Like those white lilies, luminous and cool,
Plucked from some hemlock-darkened northern stream
By fair-haired swimmers, diving where the sun
Scarce warms the surface of the deepest pool?

UNDERSTANDING THE SELECTION

1. Underline all the words in this poem that suggest heat. How many different kinds of heat (e.g.: weather, hot temper, fire) do they suggest?

2. Underline all the words that suggest coolness. How many different kinds of coolness does the poet suggest?

3. Why does Miss Wylie depict the month of August as a Negro? And why does she describe the Negro as "striding insolently"? Do you share her connotations about this summer month?

4. What type of arrangement does the poet use in the writing of this poem, time or space? Is this the most effective way to describe a part of a year? Explain.

5. Can you draw a picture of the hot part of the poem? Of the cool part?

6. Select some other month of the year and write a short paragraph (not necessarily a poem) describing it as connotatively as you can.

21 Snake in Interior

André Kertész

Photograph by André Kertész.

UNDERSTANDING THE SELECTION

1. Look at the room. Is this room part of a mansion or of a comfortable farmhouse or of an apartment? Where do you think it is located? What details lead you to your conclusions?

2. What kind of people live here? What do you infer about their ages, social status, economic status, education, interests, personalities? On what do you base your inferences?

3. Is the snake poisonous or harmless? Is it an intruder or a pet? Why is it in the room?

4. Would you feel more strongly about the picture if a person were in it? Or does part of its effect lie in the fact that no one is there but the snake?

5. Write a brief theme about the picture. Use words that will suggest as accurately as possible your feelings when you first looked at it.

Metaphor

English uses about 250 figures of speech, most of which have Greek names that are never included in daily conversation: *oxymoron, synecdoche, litotes.* As a reader, you should recognize a few of these figures of speech, since they add dimensions to the writer's meaning and, in some cases, provide the meaning altogether. A poet, for instance, is likely to use figures of speech almost entirely to express what he means.

A widely used figure of speech is *metaphor.* It is closely related to connotation because it too calls up a cluster of feelings. Although there are many types of metaphor, for our purposes it is enough to understand the general category: a metaphor compares one thing to another.

"All the world's a stage" compares our life (world) to a play (stage). "The Lord is my shepherd" points out that God cares for His people as a shepherd cares for his flocks, making sure that they get food, water, and shelter and chasing away any wolves that may lurk nearby. Less obvious are such metaphors as "She flew to answer the phone," in which the use of *flew* compares the girl to a bird, or "Fireboats greeted the *Constitution* when she entered the harbor," in which *she* suggests that the ship has feminine traits. In the last two examples the comparison is implied rather than fully stated, as it is in the first two.

A metaphor does not always consist of one or two words; whole passages may be metaphorical. Here is one by Thomas Henry Huxley, a famous Victorian writer who spent much of his life popularizing science.

> The life, the fortune, and the happiness of every one of us . . . depend upon our knowing something of the rules of a game infinitely more difficult and complicated than chess. It is a game which has been played for untold ages, every man and woman of us being one of the two players in a game of his or her own. The chessboard is the world, the pieces are the phenomena of the universe, the rules of the game are what we call the laws of nature. The player on the other side is hidden from us. We know that his play is always fair, just, and patient. But also we know, to our cost, that he never overlooks a mistake, or makes the smallest allowance for ignorance. To the man who plays well, the highest stakes are paid. . . . And one who plays ill is checkmated—without haste, but without remorse.

This metaphor, comparing life to a chess game, has also been used in Edward Fitzgerald's version of *The Rubaiyat,* which was first written by a twelfth-century Persian. The poem says we are all

> But helpless Pieces of the Game He plays
> Upon this Checker-board of Nights and Days;
> Hither and thither moves, and checks, and slays,
> And one by one back in the Closet lays.

In examining metaphors to determine what the author means, you should be sure you know what he says: What is he comparing to what? For instance, in the last line of the stanza above, what is Fitzgerald comparing to being laid back in the closet?

Before you read the selections which follow, see what you can do with metaphors. All of us use them constantly both in writing and in speaking: "He's a little tin god" or "a dead duck" or "a big wheel." Look in tonight's newspaper and collect ten examples of metaphor. The sports pages, the comics, and the advertisements will probably be the best sources.

22 There is a Garden in Her Face

Thomas Campion

There is a garden in her face,
Where roses and white lilies grow;
  A heav'nly paradise is that place,
Wherein all pleasant fruits do flow.
    There cherries grow which none may buy   5
    Till cherry-ripe themselves do cry.

Those cherries fairly do enclose
Of orient pearl a double row,
  Which when her lovely laughter shows,
They look like rosebuds filled with snow.   10
    Yet them nor peer nor prince can buy,
    Till cherry-ripe themselves do cry.

Her eyes like angels watch them still;
Her brows like bended bows do stand,
  Threat'ning with piercing frowns to kill   15
All that attempt with eye or hand
    Those sacred cherries to come nigh,
    Till cherry-ripe themselves do cry.

UNDERSTANDING THE SELECTION

1. Exactly what is the poet comparing to "her face"? Is he comparing everything in the garden to it?

2. Is the "heav'nly paradise" (line 3) being compared to her face or to a garden? Or to both?

3. Do pearls (line 8) grow in gardens? Can you think of a more appropriate metaphor for her teeth?

4. Does an ideal garden have snow (line 10)? Are the connotations of *snow* appropriate to a description of the girl?

5. What is "them" (line 13)?

6. Does the third stanza carry out the metaphor?

7. Discuss the difference it would make in your conception of the girl if the poet had used either of the following metaphors. In which version is the girl the prettiest? Best dressed? Most fun to be with? Most selfish? Most sympathetic?

> There is a kitchen in her face,
> Where angel food and custard grow;
> A spicy haven is that place
> Wherein all pleasant foods do flow.
>
> There is a city in her face,
> Where neons and shop windows glow;
> A precious Tiffany's is that place
> Wherein all pleasant jewels flow.

23 from Paper Lion

George Plimpton

1   Down on the field after a day or so, the players, who had been so many ciphers, one indistinguishable from another, began to take on identifying characteristics. Some were obvious. One was struck by the odd disparity of the football players' physiques—more than in any other team sport—from the lean, near emaciated stringiness of the defensive backs and flankers to the bulwarked heft of the linemen, many with pronounced bellies, who were set close to the ground, like cabbages. The range would be from such a player as Del Shofner, the Giants' flanker, lanky, sallow, with ulcers, who has been described as looking like a saxophone player after a hard one-night stand—from Shofner to Brown, the three-hundred-pounder of the Lions, the bulge of his thighs so enormous that to get one leg past the other produced a waddle of such distinction that the players seeing him in the locker room or emerging from the shower jawed at him about it, and imitated his walk.

2   Down on the practice field I would see Brown and the other big men endlessly circling the field after practice—distant figures against the trees, trying to remove a pound or two, so that their bulk could be moved with more agility.

3   The running styles were as different as the physical characteristics. Dick Compton, a small Texan scatback, ran with exhalations when he had the ball, *ah-ah-ah,* like piston strokes—a habit he had picked up in high school which he felt gave power to his run. He could be heard across the width of a field. The "Gasper" some of the players called him, and he was also nicknamed "Roadrunner"—after the quick-running desert bird of his home state. Jake Greer also had a distinctive run—moving his spindly body in leaps like a high jumper moving for the crossbar, high, bouncy steps, and then he stretched out fast, and when he got to the defending back he feinted with his small high-boned head, sometimes with a tiny bit of toothpick working in it. Then he'd fly on past or off at an angle, his hands splayed out wide, looking back for the ball honing in to intercept his line of flight, and then he'd *miss* it—good moves but bad hands in those early training sessions, they said—and the shouts would go up, "Squeeze that thing, baby," "Hands, man, hands." Greer would circle back, stricken, staring into his big hands as if they had betrayed him as he bent down to pick up the ball. His face would remain long and melancholy, and when his signal came up again, Scooter McLean would shout: "Look like you want it, Al, come *on,* baby."

UNDERSTANDING THE SELECTION

1. George Plimpton, a writer and sports enthusiast, joined the Detroit Lions football team in order to write firsthand a book about professional football and professional football players. This passage describing some players for the Lions is taken from Plimpton's book *Paper Lion.*

2. Underline all the metaphors you can find in this passage. Remember that a metaphor does not have to say specifically that one thing is *like* another. In the first few lines, for example, are *stringiness* and *bulwarked* metaphors?

3. Do you think all the metaphors are effective? Pick out those you think are the most effective and explain why you think so. What is wrong with the others?

4. Write a brief description of one of the following. Try to use both connotation and metaphor in your theme.

    a. A policeman directing traffic
    b. Women at a bargain counter
    c. A person going swimming in very cold water
    d. A person stalled on a freeway trying to find out what is wrong with his car
    e. Two strange dogs meeting each other
    f. A child eating an olive for the first time
    g. A young couple applying for a marriage license

h. Your instructor as he looked to you on the first day of class
i. A hippy asking for change from passersby
j. A group of people at an "encounter" meeting

24   The Silken Tent
Robert Frost

She is as in a field a silken tent
At midday when a sunny summer breeze
Has dried the dew and all its ropes relent,
So that in guys it gently sways at ease,
And its supporting central cedar pole,   5
That is its pinnacle to heavenward
And signifies the sureness of the soul,
Seems to owe naught to any single cord,
But strictly held by none, is loosely bound
By countless silken ties of love and thought   10
To everything on earth the compass round,
And only by one's going slightly taut
In the capriciousness of summer air
Is of the slightest bondage made aware.

UNDERSTANDING THE SELECTION

1. Robert Frost compares "she" to a tent. To what is Frost comparing the ropes (line 3)? The central pole (line 5)? The summer air (line 13)?
2. The tent is silken. How would the metaphor be affected if the tent were canvas? Or nylon?
3. Who is "she"? How old is she? Is she married? Does she have children? Does she have a job?
4. Are the time and place of the poem important? If you think so, do you think that they have metaphorical significance?
5. Draw a picture of the poem.

Allusion

Closely related to both *connotation* and *metaphor* is a third figure of speech —*allusion*. An allusion is a reference to some specific person or place or event. In his song "You're the Top," Cole Porter says "You're the Coliseum, . . . the Louvre Museum, . . . a Bendel bonnet, . . . a Shakespeare sonnet." Porter's descriptions of "you" are a form of connotation because they call up clusters of feelings; but they differ from simple connotative language in that they are specific references. Saying "You're the Coliseum" and "You're groovy" both call up emotions, but the allusion to the Coliseum is more precise than the simple "groovy."

Allusions are also metaphors because they compare one thing with another, but again, a writer alludes to *specific* persons, places, or things, while simple metaphors are more general. For example, notice the difference between "You're a Shakespeare sonnet" and "My life with you is one big love song."

Students frequently complain that allusions are hindrances to their reading rather than aids to understanding. "If I don't know what a 'Bendel bonnet' is," you may wail, "then what has the writer accomplished by referring to it?" You may be especially exasperated by the many Biblical allusions in literature, for modern families are not likely to study the Bible and know its images as people did in the past. Nonetheless, literature is filled with allusions to the Bible, to Greek and Roman mythology, and to equally unfamiliar images. The sentence "My English instructor is as patient as Job, but I've discovered his Achilles' heel," while it is a cliché, alludes both to the Bible and to mythology.

The good writer tries to find the precise words and images that will express his feelings. Consequently, he often feels he has to allude to a person or event a student may not be familiar with. We cannot expect the writer always to come down to our level, for he often sees the world more clearly than we do, and we turn to him for a clearer view of ourselves. It is up to the reader to discover—from the Bible, from an encyclopedia, from a history book—what it is the writer alludes to.

Since we said earlier that many allusions are to the Bible, let's trace a specific allusion that you are all familiar with. It begins with the fourteenth chapter of the Book of Revelation, verse nineteen, which is part of the description of Judgment Day:

> So the angel swung his sickle on the earth and gathered the vintage of the earth, and threw it into the great wine press of the wrath of God. (Rev. 14:19)

Julia Ward Howe alluded to this verse in the words of "The Battle Hymn of the Republic":

Mine eyes have seen the glory of the coming of the Lord;
He is trampling out the vintage where the grapes of wrath are stored;
He hath loosed the fateful lightning of his terrible swift sword;
His truth is marching on.

While Mrs. Howe's lyrics do not use the precise words of the Biblical passage, you can easily see that her work uses the exact metaphor of the earlier work.

Later on, John Steinbeck used Mrs. Howe's phrase "the grapes of wrath" as the title of his novel about migrant farmers during the Depression. While Steinbeck's book is filled with allusions to the Biblical books of Genesis, Exodus, Ecclesiastes, and the Gospels, let us examine here just one passage which continues the "grapes of wrath" idea.

Steinbeck wrote of the migrants who swarmed into California (the land of oranges and grapes) during the 1930s, when much of the country had become a giant dust bowl. He saw the plight of the "Okies" as comparable to the plight of the persecuted Israelites who were led from Egypt by Moses into Canaan (the land of milk and honey). The Okies, like the Israelites, suffered cruelty, discrimination, and bigotry. Starving, the Okies and their children looked on with staring eyes and bloated stomachs while growers destroyed food rather than sell it cheaply or give it to the hungry.

The people come with nets to fish for potatoes in the river, and the guards hold them back; they come in rattling cars to get the dumped oranges, but the kerosene is sprayed. And they stand still and watch the potatoes float by, listen to the screaming pigs being killed in a ditch and covered with quicklime, watch the mountains of oranges slop down to a putrefying ooze; and in the eyes of the people there is the failure; and in the eyes of the hungry there is a growing wrath. In the souls of the people the grapes of wrath are filling and growing heavy, growing heavy for the vintage.

In the phrase "the grapes of wrath" in this passage, Steinbeck alludes to God's anger at the harvest that men have grown for themselves; he recalls to us "The Battle Hymn of the Republic," written when the nation warred against itself, and he laments a land—like Biblical Egypt and Depression California—where man has no compassion or pity for his fellow.

To see the value of allusive writing, compare the following groups of descriptions and discuss which moves you most. See if you can find out where the allusions come from:

She's cool.	She's a Helen of Troy, a Cleopatra, a Marilyn Monroe.
He's a tool of the whites.	He's a real Uncle Tom.

English is a real ordeal for me.

When I'm in English, I feel like Daniel in the lion's den.

Professor Cobb is a tyrant.

Professor Cobb is a little Hitler.

Lawrence Welk plays corny music.

Lawrence Welk's music is really Mickey Mouse.

He pokes fun at the dean's list, but he's really green with envy.

He pokes fun at the dean's list, but it's really sour grapes.

25 Eve

Ralph Hodgson

Eve, with her basket, was
Deep in the bells and grass,
Wading in bells and grass
Up to her knees.
Picking a dish of sweet   5
Berries and plums to eat,
Down in the bells and grass
Under the trees.

Mute as a mouse in a
Corner the cobra lay,   10
Curled round a bough of the
Cinnamon tall. . . .
Now to get even and
Humble proud heaven and
Now was the moment or   15
Never at all.

"Eva!" Each syllable
Light as a flower fell,
"Eva!" he whispered the
Wondering maid,   20
Soft as a bubble sung
Out of a linnet's lung,
Soft and most silverly
"Eva!" he said.

Picture that orchard sprite;   25
Eve, with her body white,

Supple and smooth to her
Slim finger tips;
Wondering, listening,
Listening, wondering,   30
Eve with a berry
Halfway to her lips.

Oh, had our simple Eve
Seen through the makebelieve.
Had she but known the   35
Pretender he was!
Out of the boughs he came,
Whispering still her name,
Tumbling in twenty rings
Into the grass.   40

Here was the strangest pair
In the world anywhere,
Eve in the bells and grass
Kneeling, and he
Telling his story low. . . .   45
Singing birds saw them go
Down the dark path to
The Blasphemous Tree.

Oh, what a clatter when
Titmouse and Jenny Wren   50
Saw him successful and
Taking his leave!
How the birds rated him,
How they all hated him!
How they all pitied   55
Poor motherless Eve!

Picture her crying
Out side in the lane,
Eve, with no dish of sweet
Berries and plums to eat,   60
Haunting the gate of the
Orchard in vain. . . .
Picture the lewd delight
Under the hill tonight—
"Eva!" the toast goes round,   65
"Eva!" again.

1. This poem clearly alludes to the story of the Garden of Eden in the Biblical Book of Genesis. Find in the poem as many specific references to the Bible account as you can.

2. How do the accounts in the poem and the Bible differ?

3. Is "Jenny Wren" an allusion?

4. The cobra in the poem is like a stock character in many American jokes. Who is the character? Do the last two lines of the poem give you a clue to who he is? Can this similarity, which is never stated, be considered an allusion?

5. What are the connotations of "bells and grass" repeated three times in the first stanza? What are the connotations of "cinnamon tall"?

6. What do you call the figure of speech used in these lines?

> Soft as a bubble sung
> Out of a linnet's lung,
> Soft and most silverly
> "Eva!" he said.

Is it an effective use of the figure of speech? Why or why not?

26 from A Snob's Guide to Culture

Dan Greenburg

1   Culture used to be a very simple proposition. When exposed to it, all you had to do was say you didn't know much about it but you knew what you liked. It is no longer socially acceptable when speaking of culture either to know nothing about it or to know what you like. Culture has become *de rigueur;* and though it's still not necessary to actually *be* cultured, it is mandatory to look, sound and act as if you are. The following is a handy guide to building an appropriate personal image at most of the cultural events you are likely to attend.

How to Go to a Folk-music Concert

2   Be an aging teeny-bopper going to seed, or a middle-aged ex-Socialist who wears Mexican clothes. Drop names such as Blind Lemon, Bessie and Lomax. Refer to Leadbelly as "Huddie" and talk about him as though he were still alive. Speak of Joan Baez as "one of the pure ones" and reminisce about the days "at the 47 Club in Cambridge, when Joanie would sing all night for coffee money." If you're a girl, have Tom Paxton's likeness tattooed on the inside of your left thigh. In restaurants, clean your nails with a banjo pick. Have a button fly that is half open and don't give a damn. Spill paint on your best shoes and let it dry. Wear glasses with thin steel frames held together with Scotch tape or wear frames without lenses and occasionally scratch your eyelids through the holes. Know where to get great buys on at least three of the following: balalaika, koto, ukulele, dulcimer, dobro, tambourine, Norman Thomas campaign buttons and original editions of the La Guardia Report. OK comment: "When you consider that he's neither blind nor black and that he's never spent any time in jail, you have to admit he plays pretty good banjo."

How to Go to a Love-in

3   Wear one gold earring and leather Tyrolean shorts, and carry a very dirty blonde baby in a sling on your back. Or be an absolutely stacked 18-year-old blonde in tight, wide-wale corduroys from a Diggers shop who wears MAKE LOVE, NOT WAR buttons but will demonstrate a knowledge of karate if a guy makes a pass. Or be two willowy 14-year-old girls who are a little awkward now but who will grow up to be real heartbreakers, or be a 16-year-old who doesn't wear a brassiere and nobody cares, or be a fairly hip marketing trainee in gym shoes and an Army blanket whose only interest is in picking up a willowy 14-year-old girl or a 16-year-old who doesn't wear a brassiere. Carry a half-eaten loaf of French bread wrapped in a torn-out page from *The Oracle*. Give things to strangers. Burn your draft card with a pack of matches from the City Lights bookstore. Say that Emmett Grogan doesn't exist, and compare everything with "the old days, back in Haight."

How to Go to a Pot Party If You're Over 25

4   Be excessively hairy and barrel-chested and wear a scarred leather blacksmith's apron with no shirt underneath. Roll your joints one-handed from a Bull Durham sack and smoke them in a silver-filigree roach holder whose amber mouthpiece has a fly embedded in it. Develop a *Weltschmerzy* I-was-doing-this-gig-20-years-ago look. Know by heart at least six authentic marching songs of the Lincoln Brigade. Reminisce about "the good old days in Taos, when nobody knew about peyote and everybody had his own little Victory garden." Tell a long story about The Bear restaurant in Chicago, "when Dylan first got turned on." Or, if you're a girl, be an attractive, 30ish Montessori teacher, dress like an Ayn Rand heroine and sit down with a group of total strangers to talk very intensely about oral-genital sex.

How to Go to a Jazz Concert

5   Nobody goes to a jazz concert.

UNDERSTANDING THE SELECTION

1. Identify every person or place alluded to in this selection. How necessary is it to know each allusion in order to understand the article?

2. Is the writing in this selection specific or not? Find examples within the selection of each kind of writing and discuss their effectiveness.

3. Write a short paper on one of the following topics. Make it as specific as possible and make as many allusions as you can.

    a. How to go to an English class if you think the teacher is cool

    b. How to go to the library

    c. How to go to an interview for a job that you do not really want

    d. How to go to a free beach or nudist camp

    e. How to go to a draft-card burning

    f. How to go to a cocktail party that your parents are giving

    g. How to go to a Hell's Angels' weekend run

    h. How to go to a swinging bar if you are under eighteen

    i. How to go to a swinging bar if you are over eighteen

    j. How to go to the doctor to get excused from physical education

27   Hope Deferred
Roger Malloch

Photograph by Roger Malloch. © Magnum Photos, Inc.

UNDERSTANDING THE SELECTION

1. Most of the photographs in this text tell a story or make some kind of statement. They are not merely records of family reunions or embarrassing reminders of your childhood. This photograph makes a statement which depends largely on allusion. To what does the photographer allude in this picture?

2. Would the photograph have been as effective if the boy had been at the feet of a statue of, say, Richard Nixon? Of Robert E. Lee? Of the Statue of Liberty? Why or why not?

3. The title of this photograph —"Hope Deferred"— is also an allusion. See if you can find where the title came from and what the entire quotation is. Is the title an appropriate one for the photograph?

Symbol

A figure of speech which should be discussed separately is the *symbol*. A symbol represents both itself and something else. For example, Cinderella is a young girl with a horrid stepmother, horrid stepsisters, and a dear, sweet, kind fairy godmother. In addition to being a girl, however, she is the symbol of someone who goes from rags and menial chores tochinchilla and servants, probably including a press agent.

A frequent symbol in literature is that of the journey which represents life. We use this symbol when we speak of "the path of life" or say, "It's a long road that has no turning." Folk songs like "Poor Wayfaring Stranger" and fairy tales like "Little Red Riding Hood" use it. So do such works as *The Odyssey, The Divine Comedy, Don Quixote, Gulliver's Travels, Peer Gynt, The Grapes of Wrath,* and *On the Road:* in all these the journey and its adventures symbolize life and the events that happen to man throughout his life.

Many students—and too many teachers—make the mistake of "seeing" symbols where none is intended by the author. To find symbols in every picture drawn by an author is to be guilty of a kind of superstition. When an author writes, he does not ask himself, "Now what can I use to symbolize life?" Or love. Or goodness. Or evil. To do that would blur what he is trying to say. He starts with something he wants to say, and he looks for a way to say it that will make it clearest to his readers. Sometimes a symbol—a person or thing which represents both itself and something else—is the easiest way to communicate with an audience.

What are these things symbols of?

1. love beads	6. a black cat
2. the Eiffel Tower	7. Uncle Sam
3. a Rolls-Royce	8. roast turkey
4. a billy club	9. Don Juan
5. the lion	10. pink

What are appropriate symbols for the following?

1. Mother	6. a majorette
2. St. Francis	7. San Francisco
3. the Olympics	8. New Year's Eve
4. the theater	9. good
5. a detective	10. evil

28   Desk Lamps

Anthony

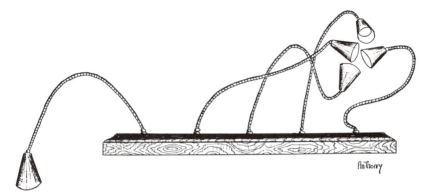

UNDERSTANDING THE SELECTION

1. What do the lamps symbolize? Why do you think so?
2. Do they make an effective symbol? Why or why not?
3. Would you expect them to be used as a symbol?

29   The Blind Men and the Elephant

A Hindoo Fable

John Godfrey Saxe

It was six men of Indostan
  To learning much inclined,
Who went to see the Elephant
  (Though all of them were blind),
That each by observation   *5*
  Might satisfy his mind.

The *First* approached the Elephant,
  And happening to fall
Against his broad and sturdy side,
  At once began to bawl: *10*
"God bless me! but the Elephant
  Is very like a wall!"

The *Second,* feeling of the tusk,
  Cried, "Ho! what have we here

So very round and smooth and sharp?   15
  To me 'tis mighty clear
This wonder of an Elephant
  Is very like a spear!"

The *Third* approached the animal,
  And happening to take   20
The squirming trunk within his hands,
  Thus boldly up and spake:
"I see," quoth he, "the Elephant
  Is very like a snake!"

The *Fourth* reached out an eager hand,   25
  And felt about the knee.
"What most this wondrous beast is like
  Is mighty plain," quoth he;
"'Tis clear enough the Elephant
  Is very like a tree!"   30

The *Fifth* who chanced to touch the ear,
  Said: "E'en the blindest man
Can tell what this resembles most;
  Deny the fact who can,
This marvel of an Elephant   35
  Is very like a fan!"

The *Sixth* no sooner had begun
  About the beast to grope,
Than, seizing on the swinging tail
  That fell within his scope,   40
"I see," quoth he, "the Elephant
  Is very like a rope!"

And so these men of Indostan
  Disputed loud and long,
Each in his own opinion   45
  Exceeding stiff and strong,
Though each was partly in the right,
  And all were in the wrong!

    Moral
So oft in theologic wars,
  The disputants, I ween,
Rail on in utter ignorance   50
  Of what each other mean,

And prate about an Elephant
Not one of them has seen!

UNDERSTANDING THE SELECTION

1. What do the blind men symbolize?
2. What does the elephant symbolize?
3. Can you think of other equally effective symbols for the same things?
4. Does the poet imply that all men are—symbolically—blind? What blinds them?
5. What does the poem imply about truth? Is it possible for any man to know the truth?

30   I Lift My Lamp

Bruce Davidson

Photograph by Bruce Davidson. © Magnum Photos, Inc.

UNDERSTANDING THE SELECTION

1. Is the Statue of Liberty a symbol? If so, what does it symbolize in general? In this picture?
2. Are TV antennas symbols? If so, what do they symbolize in general? In this picture?
3. What does the whole picture symbolize?

31 from The Black Arts

Richard Cavendish

1   The driving force behind black magic is hunger for power. Its ultimate aim was stated, appropriately enough, by the serpent in the Garden of Eden. Adam and Eve were afraid that if they ate the fruit of the Tree of the Knowledge of Good and Evil they would die. But the serpent said, "Ye shall not surely die: for God doth know that in the day ye eat thereof, then your eyes shall be opened and *ye shall be as gods,* knowing good and evil." In occultism the serpent is a symbol of wisdom, and for centuries magicians have devoted themselves to the search for the forbidden fruit which would bring fulfillment of the serpent's promise. Carried to its furthest extreme, the black magician's ambition is to wield supreme power over the entire universe, to make himself a god.

2   Black magic is rooted in the darkest levels of the mind, and this is a large part of its attraction, but it is much more than a product of the love of evil or a liking for mysterious mumbo-jumbo. It is a titanic attempt to exalt the stature of man, to put man in the place which religious thought reserves for God. In spite of its crudities and squalors this gives it a certain magnificence.

3   The great fascination of magic is in the type of thought on which it is based. Magical thinking is not random, it has its own laws and its own logic, but it is poetic rather than rational. It leaps to conclusions which are usually scientifically unwarranted, but which often seem poetically right. It is a type of thinking which has been prevalent all through the history of Europe, which lies behind huge areas of our religion, philosophy and literature, and which is a major guide-post to the regions of the spiritual and the supernatural, the regions of which science has nothing to say. There is no necessity to accept it, but it rings many a far-away, summoning bell in the depths of the mind.

4   It is natural to think of magic as a thing of the past, which must have withered to dust under the hard light of modern science and scepticism;

but, in fact, this is not the case. Magical thinking is still deeply embedded in the human mentality. Magic has been practised throughout European history, down to and including the present day, and it has attracted more interest and support in the last hundred years than at any time since the Renaissance.

5   No one is a black magician in his own eyes, and modern occultists, whatever their beliefs and practices, think of themselves as highminded white magicians, not as sinister Brothers of the Left-hand Path. In October 1964 the Los Angeles police arrested thirty-nine gipsies on charges of for-tune-telling. The gipsies immediately accused the police of violating their religious freedom. They were not telling fortunes, but giving "spiritual read-ings." "Gipsies are born with the power to look into the future. It's part of our religion. We are members of the Palmistry Church." About a year earlier the British witch covens celebrated one of their great annual festivals, All-Hallows Eve, with rites involving the magic circle, the magic knife, incanta-tions, nudity and frenzied dances. One of the St. Albans witches, naked except for a string of beads, is reported as saying, "We are not anti-Christian. We just have other means of spiritual satisfaction."

6   The most notorious and most brilliantly gifted of modern magicians, Aleister Crowley, was regarded as a black sorcerer by many other occultists, and his rituals are saturated with sex and blood to an extent which, to put it mildly, scarcely fits the normal conception of white magic. But he him-self professed nothing but contempt for black magicians. Among them he included Christian Scientists and Spiritualists, as well as those of his fellow occultists who disapproved of him.

7   In the same way, the writers of the old grimoires, or magical text-books, which instruct the reader in methods of calling up evil spirits, killing people, causing hatred and destruction or forcing women to submit to him in love, did not think of themselves as black magicians. On the contrary, the grimoires are packed with prayers to God and the angels, fastings and self-mortifications and ostentatious piety. The principal process in the *Grimoire of Honorius*, which is usually considered the most diabolical of them all, overflows with impassioned and perfectly sincere appeals to God and devout sayings of Mass. It also involves tearing out the eyes of a black cock and slaughtering a lamb, and its purpose is to summon up the Devil.

8   It is not merely that people are naturally disinclined to pin nasty labels on themselves and that the human mind can always find excellent reasons for evoking the Devil or killing an enemy or causing harm and destruction. The magician sets out to conquer the universe. To succeed he must make himself master of everything in it—evil as well as good, cruelty as well as mercy, pain as well as pleasure. Deep at the heart of the magical outlook is the pagan but not ignoble conviction that everything has its place and function in the order of the universe and that all types of experience are

potentially rewarding. The complete man, which is what the magician attempts to be, is the man who has experienced and mastered all things. This conviction is closely related to the magical theory of the relationship between God, man and the universe. . . .

9   Magic is sometimes said to be a primitive form of science, but it is very much nearer to poetry than to even the most rudimentary science and, like poetry, it relies extensively on the use of analogy. The whole magical universe itself is built on the analogy of the human body. Imitative magic, which depends on the principle of analogy, the law of like to like, is only one more example of this tendency. Magic makes use of all kinds of associations and connections between things whose relationship to each other is a matter of similarities and parallels. For instance, things which are backwards or upside down—an inverted crucifix or saying the Lord's Prayer backwards—are linked with evil and the Devil because they reverse the normal and proper order of things and the Devil is the arch-rebel who seeks to overturn the order established by God.

10   This is a natural parallel for the mind to draw, but in occult theory the connection between evil and things which are reversed is not merely symbolic but real. Man is a tiny replica of the universe. If two things are naturally associated together in the human mind, which is an image of the "mind" of the universe, this is evidence of a real connection between the two things in the universe. Many of the important magical analogies and connections are not natural to most people's minds today, but have been handed down by tradition from the remote past. This enhances their value for occultists, who believe that humanity was a great deal wiser in these matters in the remote past than it is now.

11   An example is the magical use of salt to ward off demons. All devils are supposed to detest it and no salt should be used in ceremonies designed to attract them. Salt is anti-demonic because it is a preservative. Demons are creatures which corrupt and destroy. Anything that has preservative qualities is contrary to their nature, and disagreeable to them. Iron can also be employed against demons, because men discovered and used meteoric iron long before they found iron ore in the earth. Since it first came from the sky, iron is "heavenly" and devils fear it.

12   On the other hand, the left is associated with evil. Black magic is "the Left-hand Path." Moving to the left in magic is done with evil intent and attracts evil influences. Some spells will only work if you move to the left while repeating them. The tendency to connect the left with evil is very old. When the Babylonians drew omens they usually considered the left side bad and the right side good. In Homer birds flying to the right are a favourable omen, but birds which fly to the left are unfavourable. "Sinister" was the Latin word for both left and evil and has kept the double meaning in English (it still means left in heraldry).

13   The probable explanation of this general disapproval of the left is the fact that the right hand is normally the stronger and the left hand the weaker. The word "left" comes from the Anglo-Saxon word *lyft,* which meant weak. To be left-handed is peculiar and suspect, a reversal of the proper order of things, and so the left is associated with the powers of evil which rebel against God. Some modern psychologists say that left-handedness is often a characteristic of men who are sexually abnormal—homosexual or perverted. A stock example is the Emperor Tiberius, a notorious pervert who was left-handed.

14   A more obvious but equally ancient connection is the link between blood and life. Primitive people who observed that as a man loses blood he weakens and eventually dies came naturally to the conclusion that his blood contains his life. But the magical connection is not merely the physical one. A man's life includes all his experiences, characteristics and qualities, and these are contained in his blood. A classical cure for epilepsy is to drink the blood of a slaughtered gladiator, which conveys his strength and healthy vitality into the epileptic's body. The gladiator should be freshly killed, because the energy in his blood will dissipate quite quickly. Pliny's *Natural History* says that some epileptics found it most effective to reach the gladiator before he was actually dead and gulp the invigorating blood down as it came warm and bubbling from the dying man's wounds.

15   The sadistic Hungarian Countess Elizabeth Bathory bathed regularly in human blood to preserve her looks. Her supplies came from peasant girls who were kept in chains in the cellars of her castle and whose fresh young blood was expected to give the Countess's skin a youthful bloom. When she was arrested in 1610 the dead bodies of about fifty of these girls were found. She once wrote to her husband, "Thorko has taught me a lovely new one. Catch a black hen and beat it to death with a white cane. Keep the blood and smear a little of it on your enemy. If you get no chance to smear it on his body, obtain one of his garments and smear it." The magical theory behind this is that the hen's life, which was characterised by an agonised death, has been transferred to the enemy in the hen's blood. His death in the same agony will follow. Beating the black hen to death with a white cane is an interesting example of a reconciliation of opposites.

16   The blood of an executed criminal is a strong protection against disease and misfortune, because it carries the vigorous energy of a man cut off in full health and the powerful force of his resentment and fury at the fact. Spectators at executions, including those of Charles I of England and Louis XVI of France, struggled to dip cloths and handkerchiefs in the dead man's blood. When John Dillinger, the notorious gunman and bank robber, was shot down and killed by F.B.I. agents in Chicago in 1934, people gathered round and soaked their handkerchiefs or pieces of paper in a pool of his blood on the sidewalk. Some of the women dipped the hems of their skirts in it. The blood was quickly used up, but enterprising local tradesmen sold large quantities of fake Dillinger blood.

17   A sidelight on the belief that you can absorb a man's qualities by drinking his blood or eating part of his body is provided by recent experiments with flatworms at the University of Michigan. The worms are conditioned to respond to lights and to negotiate a maze. A conditioned worm is then killed and fed to an untaught worm. In some cases the untaught worm acquires the conditioned worm's ability to respond to the lights and the maze simply by eating it. The tentative explanation is that the conditioned worm's memory is connected with a chemical, possibly ribonucleic acid, in its body, but other experimenters have not obtained the same results.

18   Most of us do not associate the colour green, copper, the number 7, the dove, the sparrow, and the swan together in our minds, but in magical theory these things are linked because they are all connected with the force of Venus, the universal current of love. These connections are part of what is called a "system of correspondences." From the earliest times men tried to understand the way in which the world is constructed by classifying all the features of the universe in terms of the gods who controlled them. Magicians have followed suit, substituting the great driving forces of the universe for the gods. Everything is classified in terms of the force with which it is connected.

19   The system is extremely detailed, but the oldest and most important part of it is the set of links between planets, metals and colours.

Planets	*Metals*	*Colours*
Sun	Gold	Gold, yellow
Moon	Silver	White
Mercury	Quicksilver	Grey, neutral
Venus	Copper	Green
Mars	Iron	Red
Jupiter	Tin	Blue
Saturn	Lead	Black

These correspondences are vitally important in magic because magicians use them in their attempts to control the great occult forces. In a ceremony of hatred and destruction the magician uses things which are red or made of iron. He drapes the room in which he is working in crimson hangings. He wears a scarlet robe and a ruby in a ring on his finger. The ring is made of iron and he uses a magic wand made of iron. The number 5 also corresponds to Mars and the magician lights five candles and has pentagrams (five-pointed stars) drawn or embroidered on his robe. These things arouse and control the force of Mars because they are connected with it in the universe, as if it was an animal on the end of a chain made of red, iron and five.

20   The reasons for linking these particular things together are hidden far back in antiquity, but the logic behind most of the connections seems clear. Gold and yellow go with the sun because the sun is golden or yellow in colour. For the same reason silver and white belong to the moon. In the ancient world the sun and moon were believed to be the most important of the heavenly bodies and were distinguished from the others. They were the two which gave light and were therefore the most valuable to men, and it was natural to connect them with the two most important metals, gold and silver.

21   Blue is the colour of Jupiter because it is the colour of the sky, and Jupiter, the ruler of the gods, was lord of the sky. Tin may belong to Jupiter because the planet has a silvery appearance like tin. This link seems to be very old. The Sumerian term for tin was "metal of heaven," which suggests that they already connected it with the ruler of the sky and possibly they thought the sky was made of tin. Quicksilver belongs to Mercury (and is called mercury) because it is the most mobile of the metals and Mercury is a particularly fast-moving planet, which shoots across the sky at great speed, as is suitable for the god who carried the other god's messages.

22   Lead, the darkest and heaviest of the metals, was naturally assigned to Saturn, the dimmest and slowest-moving planet, which trudges heavily through its slow path round the sun. In the old cosmology Saturn is the farthest planet from the sun, the ruler of life, and is the lord of death. The analogy between death and night was drawn very early. Black is the colour of night and the colour invariably associated with death in Western countries.

23   Copper is the metal of Venus, probably because Aphrodite, the Greek Venus, was closely associated with Cyprus and Cyprus was the classical world's chief source of copper. The cult of Aphrodite ("the Cyprian") seems to have spread to Greece from the Near East through Cyprus, from which copper was also imported, and one of her principal shrines was at Paphos in western Cyprus, where she had been born from the sea. Venus is not only the ruler of love but also the mistress of Nature and the characteristic colour of Nature is green. In most languages the word for green is connected with words for plants, leaves and grass. Our "green" comes from the Germanic root *gro,* which probably meant "to grow" and also appears in "grow" and "grass."

24   The most interesting of correspondences is the link between Mars, iron and red. Iron became the metal of Mars when the superiority of iron

weapons over bronze weapons was discovered. The Hittites were the first people to develop the use of iron weapons. (They were also noted for the use of horses in battle and the horse is a beast of Mars in magic as a result.) The Assyrian army was equipped with iron weapons by 800 B.C. and dominated the Near East for two hundred years. The Dorians brought the Iron Age to Europe when they invaded Greece and defeated the bronze-wielding Achaeans.

25   Red is connected with Mars through several chains of association. The planet has a reddish look and the Egyptians called it "the red star." Red is the colour of blood and Mars was the god of bloodshed and war. The war-chiefs of Rome in early times painted themselves bright red with vermilion and the same custom has been found among other primitive peoples. Red is the colour of energy and vitality and in astrology Mars rules all forms of violent energy and activity.

26   The word for red in most languages is based on the fact that red is the colour of blood. Our "red," Greek *eruthros* and Latin *ruber* and *rufus* are all akin to Sanskirt *rudhira,* "blood." In primitive belief, the blood contains the body's life and so red becomes the colour of vigour and vitality. This is probably the explanation of the prehistoric custom of colouring corpses red. In a prehistoric graveyard near Nördlingen in Bavaria thirty-three human skulls were found embedded in red ochre (and all facing west, where the sun "dies" in the evening). Finds at Grimaldi in Italy included a boy's skeleton stained red with peroxide of iron, three bodies in a grave lined with red ochre and the scarlet skeleton of a man whose bones had been covered with powdered haematite. The intention was probably to keep the body in a usable condition in case its owner might need it again, by painting it with the colour of life and vitality.

27   The connection with blood and death gives red some sinister overtones. An ancient Egyptian papyrus contains a prayer to the goddess Isis— "O Isis, thou great magician, heal me and save me from all wicked, frighful and red things." The Egyptians had the curious custom of jeering at red-headed men on certain religious occasions. They connected red with Typhon, a demonic dragon and evil power. In Scotland and Ulster until fairly recent times a fisherman who met a red-headed woman on the way to his boat would turn back because he would have no luck with his fishing that day. If a woman with red hair came into a house where the milk was being churned it was thought that her presence would spoil the butter.

28   Because it carries a current of energy and vigour red can be used to make a particular powerful poison. In 1580 an epidemic broke out at Aix in France and an English doctor named Thomas Flud said it was caused by Jews who had gone about rubbing poison on the town's door-knockers. The poison was snake venom, but it was made peculiarly virulent by being

strained through people with red hair. Flud said that the Jews kidnapped a red-haired man and tied him to a cross, keeping his mouth open with a wedge of wood. Then they stung him with adders and collected the poisonous froth from his mouth. Others stripped a red-headed woman, buried her in the ground up to her middle, stung her breasts with adders and drained the slaver from her lips.

29   People's reactions to colours today seem to match their traditional occult significance remarkably neatly, whether because colours really do have their own innate force or simply as the result of the association of the same ideas with them for centuries. Green, which is traditionally the colour of Venus, the force of love, peace and harmony, does exert a peaceful, pleasant, tranquillising influence. Blue has a subduing effect which is an appropriate reaction to the colour of Jupiter, the ruler of all things. Red, the colour of energy and vitality, has a highly stimulating and exciting influence. B. J. Kouwer found that the ideas which people tend to associate with red are passion, emotion, temperament, action, rebelliousness, force, sexuality, tension, love, spontaneity, victory, shame. Most of these fit very well with the magical and astrological character of red as the colour of Mars, the planet of force, battle, action, energy, vitality, and connotations of violent emotion, passion and sexual vigour. Ovid in his *Fasti* called Priapus, the god of the phallus, "red Priapus", and it is the red light which marks the brothel. Similarly, Kouwer found that the ideas generally associated with black, the colour of the grim and ominous Saturn, are death, night, murder, anxiety, defeat.

UNDERSTANDING THE SELECTION

1. This selection should help you to understand how symbols develop. For example, Cavendish points out in his final paragraph that people seem to associate certain feelings and ideas with colors. After such an association has continued for centuries, the colors become *symbols* of the things people associate them with.

   What associations do you have for the following colors: brown, purple, pink, turquoise, white? Are these colors symbolic in any way?

2. Yellow is traditionally linked with the sun and gold, both good. How, do you suppose, did it come to stand for cowardice, too?

3. In paragraph 1, Cavendish explains that magicians seek knowledge which will give them the power of gods. Does knowledge bring power? Is unlimited knowledge a good thing? Consider such things as the H-bomb, cryonics (which claims the ability to freeze a man when he dies and bring him back to life at a time when he can be cured), space exploration, and heart transplants.

4. In the light of this selection, what do you make of the old custom of throwing salt over your left shoulder when you have spilled it?

5. Do the flatworm experiments at the University of Michigan (paragraph 17) suggest anything to you about cannibalism? Why is cannibalism practiced in some tribes? Has it any connection with the rite of Holy Communion?

6. Do we still believe that blood somehow "contains . . . life"? Is the heart the most vital organ? Is it symbolic of life?

Do we still disapprove of left-handed people? Of red-haired people?

32 The Death of Tommy Grimes

R. J. Meaddough III

1   Tommy had become part of the ground. At least he felt that way as he watched the dew and the daylight make giant shiny cobwebs of the treetops. The sun had not yet risen and a mist lay over the ground, which made the forest seem rather spooky to him.

2   His nose itched and he longed to scratch it, maybe just nudge it a little, but Pa said don't move, don't twitch, don't even breathe hard. Not one arm, one hand, even one finger, he said. "He knows the woods," Pa told him; "you'll never know he's there; suddenly he'll just *be* there looking at you, just looking."

3   It started so long ago, Tommy remembered, almost a year, when he was just eleven. That night, in the hen-yard, with the weasel's eyes glistening in the flashlight. He never even fired a shot, just stood there with his mouth open, foolish, while the weasel dashed into the woods.

4   And Pa knocking the rifle from his hands and asking, "Why didn't you shoot? What you waiting on? What's wrong with you, boy?"

5   "Pa, I . . . I couldn't, Pa. I just couldn't."

6   Pa hunkered down and pulled on a blade of grass. He didn't say anything for a minute, just knelt there chewing on that grass.

7   "You never did like to kill nothing did you, boy? Even when you was small."

8   Tommy looked at the ground without saying anything and his father sighed, "Tommy, dammit, a man *always* dies a little when he kills something, but it just plain has to be done. Some animals just ain't no damn good and got to be *killed*. Understand?"

9   He nodded without answering, still looking at the ground, and Pa stood up with a groan and they walked into the hen-house without speaking. They counted forty-three dead pullets, lying in red and white patches of feathers, blood and confusion.

10   So he began to practice with the rifle, shooting at moving targets, and the rifle became part of his arm. It seemed so long that Pa practiced with him, so long. Again and again he would take a deep breath, let some out, then squeeze the trigger. So long, so very long.

11   Tommy felt beads of sweat form on his forehead despite the chill that remained in the forest air. Soon the beads would form into droplets and run down his face and burn his eyes. There was a handkerchief in his coat pocket just a few inches away but he could not, dare not reach for it. But soon it would be over. Soon.

12   It got so that he could hit anything he aimed at, even things a good bit out. And sometimes, when he turned real quick, he would see pride in Pa's eyes. But then Pa would always make his face blank and say, "We-e-ell, Tommy," real grim-like, "you're getting better but you need more practice."

13   Pa taught him how to track animals and how to lead quail, and how to lean into the rifle to take up the recoil. And Pa showed him how to lie quiet so the forest forgot he was there and Nature went on about her business.

14   And the time came last night when Pa came home and mentioned that some of the men were going into the forest to get a buck; and how it might be some good shooting because bucks were fast, real fast.

15   He bent his head to eat his beans, yet he knew without looking that his father was watching him, way out of the corner of his eye. He knew, too, that Pa wouldn't have said a word if Ma was there—she was always saying he was too young for something or other—but she was visiting overnight up in Colliersville. And he thought how it must be for Pa when the other men bragged about their boys, and him so scared to kill a weasel, and he knew what he had to do.

16   "Pa," he murmered, "think maybe I could go a time at that old buck?"

17   "Boy, this ain't no old buck, it's a young one," Pa said, making like he was surprised. "Boy, you might get hurt."

18   "Some time, I think I'd like to take my turn," he answered, face even closer to the beans.

19   "Well I'll think about it, boy," Pa mumbled, but he couldn't hide a gleam in his eye.

20   Tommy slowly, ever so slowly, rubbed his forehead along his sleeve and watched the gloom in front of him. Somewhere out there Pa had circled around and was trampling through the woods, scaring everything away, away toward the clearing where he lay waiting.

21   He laughed in his mind when he thought of the last time when Pa had gone down to the Hut for a drink with the "boys," as he called them. And when he came out his eyes were gleaming like the mischief and he wob-

bled into the yard like he didn't know how to walk. He had gone downstairs in his pajamas and they sat on the back porch and listened to the crickets and looked at the stars. Maybe afterwards Pa would let him go into the Hut and talk with the men and drink liquor. But right then he had to be satisfied with listening to Pa tell stories that he had heard at the Hut and then squeeze his arm at the end and laugh, oh my, how he would laugh. Then he filled his pipe and stared out across the backyard toward the north pasture.

22   "Dawn in the forest is a beautiful thing, boy, beautiful. All the colors and wild flowers, fresh streams, cool breeze, you feel like, boy, feel it! Even though there ain't a sound you feel it. You see a flash of white and you know some rabbit's going home. Or you might see a chuck burrowing in. And the trees," he whispered, "they just stand there watching you. Been there before you came, be there after you gone."

23   "Gee, Pa," he murmured, "you make it sound so nice I don't know's I want to *hunt* tomorrow."

24   Pa smiled. "It *is* nice, boy, real nice, but things got to be done to keep it that way. Fox eats a rabbit, he keeps the rabbit population down, else they'd overrun the land. Same here. You hunt 'cause you hungry and got to eat, that's one reason. Then you might hunt for the sport—pit your mind against animal cunning—'course I don't hold much with that, but some do. Some do. But there's some varmints that do damage and just plain got to be killed. Understand?"

25   "I . . . think so. But what about what you said about a man dying when he kills something?"

26   "Man kills once and he starts to get callous. Next time it ain't so hard. Then you get so's you make a decision that something's got to die and you kill it, just like that. Then you dead, boy. You got no feeling no more so you just as good as dead. You just ain't had time to lay down."

27   Tommy wiggled his toes and got no response. They felt like sticks of wood, stilts that somebody had glued on his legs. An ant left the ground and started climbing his arm until he blew, softly, blew the ant into some brave new world. The mist was thinning and the sun began to shine dully through the trees. Pa was right, he thought. Seems as if everything had a place in the scheme of things. Birds ate worms they found on the ground. Then they got eaten by bigger birds. Rabbits got eaten by foxes and foxes by bobcats, and bobcats by bears or something all the way up to elephants. And elephants were killed by man. Pa said that man preyed on himself, whatever that meant, but everything had a place, and when they got out of place they upset the balance. Like too many rabbits or squirrels or anything.

28   A twig snapped like dynamite and he froze on the ground and swiveled the gun to the left and waited. Slowly, clumsily, with three blades of

grass waving like pennants ahead of him, a porcupine strolled into view, made his way through the sunlight, and vanished into the grass. Tommy laughed, out loud almost, he could hardly keep from blowing up he was so relieved, so happy. Instead he settled down again to wait.

29   But things had changed somehow. The sunlight was duller, almost disappearing and he felt a chill again as he had before the sun came up. And the silence somehow nettled him . . . *the silence!* Not a sound! No crickets, no chirping, no rustling, nothing. There was something out there! The happy-scared feeling ran up and down Tommy's back and his breath came in painful gasps. His chest hammered, almost pushing his lungs into his mouth with its rhythm which seemed to be saying: *Soon! Soon! Soon they would be calling him Tom Grimes like his father. Soon he would be able to go into the Hut and drink liquor with the rest of the men. Soon the waiting would be over. Soon he would be grown. Soon. Soon. Soon. Soon! Soon! Soon!*

30   There! In the bushes! A little pinch of color behind the bramble bush moving light and easy, so very easy, behind the bushes. He slid down still further behind the gun and spread his feet wide, toes digging into the soft earth. "Put the whole side of your body behind the gun to take the recoil," Pa had said. "Spread your legs wide to brace yourself. Make the gun, your arm, your hip, your leg into one long line." Tommy drew his breath in and nearly gagged trying to hold it, sighting along the clean black ridges of the rifle. The outline was clear behind the bush, creeping, sniffling, gliding along.

31   "You won't see it, or hear it, or smell it, or anything," Pa had told him. "You'll just feel it, and it'll be there."

32   Tommy breathed out and in, let some of the air out and chokingly began to squeeze the trigger. Would it never go off, his mind asked, reeling and stumbling and clinging desperately to reality, and the earth stuttered. The light blinked. His ears rang. His nose reacted to the smell of smoke and the taste of ink crept into his mouth. There was a rustling sound in the bushes and a thrashing, a terrible thrashing and rattling, but it stopped. Suddenly it stopped. Tommy blinked. It was over; just like that, it was over.

33   He got to his feet and the stiffness forced him to lean against a tree trunk. Before there had been nothing, then suddenly there was something, a small patch of color the same as Pa's jacket. Tommy blinked and listened for the crashing sound of someone coming through the forest—but there was nothing. Nothing. He strained his ears and heard new-sprung crickets and birdcalls, but no crashing, no rustling, no voice, and he started for the bush and then stopped, trembling.

34   "Pa?" he whispered, "Pa-a-a?" There was no sound except his own voice, twisted and shapeless and mocking, twirling through the trees like vapors in the dull, chilly air. "Pa! Pa! Pa!"

35   Then came the rushing and the crashing to the left and the tall husky figure coming out of the gloom saying, "Boy? What's wrong, boy?" And Tommy ran over and slammed his head against his father's chest. "Pa! I thought I killed you, Pa, I thought I killed you, Pa, I thought I killed a man!"

36   "Now, Tommy, it's all right, everything's all right," Pa said, walking behind the bush and kneeling and then rising and coming back.

37   "See?" he said. "What did I tell you? Right through the heart. Now that's good shooting. Come on over here and look; come on, now."

38   So he looked, and then it wasn't so bad.

39   Later, much later, they walked the mile from town to the Hut and walked inside together. There were some men sitting at tables and they looked up as Pa hoisted him onto the bar, running his fingers through his dark, blond hair.

40   "Boys, I wanna tell you my boy became a man today. Yessir, killed his first nigger."

41   "No!" a man said. "Who?"

42   "Swamp-buck got away from the chain gang yes-tidy."

43   "Git out!" the man said.

44   "Yessir, got him right through the heart."

45   The man grabbed Tommy and hugged him around the knees. "You a man now, boy!" he yelled, "you a real live honest-to-goodness 'fore God man!"

46   And Pa, his blue eyes agleam, yelled out, "Bartender! Don't just stand there! Give this man a drink!"

47   The man sat Tommy down on the bar and the liquor made him cough a bit as it coursed down his throat and it made his ears ring like the tolling of bells. But he smiled happily as the feeling of warmth like Mississippi sunshine spread through his insides. For now he belonged.

UNDERSTANDING THE SELECTION

1. Why do you supposed the story is entitled "The Death of Tommy Grimes" since Tommy did not die?

2. What connotations does Tommy's last name have for you?

3. The next to the last sentence of the story reads, "But he smiled happily as the feeling of warmth like Mississippi sunshine spread through his insides." Discuss metaphor, allusion, and symbol in this sentence.

4. Discuss "Pa," the "boys down at the Hut," and Tommy as symbols.

5. What other symbols does the writer use?

6. In paragraph 27 occurs this sentence: "Pa said that . . . everything had a place, and when they got out of place they upset the balance." What does Pa mean? Did you understand his meaning when you first read the story? If not, what did the sentence mean for you?

7. The jolting effect from this story comes from your recognition only at the very end of the story of what it was that Tommy shot. Yet the author actually tells you quite early in the tale what was being hunted. The surprise in the story hinges on the different meanings—both denotative and connotative—of a single word. What is that word? What are its connotations for Tommy? For you?

8. The author of this story is a young New York Negro. Does knowing this fact influence your judgment of the story in any way?

33   The Flea

John Donne

Mark but this flea, and mark in this
How little that which thou deny'st me is;
    It suck'd me first, and now sucks thee,
And in this flea our two bloods mingled be.
    Thou know'st that this cannot be said   5
A sin, nor shame, nor loss of maidenhead;
    Yet this enjoys before it woo,
And pamper'd, swells with one blood made of two,
And this, alas, is more than we would do.

O stay, three lives in one flea spare,   10
Where we almost, yea more than married are.
    This flea is you and I, and this
Our marriage bed and marriage temple is;
    Though parents grudge, and you, we're met
And cloister'd in these living walls of jet.   15
    Though use make you apt to kill me,
Let not to that, self-murder added be,
And sacrilege: three sins in killing three.

Cruel and sudden, hast thou since
Purpled thy nail in blood of innocence?   20
    Wherein could this flea guilty be,
Except in that drop which it suck'd from thee?
    Yet thou triumph'st, and say'st that thou
Find'st not thyself nor me the weaker now.
    'Tis true. Then learn how false fears be: 25
Just so much honor, when thou yield'st to me,
Will waste, as this flea's death took life from thee.

UNDERSTANDING THE SELECTION

1. John Donne wrote in the early part of the seventeenth century. His youthful work consisted mainly of a number of cynical poems about men and women, and a few tender love poems. In his middle age he was ordained into the Church of England, became the most famous preacher of his time, and wrote some very powerful religious sonnets. "The Flea" obviously belongs to his early work.

2. Who is the speaker in the poem? Describe him as fully as possible. To whom is he speaking? Describe the listener as fully as possible. Describe where they are, what time of day it is.

3. The speaker is arguing with his listener. What point is he trying to make? Express it in your own words.

4. What does *this* in line 7 refer to?

5. You may have trouble understanding lines 16 through 18. *Use* means "custom." *Apt* can mean both "likely" and "quick to learn." *To kill* means "to murder," but it also refers to a slang expression of Donne's day: people called having sexual intercourse "dying." *That* in line 17 refers to "kill me." What are the *three sins* and who are the three who are killed?

6. Who or what is *cruel and sudden* in line 19?

7. Is the flea a symbol in the first stanza? In the second? In the third? If so, what does it symbolize in each? Is the flea a real flea anywhere in the poem?

8. Do you think the speaker convinced his listener that he was in the right?

Stereotype

Another element of writing is the *stereotype*. Whereas a symbol clearly and succinctly uses something simple (a journey) to express something complex (life), the stereotype inaccurately and too simply describes all the parts of a group. To talk of the shamrock in connection with Ireland is to use a symbol; to talk of "the Irish peasant" as if everyone in Ireland had gnarled laborer's hands, spent his time digging peat moss, and believed in leprechauns is to resort to a stereotype. A stereotype, then, is a generalization about a group which may not describe accurately a single member of the group but which many of us accept without thinking. Stereotypes also indicate approval or disapproval of the group. For example, we tend to accept the notions that all redheads have fiery tempers, all Scotsmen are thrifty, all Italians love opera, and all cowboys are big, simple, honest, and gentle. In actuality, many redheads are mild, some Scotsmen are spend-thrifts, a few Italians are tone-deaf, and there are cowboys who are nothing but hoodlums on horses.

In spite of their oversimplification, stereotypes abound in all kinds of writing; some authors use them deliberately, while others are unaware they have employed them. In order to understand the meaning of a piece of writing, you often must recognize the stereotypes in it.

To see just how widespread stereotyping is, list the characteristics which you feel describe the following groups. Then compare your lists with those made by others in your class. If you find that your descriptions are almost identical with the descriptions your classmates give, you probably all subscribe to a stereotype.

1. Hollywood starlets	6. New Yorkers
2. waitresses	7. Lithuanians
3. class presidents	8. sports-car owners
4. American Indians	9. poets
5. labor leaders	10. scientists

34   Dog

Anthony

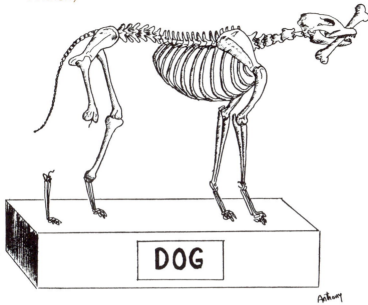

UNDERSTANDING THE SELECTION

1. The man who mounted the skeleton had a stereotyped notion of what a dog should resemble. What was his stereotype of a dog?

2. Do stereotypes always produce results as illogical and inaccurate as this   skeleton?

35   To My Mother

George Barker

Most near, most dear, most loved and most far,
Under the window where I often found her
Sitting as huge as Asia, seismic with laughter,
Gin and chicken helpless in her Irish hand,
Irresistible as Rabelais, but most tender for   5
The lame dogs and hurt birds that surround her,—
She is a procession no one can follow after
But be like a little dog following a brass band.

She will not glance up at the bomber, or condescend
To drop her gin and scuttle to a cellar,   *10*
But lean on the mahogany table like a mountain
Whom only faith can move, and so I send
O all my faith, and all my love to tell her
That she will move from mourning into morning.

UNDERSTANDING THE SELECTION

1. In what period of time does the poem take place?
2. What does "seismic with laughter" mean?
3. What does the mother look like?
4. How do people feel toward her?
5. What qualities in his mother does the writer most admire?
6. Do you feel that mothers "ought" to have certain qualities? In other words, have you a stereotype of mothers? Does this mother fit it?
7. Pick out and explain the allusions in this poem.

36   *The Wastrel*

Reginald Wright Kauffman

Once, when I was little, as the summer night was falling,
   Among the purple upland fields I lost my barefoot way;
The road to home was hidden fast and frightful shadows, crawling
   Along the sky-line, swallowed up the last kind light of day;
     And then I seemed to hear you   *5*
     In the twilight, and be near you;
   Seemed to hear your dear voice calling—
   Through the meadow, calling, calling—
     And I followed and I found you,
     Flung my tired arms around you,   *10*
And rested on the mother-breast, returned, tired out from play.

Down the days from that day, though I trod strange paths unheeding,
   Though I chased the jack-o'-lanterns of so many maddened years,
Though I never looked behind me, where the home-lights were receding,
   Though I never looked enough ahead to ken the Inn of Fears;   *15*

Still I knew your heart was near me,
That your ear was strained to hear me,
That your love would need no pleading
To forgive me, but was pleading
Of its self that, in disaster,   *20*
I should run to you the faster
And be sure that I was dearer for your sacrifice of tears.

Now on life's last Summertime the long last dusk is falling,
    And I, who trod one way so long, can tread no other way
Until at death's dim crossroads I watch, hesitant, the crawling *25*
    Night-passages that maze me with the ultimate dismay.
        Then when Death and Doubt shall blind me—
        Even then—I know you'll find me:
    I shall hear you, Mother, calling—
    Hear you calling—calling—calling: *30*
        I shall fight and follow—find you
        Though the grave-clothes swathe and bind you,
And I know your love will answer: "Here's my laddie home
    from play!"

UNDERSTANDING THE SELECTION

1. What is a *wastrel?*
2. What kind of person is the man who speaks in the poem? How old is he? What do you think he has done in his lifetime? How does he feel about himself? How mature a man is he?
3. What symbol does the poem use to represent the speaker's life?
4. Compare the mother in this selection with the one in "To My Mother" (Selection 35). Is the mother of "The Wastrel" what a mother "ought" to be like? Can you draw a picture of her? In what ways are the two mothers alike? Unlike?
5. If you were asked to judge "To My Mother" and "The Wastrel," which would you say is the "better" poem? Why?

37   Domestic Interior

Leslie Krims

Photograph by Leslie Krims.

UNDERSTANDING THE SELECTION

1. You have probably seen many pictures in Sunday supplements or in women's magazines which show the interiors of mansions, apartments, beach houses, remodelled barns, and the like. From such pictures you can deduce a number of things about the people who live there. Does the woman in the picture live in this room? Does she live here alone or has she a husband? Has she children? What is her social, educational, and economic background?

2. Is the room a sterotype? Consider such things as the furniture and its arrangement, the accessories, the pictures.

3. Is the woman a sterotype? Consider such things as her pose, her age, her hair, and, of course, her nudity.

4. Do you think she is a mother? If so, does she fit your idea of what a mother "ought" to be like? Compare her with the mothers in "To My Mother" (Selection 35) and "The Wastrel" (Selection 36).

5. What would your mother think of the woman in the photograph? What do you think of her? What does the photographer think of her? Give reasons for your answers.

6. Is this photograph effective? Why or why not?

38 Quiet Night

Elizabeth Seifert

1   Fifty years old. In thirty years of nursing, how many buttons had she put into clean uniforms, and how many of the pesky little bars had she run under her fingernail? Now she'd have a sore thumb for days. If she were still on operating or delivery duty, she'd have to report that puncture. It didn't matter with a floor head.

2   A fiftieth birthday, for a nurse, was like a baseball player's fortieth; few celebrated them on the field. But Grieder felt that she was good for another ten years. She hoped that she was. What night duty would do without her—Why, even her day off once a week, her two weeks' vacation each year, put things in a mess. The substitute head couldn't even get feedings on time.

3   There! A pin through her cap, and she'd be ready—five minutes to spare. The kids laughed at Grieder's cap. The little hospital where she'd trained had been out of existence so long that nobody ever saw another cap like Grieder's. But she was still proud of its bulbous whiteness. She remembered the first time she'd put it on: It had set up on a round pompadour then. Her high collar had fastened with a gold-washed collarbutton, like a man's, and her skirts had touched her insteps. Regulations had said two starched petticoats and muslin drawers. Just last week Dr. Tallen had asked her what was wrong with a new Special's uniform. Grieder, looking at the girl, had discovered that a pink slip was showing through the starched white poplin of her dress. . . .

4   She went downstairs and walked across the lawn toward Maternity. There were cherries on the little trees, and two training nurses eating them, though they weren't ripe.

5   "If you kids aren't careful, we'll have to send for a doctor," Grieder said dryly, continuing on her way. A little new moon swung in the exact center of the pale sky. It was spring in Missouri.

6   Supper was Grieder's best meal; she was always tired at morning breakfast, but she enjoyed supper. She ate steadily, listening to the young girls complain of the plain, hearty food. Well, it would take more than their talk to spoil her appetite. "Thank God for a good digestion." That made her best grace before meat.

7   Haskell came in. She was on eight-hour Special, the soft seven-to-three trick. Trust Tallen for seeing she had that! Tonight she was dressed to the nines, and was cross.

8   "Going out?" Grieder asked.

9   "M-hmmm. Heavy date. Been trying to sleep—but the Dorm's a hell."

10   "Your age, you ought to sleep through thunder."

11   Haskell glared. She wanted people to think she was much younger than thirty-five. Just as she went around lying about her weight. What difference did it make? Ten pounds. Haskell was a darned good-looking woman. Men like Tallen—men she wanted to attract—admired a well-set-up woman of thirty-five.

12   "How's the schedule?" Grieder asked, buttering a biscuit.

13   "I should care. I'm on Special."

14   "I thought, maybe, your date was with—er—some one it did matter to if something important turns up. Like the Srenco case."

15   Two kinds of deliveries intrigued Tallen. The showy, difficult ones he could be dramatic about, and the babies of Big Names. Like Srenco, the movie man, one of the richest men in the little city of Darbridge.

16   "Srenco kid born this morning. I wish I'd been free to take it."

17   "Greeks aren't generous. Wife's only seventeen. Probably spoiled."

18   "How do you know so much?"

19   Grieder looked at the handsome, auburn-haired woman across from her. "A thing you ought to learn, Haskell, is that it may be important to keep your eyes and ears open even if you're not paid to do it. You Special eight hours a day. But at three o'clock you drop everything—baby crying, mother on the nest—and you don't think another thing about nursing until you come on duty five minutes late the next morning."

20   "So what? I should spend my free hours worrying about my patient's after-pains? Or wrapping bandages for the Sisters?"

21   Grieder had been guilty of both charges. "You might," she agreed.

22   Haskell pushed back her chair—stood smiling down at Grieder. "I spend my free hours lightening the cares of the Chief," she said boldly.

23   Grieder nodded, not shocked one bit as Haskell had thought she would be. "And you ought to be old enough, too, to know that that's bad business. Tallen won't marry you. And when he gets tired of playing around with you, he won't want to see you around the hospital. You'll be out, Haskell."

24   She would be, too. Grieder had seen it happen a hundred times.

25   She went upstairs and checked in, ten minutes early. While she stood chatting to Sister Mary Joseph, a taxi pulled up at the broad steps, and the driver helped a heavily burdened woman out of the cab. Grieder went to meet the case. She was just a girl, big-eyed, scared. She had only a shabby suitcase. The purse from which she paid the driver was thin and torn.

26   "I—" She spoke to Sister. "Dr. McHendry said it was time to come."

27   "Yes. Are you registered?"

28   Grieder turned away, walking along the hall with a third-year girl who went on duty with her for the night.

29   "Ward case," the girl said. "She isn't married."

30   "What of it? They have the baby the same way. And usually a pret-
tier baby than the ones that come through a wedding-ring."

31   "O.K. O.K."

32   "What did you say?" Miss Grieder was Head; and this girl should
remember that fact.

33   "Yes, Miss Grieder." The girl stepped back respectfully to let the
Head enter the elevator first. Grieder saw the face that was made at her
shoulder blades. The back of the elevator was a mirror. At the same age
as this girl, Grieder would have had the sense to remember that.

34   The first half-hour of duty was always busy. Nurses reporting on
and off duty. Night corps to be inspected. Night orders to be read, but not
marked up yet on the charts. Rounds with the night interne, an earnest
youngster, with gold-rimmed glasses. Grieder liked internes as she had never
liked them when she was younger. But she still dealt firmly with them. They
must not be allowed to indulge in "monkey business." That term was an
elastic one, covering a multitude of sins: smoking on the fire escape, dally-
ing with the nurses, a half-hour nap stolen in an empty room. This young
man followed her respectfully. Stood patiently if she chose to chatter for
a minute with a mother. She cut short her description of Nelson Eddy in
Maytime because of his patience. More than one mother, knowing her weakness, asked her what film she'd seen that afternoon. Well, she could do
worse things than spend her off hours decently in a movie.

35   This interne—Hunter, his name was—would make a good doctor.
He let a patient argue him into giving her a pill tonight instead of oil in the
morning, and didn't make a crack about no oil being ordered for her. Mothers of experience usually worked up a temperature over the oil they knew
they'd probably get the third morning. It was nice when they didn't have to
have it.

36   Back at her desk, the charts must be gone over carefully, the night
orders written in, the evening readings recorded. Grieder liked to make
the neat figures and lines on the charts; she liked the smack of each board
being pushed into the proper slot. Doing this job, she was pleasantly aware
of the visitors in the corridors. Grieder liked the beaming young fathers,
the important new grandmothers. There were always flowers in Maternity,
and noise didn't matter. Yes, Maternity was far more cheerful than Surgical
or Medical.

37   A walking case came to the door of the Head's cubicle and asked
if she might telephone. "I live out of town. I was waiting for the night rates
so I could phone my husband. I think it's all a mistake. I might as well go
home for a few weeks."

38   Grieder got up, smoothing her uniform. "You can phone if it'll help you. But I expect your baby isn't far off. I wouldn't plan to go home."

39   "But—if it runs the bill up so big—"

40   "I wouldn't worry about that—if you can help it."

41   Grieder led the way down the corridor. The woman wore a robe of brown corduroy, plain and new. Grieder could estimate the financial ability of a patient by her negligee. This woman was a good manager, paid her bills, on a small income.

42   The outside telephone was in a little cubby at the farthest end of the hall, past the delivery room, where the nurses were busy over the girl who had come up an hour ago, the bathroom and sterilizing rooms and the doctors' scrub-up room and lockers. In the cubby, a pale young doctor was climbing into white trousers. He flushed when he saw the Head and the patient. "I'm Dr. McHendry," he said unhappily.

43   "Good evening, Doctor. You can keep your things in a locker in yonder."

44   He should have spoken to the Head before this. Obviously, he was one of Public Health's men, strange to this hospital. Grieder hoped he knew his business.

45   She asked the mother in brown corduroy if she could get back to her room. "You know the number?"

46   "Yes—88. And—thank you."

47   It was almost eight-thirty. Time to begin warning the die-hards. The worst would be 52. A week ago, Grieder had had to call the interne to put this father out. All rules to the contrary, he was determined to stand guard; he'd heard some fine stories of women mistreated, babies mixed up. He still tried to stay overtime.

48   This was a twelve-dollar room, the baby sleeping in a bassinet at the foot of the mother's bed. Usually these patients had Specials; 52 didn't. Grieder marched in.

49   "Good evening, Mother. Good evening, Father."

50   "Good evening. Nurse, can my wife have a cup of coffee?"

51   "Not at night."

52   "It quiets her. She isn't like most people."

53   "I'll get her some hot milk if she can't sleep." Last night the floor nurse had had almost to club 52 awake at ten-o'clock feeding. "How's the baby?"

54   "Will you see if he's dry, nurse? He sleeps so steadily, and I don't want him—"

55   "You'll learn to let 'em sleep when they will. Anything hurting him, he'd yell."

56   "And how he yells!" the mother said smugly. "Not a little kitten-mew like the one across the hall."

57   It was against the rules to discuss one case with another. The baby across the hall had a paralyzed face. "That mother had long hard labor—she wasn't lucky enough to have an easy time like you."

58   "Easy! A lot you nurses know! I suffered agonies!"

59   "I guess you nurses get pretty hard-boiled, seeing so much pain," the father said.

60   "Well, maybe we do. Good night, Father."

61   To her pleased surprise, he left. Grieder went across the hall to turn 89's pillow, and show joy at the news that the baby had nursed a little that day. "He'll get over it, won't he, nurse?"

62   "Sure, he'll get over it."

63   Eight-thirty, and visitors trooping down the halls, chattering at the elevator. Grieder spoke sharply to the nurses; they must have their charges ready and quiet within half an hour. The delivery room was busy.

64   Things were going along busily in the hall. More than half the lights burned red; bedpans clanged in the lavatory; a kid spilled a pitcher of hot lysol water on the floor. Sister came sailing down the hall, her cap wings trembling, her gown belling out about her.

65   "Get a mop and clean it up," Grieder told the young nurse. "You're going to be late to bed, Sister Raymond."

66   Sister's eyeglasses flashed. She glanced at the flustered kid. "Late? Ah, no, Miss Grieder. I've still time for a jig and then get to bed on the dot."

67   "I'd like to see the jig," a Special laughed, waiting for the mess to be cleaned up.

68   Sister Raymond cast a quick look down the hall—grasped her full skirts in both hands, pointed the toes of her heavy black shoes, did an expert cut and shuffle, and was demurely off down the hall again as Mother Superior came around the corner for night rounds. Grieder glared at the Special and at the kid; they mustn't give Sister away by laughing.

69   Nine o'clock. Grieder herself went to the switch and dimmed the lights. Those in the delivery room blazed. She'd go there as soon as the nurses going off duty had reported. Delivery-room Head hated her snooping around, but she'd go, anyway. This floor was her responsibility. She'd have a look at that young Public Health man. Sometimes these unwed mothers didn't want their babies bad enough to work for them.

70   Miss Wiley, Delivery Head, looked up sharply at her entrance. The patient lay inert on the table; the young doctor was washing his hands.

71   "Did you want something, Miss Grieder?"

72   "How are things going? I was about to report to Dr. Tallen."

73   "Is Dr. Tallen in the hospital?" The young doctor turned sharply, hope lighting his pale face.

74   "No. But I phone him each night about this time." She didn't, unless he was needed. She saw Wiley's eyebrows go up.

75   "Office asks us to economize on cotton, Miss Wiley," she said firmly. One new roll had fallen to the floor, a dead loss. You could almost always catch a "smart" nurse out if you wanted to. "Have you any word for Dr. Tallen, Doctor?"

76   "Why, I'm Dr. McHendry, of Public Health. He doesn't know me. . . . But tell him I'd like his advice on this case. Very little prenatal care."

77   "I'll tell him."

78   She would tell him all of that, and a few things she could think up for herself. She was pretty sure Haskell's evening would be a short one. One thing she must grant Tallen; he respected Grieder's estimate of trouble in the delivery room.

79   Ten o'clock. For fifteen minutes the babies had been tuning up for feeding time.

80   The nursery was well filled. Spring was rush season in Maternity. Grieder inspected the new ones, arrived since last night. She nodded to the masked nurses behind the glass, gestured toward the carts and the clock, and went into the hall again. She could smell coffee—evidently Tallen had come.

81   The Srenco baby in 54 was crying. Grieder peeked around the swinging half-door. The Special was sound asleep; the room was a welter of flowers, and no window open. A wonder everybody wasn't yelling, or smothered. The mother was pretty; black hair spilled richly upon the pillow, white satin and blue ribbons puffed about a round, creamy arm. Regulations said hospital shirt for the first three days. Rich as the Srencos were, regulations be hanged! But the Special shouldn't sleep with the baby crying; and these flowers—Lord, the things Grieder didn't have to see to! She was the one who had a right to be cross, not the lazy Special. Eight-hour duty was a cinch. One mother, one baby—was that work?

82   Grieder went on down the hall. In Delivery she could see Tallen's huge back. His gown was never tied below the neck, and his undershirt and belt were displayed. A good doctor, though—when he wanted to be. A doctor probably hadn't the right to "want" or not "want" to be.

83   She went into Diet and got some fruit for 67, who couldn't have milk or cocoa—because she had too much milk anyway, without a baby to nurse it.

84   A sweet person 67 was—anxious not to make trouble. Tallen had worked hard to save her. He couldn't make it with the baby. Too bad; at six months it had been a little wax doll, had lived five hours, and cried.

85   Grieder put the plate of grapes and oranges on the bedside table—and examined the bandages she herself had wrapped around these useless breasts. The mother smiled at her weakly: "I'm feeling much better. My husband brought me a box of candy; if you'd like a piece—"

86   Against the rules, but Grieder selected a fat chocolate, and took her time eating it. It seemed to please the mother.

87   Grieder told her about *Maytime.* "I cried buckets. Sort of relaxes you to cry when you know it isn't real trouble."

88   "Yes, I know. Is there a baby being born?"

89   "Always a baby being born around here."

90   "Dr. Tallen stuck his head in my door and made a face at me. He's wonderful, isn't he?"

91   Grieder grunted. Tallen was a whale. He looked like one of his own pink-and-white babies. But most of the mothers fell in love with him. He'd treat this woman as if she was the most important case he had. When she'd come back for her six-weeks' check-up, he'd hardly remember the case. They always resented that, the mothers.

92   Feeding time was the most restful period of the night. Grieder had a few minutes to examine tonight's backache, to talk about it a little to the nursery girls who were waiting with their carts. . . .

93   They had diarrhea up in Children's free nursery. And the Supe was worried for fear the papers would get word of it. Papers could always stir up bad publicity about a hospital. They ought to make news of the good things that went on all the time.

94   Grieder told the girls to be careful. Diarrhea didn't spread except by diapers, and nurses' hands.

95   "What starts it?" the youngest girl asked impudently. She was like a Dutch doll, with smooth blond hair cut square, wide blue eyes. She would bear watching.

96   "Things being quiet," Grieder told the older girl, "I'm running up to Children's. They have a substitute Head—she's young."

97   She heard the Dutch doll ask innocently if you had to be a hundred years old to be trusted around here. Yes, that girl would bear watching. . . .

98   Grieder's eye was caught by something white and strange out in the shadowy hall. The baby-carts had gone up several minutes ago. She stepped to the door. A woman in a short hospital shirt, tied at the neck, floating away at the side, was wandering barefooted down the hall. Grieder had had one or two experiences with sleepwalkers. Why, it was the mother with the corduroy robe. Or rather, without it! Her costume was nothing for a promenade—good thing she hadn't done this during visiting

hours. If Grieder could get her back without Tallen seeing her. . . . It was the sort of thing he'd make a joke of.

99   She put her strong arm about this half-conscious mother. "We go this way, dear." Docilely the woman turned, let Grieder guide her. Tallen was telephoning. In 88, Grieder put on the call-light, helped the mother into bed. So far, so good, but she'd have to be watched. And no money for a Special. Well, the floor nurse could sit here as well as at the call-desk. Baby in the morning, probably. Poor dear.

100   Twelve. Lunch to get for herself, her two assistants, Tallen and the delivery crew. Grieder had most of it to do herself, because she'd put the floor nurse in 88, and the second girl was too young to know anything about the diet kitchen. Coffee was started. Milk. Creamed eggs. Toast for this gang took plenty of time.

101   Tallen came in, talking to Miss Wiley.

102   The youngster on Delivery came flying down the hall. That was bad. When patients heard some one running, it scared them. Tallen got up and went down the hall.

103   "I guess she wasn't fooling," Grieder heard him say. "It'll be here before my eggs get cold."

104   Grieder didn't want to go down; but she was right behind Tallen. There wasn't time for much ether. . . . Even Tallen showed that he was worried.

105   After it was over, Grieder went back to her desk. Nodded to the floor nurse. "Boy."

106   Grieder sat down heavily in her chair. She was tired.

107   The girl turned and went out. At the door she gave a muffled scream, then giggled. Grieder went to see what was up.

108   She was a little startled, too. Dr. Tallen was sitting in the wheelchair, pretending sleep or unconsciousness, his pink hands folded across his round belly. Balloon-like in his white gown, he looked like a patient.

109   A few minutes later he came into her cubicle, sat down and regarded the floor layout. Checked her night report, so far as it went. "Remind me to have Bragg look at 54," he murmured.

110   "Nice baby."

111   "Yes. They'll have some specialist. Might as well be Bragg. How's the new interne?"

112   "Good. Does the work he's supposed to do. Most of them leave it to me."

113   "Your fault. You're an old-fashioned nurse, Grieder."

114   "A good thing for Anna Memorial that I am."

115   Together they went into the diet kitchen. The Delivery crew, Hunter, the floor nurse, the nursery girls, were gathered around the long table. Tallen told about the time Mother Superior had rewarded the doctors and nurses on a complicated operation with tall glasses of citrate of magnesia. "Good as lemonade," he chuckled, "and did us all a world of good. Took her a few days to check the shortage in pharmacy. Hunter, you see if 88 is comfortable. Give her aspirin and soda bicarb. Order tea in six hours. I'm going home. Any new case, Miss Grieder, call Vestby. Why didn't you call Vestby tonight?"

116   "I thought you were the one needed."

117   "Thanks. For nothing. Public Health cases are always a pain in my neck. All that girl needed—and her doctor, too—was a little guts. Wish some pathologist would invent a hypo to that effect."

118   The hall quieted. Grieder got a shawl out of her desk drawer and folded it around her shoulders. The nurses at the call-desk nodded over their double solitaire. The shaded lamp made their young faces beautiful. The dark green linoleum lay glimmering between pools of light like a leaf-shaded lane.

119   When Grieder had been as young as those yonder, she had spent these minutes of suspension dreaming about the future, young dreams of marriage and a home. Marriage to almost anybody. The interne—the chief surgeon—the engineer in the basement. All sorts of homes: bright little flats with a pink bedroom, or two rooms in a boarding-house a block from the hospital till he established his practice. A magnificent home out in the country, with two maids. And children. Only for the last few years had Grieder given up entirely her dream of children.

120   Two o'clock feeding. Not so noisy. About half the babies got formulas at this hour. Grieder made the rounds again.

121   Her phone buzzed. A new patient coming up—walking.

122   Grieder went down toward the elevator, speaking to the floor nurse and to the interne as she passed them. Almost the last of the private rooms—66.

123   The mother was frightened. "I can't walk far," she wailed.

124   Grieder watched alertly.

125   "It will help to walk. We'll go slowly. First baby?"

126   "Yes." Her long upper lip drew down to emphasize this bid for attention.

127   Grieder turned 66 over to the nurses. "You come with me," she told the husband. "Wait in here until they get her to bed; then you can see her for a minute and—"

128   "I'd like to stay with her. I think I should share this—"

129   "Against the rules. If you stay in the hospital, you'll have to wait downstairs. I think it may be some time." She looked up at the interne. "After you've been in, I'll call Dr. Vestby if you say so. Just send word."

130   "Yes, Miss Grieder."

131   Hunter grinned and went out.

132   There was no rush about 66. The husband went downstairs. Grieder got a handful of crackers and settled down to read the evening papers. She didn't get sleepy, but she did get tired, these dull hours of the night. Sort of discouraged-feeling; her fifty years ached in her bones. Fifty was too old for active duty. She'd better hunt for a cushy job.

133   In the street fire sirens shrieked. She hoped, dear God, it was not the hospital. She got up and looked down into the street. The long red trucks were pulling up in front of the apartment hotel across the street; the men were running into the court. . . . More trucks screamed up—they'd have every patient in the hospital on edge. Sure enough! Almost half the call-buttons were on. She'd go along the hall and quiet the mothers.

134   "Grieder—89's having hysterics. She's trying to get out of bed."

135   Grieder hurried—89 mustn't get out of bed. "The fire is across the street. This building is fireproof."

136   "I want my baby. I must have my baby. He may be hurt—smothered. I—let me up!"

137   Grieder held her shoulders down with firm hands. "Get her baby," she said to the youngster.

138   "But—if all the mothers—"

139   "*Get her baby!* I said."

140   The youngster ran—brought the paralyzed baby that would never talk well, nor hear. The mother held him tightly. She couldn't have taken a dozen steps to save herself; but she could do anything for her baby. Motherhood!

141   They had a busy fifteen minutes. The husband of 66 came charging up the stairs. Long after the firemen had extinguished the rubbish fire, feet hurried along the halls of Maternity; mothers talked excitedly. It would take forty-eight hours to correct the effect of those sirens.

142   Almost on top of that—call-buttons were still blooming rosily on the board—came the crashing four o'clock gong which wakened the Sisters. Grieder had a little routine profanity for that gong. Used to it as she was, it made her jump and quiver every time. Senseless to startle everyone. Mothers who returned to the hospital for a second, a third baby, told Grieder that their children almost never lost the habit of waking at four o'clock. Small babies supposedly could not hear, could only feel vibrations. Well, a racket like that had plenty of vibrations. It wakened everyone—this hospital could take four o'clock temperatures. Grieder marked the charts with firm strokes of her pen. The longer she nursed, the fancier hospitals became, the more complicated became the ritual of delivery and nursing care. Did the mothers benefit by all these new ideas and stunts? Perhaps. The mortality rate was much lower than it had been thirty, twenty years ago. So far, so good. . . .

143   Sister Raymond came on the floor, followed by the little priest who served the hospital. Grieder gave him the list of babies which had been born since yesterday morning.

144   "Too many boys," Sister told Grieder severely.

145   "Twin girls in 90B."

146   Sister giggled. "I know. She wanted a boy. She came in before evening prayer. I told her I'd pray for her. Yesterday she told me I hadn't prayed hard enough. I said I hadn't prayed *soon* enough."

147   The priest put a thin hand over his mouth to hide his grin. Grieder nodded. "You're always interfering with nature, Sister—or trying to."

148   They went off, Sister's skirts a blue balloon around her swift feet. She was a good woman, strong and vigorous; she'd have made a wonderful mother.

149   The phone buzzed. Hunter lifted his head from his arms. "Another?"

150   "Maybe. How's 66?"

151   "Asleep."

152   She took up the phone, listened, set it back. "Coming up," she told the interne. "I'll have to put her in 89B. I'd have liked A to have the room alone."

153   "Usually they are better for company."

154   "A's baby is a misdeal. Be hard on her if the other one is a good one. Mothers brag so about their brats."

155   Hunter looked bewildered. Grieder heard the elevator and hurried into the hall. Heavens—a millionaire! Three big bags. In a two-bed inside room!

156   She shooed the father away. The mother had childish, curly hair; she leaned heavily on the nurse's arm. She was almost ready. Grieder set the screens—spoke softly to 89A. She told the nurse to bring the patient quickly to the anteroom. She went out to call Dr. Vestby; she could see he'd be needed.

157   She was making out the new chart when the training nurse came to her. "She hasn't any safety pins."

158   "Who hasn't?"

159   "New case in 89."

160   "All that baggage, and no safety pins?"

161   The girl giggled. "She's got black lace underwear, and has each of her gowns wrapped separately in tissue paper, but no safety pins."

162 Grieder sighed. The mothers were given a careful list of things to bring to the hospital. "Borrow them around," she directed. "But not from 67."

163 "Why not? She'd have plenty."

164 "Sure she'd have plenty—because her baby died. Be sure to explain that to her when you go to ask for 'em!"

165 Grieder was so angry, so tired, she felt herself tremble.

166 "Aw—Grieder."

167 "What? Since when does a training girl fail to speak respectfully to the head nurse?"

168 The girl mumbled something and ran down the hall. Grieder went back to her desk work. She was weary to her bones' core. There was too much work on Maternity, too much life—the cumulation of it weighted her shoulders and her limbs.

169 Dawn was beginning to streak the east. The lights in the hall drew up from the floor and the walls, became little blobs of dim radiance. Grieder went to the switch. The cart came down the hall from 89B. She hoped the night Delivery crew would miss this; there was always a row when they got caught by a few minutes and had to work several hours.

170 Six o'clock. The noisiest feeding of the night, and all the mothers wanting attention at the same time. Rounds to make to complete her night report. Hardly any mother would claim she'd had a good night. Grieder had to decide that fact from circumstantial evidence. Grieder must see for herself that the sterilizers for Delivery and Operating were started.

171 Things piled up these last minutes. The night nurses were hurrying to get their tasks done before the day crew came on at seven. The hall freshened its smells. Ether from Delivery—Dr. Vestby had hurried through the hall fifteen minutes ago. Toothpaste. Lysol. Bacon and toast.

172 Grieder took the keys for the floor pharmacy cupboard. The nurse brought her tray of glasses. Grieder measured out the oil. Hateful stuff. She didn't blame the mothers for objecting. It nauseated her to smell it. But she sharply rebuked the young nurse for the face she was making. Gave her a good lecture on the psychological methods of administering medicine.

173 The day girls were coming down the hall. Grieder hurried her last reports, made out her own sheet, ending stanchly with a clearly written: *"Quiet Night."*

UNDERSTANDING THE SELECTION

1. What do you expect a head nurse to be like? Was Grieder what you expected?

2. What do you expect student nurses to be like? Were the ones in the story what you expected?
3. Why is 89 more upset than the other mothers when she hears the sirens? Does she act as you would expect?
4. Was Dr. Tallen what you expected?
5. Did you learn anything new about human nature from the story?
6. List as many stereotypes as you can find in the story.

39 from Intern

Doctor X

1   On top of the OB work a distressing thing happened on the medical service Monday night, one of these things that you can find all sorts of rational excuses for, but still leave you sick and disgusted with yourself. Around 10:30 P.M. the nurse on the fifth floor called to tell me that old Mr. Dorcas in 513 was having trouble with his breathing again. Mr. Dorcas was a patient of Stern's and Compton's, a diabetic of long standing who also had some heart trouble. I'd never seen Mr. Dorcas, but I had sure heard about him from the interns and residents and even Dr. Compton himself. Apparently Mr. Dorcas was regarded by general acclamation as the biggest pain in the ass in the whole hospital.
2   Every now and then a patient turns up that nobody can stand, not even his own attending physician; these are the ones that the profession speaks of as the "crocks"—usually old, cantankerous, complaining, uncooperative people who seem to go out of their way to make themselves especially repulsive to everybody. Mr. Dorcas had won the title of "The Patient We'd Most Like To See Go Home," as Ned Stern remarked sourly one evening. His diabetes had gotten out of control, mostly because he had decided unilaterally that he didn't care to take his insulin any more; he got hauled to the hospital in acidosis at 3:00 one morning. Once he was out of immediate danger, he started a campaign to fight his doctors and the nurses and the house staff and everybody else who was trying to help. He would refuse to take his insulin unless Compton himself came in and coaxed him to take it, and then would dump his breakfast tray upside down on the floor on grounds that since he hadn't had any insulin he couldn't eat anything. Then when his blood sugar got up to 500 or so and he started feeling bad, he'd accept the insulin but stuff his dinner into his pillow case, telling the nurses he had eaten it, and then go into insulin shock at 4:00 in the morning and stir half the house staff out of bed to get him bailed out of it.
3   When I first heard about this nonsense from Hamilton, I thought

the old guy must be off his rocker, but Hamilton said, no, he was lucid as could be, just doing his damnedest to annoy everybody he could annoy. He had long-standing bronchitis, and brought his own oxygen equipment to the hospital with him, but he wouldn't use it when the intern ordered it, and then would run the nurses and interns ragged all night because he couldn't breathe.

4   Well, just when everybody already had a gutful of Mr.Dorcas, one of the X-ray boys thought he spotted a lesion in the old man's lung on a chest plate, and, sure as hell, more films showed that Mr. Dorcas had a tumor in his lung. Dr. Richards had the joy of opening his chest a week ago to try to remove whatever it was, and now Mr. Dorcas was postoperative as well as an uncontrolled diabetic, and now he *really* had episodes of shortness of breath, which he rode to the ground, complaining constantly.

5   I noticed on his chart that he had had the intern out twice or three times per night every night all week. Hamilton had seen him the night before and left a sort of frustrated, disgusted 3:00-in-the-morning note in the chart to the effect that if Mr. Dorcas would only just leave the oxygen valve in his tent alone he might have less trouble breathing and be able to sleep.

6   I went down to see the guy, a little beady-eyed, bald-headed gnome who greeted me at the door with "Well, do something! I can't breathe!" He didn't look very good, but his cheeks were pink enough, and when I listened to his chest in front (he wouldn't sit up for me to listen in back), I could hear air moving on both sides. The nurse was saying that he'd been ringing his call bell constantly since she'd called me, saying he couldn't breathe, he couldn't get comfortable, he wanted to vomit, and so on. Earlier in the evening he had gotten a little shocky from his insulin, and she had finally talked him into eating a little sugar after he refused to drink any of the orange juice they keep on hand for such occasions.

7   Well, I couldn't see any immediate reason for him to be short of breath, and I could just see spending the rest of the night up and down trying to humor this old fart. I reassured him that he was going to be all right, and ordered the oxygen to be left on all night so he could get some sleep. Ordered a capsule of Seconal for him, and then went down for midnight supper. Found Milt Musser there and thought he might have some ideas, but all he said was: "Oh, Christ! I don't know why Stern doesn't just give that bastard about 5 grains of morphine all at once and cure his breathing troubles for good."

8   So I went up to the OB floor and turned in for sleep about midnight. At 12:30 the night nurse on Fifth called to tell me that Mr. Dorcas was just having a terrible time, he was all upset and couldn't breathe, and wasn't

there something I could do? I was afraid to order any more sedative, so I asked if he was still getting the oxygen. "Oh, no, he turned that off himself an hour ago!" So I told her, for Christ's sake go turn it on again, and maybe try to get him to eat a little more sugar in case he was still shocky. She asked if I didn't want to come down and see him, and I told her I'd just seen him an hour or so ago and that she'd better just try to manage the situation by herself.

9   Well, that was fine until 2:30 A.M. when she called again and this time *she* was practically hysterical. Said Mr. Dorcas wasn't breathing right, he was ringing his buzzer every two minutes and just having a terrible time, and couldn't I please do something? She woke me out of a dead sleep to tell me this. By now I was so pissed off at Mr. Dorcas *and* the nurse that I was damned if I was going to crawl out of bed and go down and see him. I told her to go ahead and give him another Seconal, and she said he'd refused to take the first one I had ordered because he was afraid he might go to sleep. Well, that blew it. I told her for my money I was afraid he might not, and for her to go down and give him two grains of Luminal by hypo whether he happened to like the idea or not, and then to quit bothering me. If she couldn't get the old goat to quiet down, she would just have to put up with him, that was all, because I wasn't coming down there just to humor her *or* Mr. Dorcas.

10   I slammed the receiver down, and then lay blinking at the ceiling and getting madder by the minute; I kept thinking, Jesus, maybe I'd better go down and see what's going on, and then I'd think, the hell with it, all I'd find was what I found when I saw him earlier, namely, nothing. So I just lay there wide-awake, cursing Mr. Dorcas up, down and sideways and generally feeling very bitter about it all.

11   I guess I succeeded in intimidating the nurse because there weren't any more calls from the fifth floor until 6:15 when Miss Wood called with her chipper, cheerful, early-morning voice and told me she thought I'd better come down to 513, it looked as if Mr. Dorcas had just expired . . . .

12   I got my clothes on in a cold sweat and got down there, and, sure as hell, Mr. Dorcas had "ceased respirations." He was very dead indeed. The night nurse just glared at me and stomped off without a word, and I sat there at the desk looking at his chart and trying to figure out just what the hell to write in it about the evening's events. I could just hear the nurse telling all the girls how she had begged me to come see this poor dying man and all I had done was swear to her. To top it off, when I called Ned Stern to tell him Mr. Dorcas had died, he said, "Died! What happened?" which made me feel even more delightful, and then I had the joy of calling Mr. Dorcas'

sister to tell her he had died. All in all, I was feeling like a first-class shit about the whole thing.

13   I saw on the chart that the nurse had called Pete Carey about 3:30, in desperation, I guess, and Pete had ordered some Demerol for the man but had also refused to come over and see him. Dr. Richards said later that at surgery he had found Mr. Dorcas had an extensive lung cancer all over the inside of his chest and extending up the esophagus and down into the abdomen, totally inoperable, and that all he had had ahead of him was three or four bad months anyway. Which was comforting to know, in a way, but doesn't really excuse my own negligence. Maybe I couldn't have done much. You could argue that the man had just called wolf once too often; certainly you could argue that it was just an error in judgment on my part, assuming that all the hullabaloo was just a matter of Mr. Dorcas' crock-ism when he was, in fact, choking to death. Still, my job here is to be on call and see people when they need attention whether I'm annoyed at them or not, or tired or not, or inconvenienced or not. Strip it down to the bone and the fact was that I was just too lazy and irritated and stubborn to drag my fat ass out of bed and walk down two flights of stairs to see the man. I depended, instead, on a snap judgment that just happened to be wrong. I feel lousy about it, and so does Pete, but there you are. Maybe I've learned something.

UNDERSTANDING THE SELECTION

1. *Intern* is the record kept by an anonymous doctor of his "most critical year," the first year he actually was responsible for the lives and deaths of patients. *Intern* was tape-recorded at irregular intervals during this crucial year, and because it is outspoken and candid, its author has not revealed his identity.

2. In "Quiet Night" (Selection 38), Grieder's views of interns are given in paragraphs 34 and 35. Would she approve of Doctor X?

3. Does Doctor X behave as Grieder would expect him to behave? Does he behave as you would expect him to? Consider not only his actions but his attitudes and the way in which he expresses them.

4. Have you ever been in the hospital? If so, did you find that the doctors and nurses behaved as you expected them to? Did patients behave like Mr. Dorcas?

5. Compare all of the characters and situations in "Quiet Night" and this selection. Which selection would you say gives the layman a better view of what it is like to work in medicine? Why?

6. Both of these selections were written in part to allow readers to evaluate better the members of the medical profession. Studies of comparative incomes indicate that doctors as a group receive the highest income in the nation. Do you think they earn it? Do you think they deserve it? Does either of these two selections enable you to make a more confident judgment?

Tone

An author's attitude toward his audience or his subject is called *tone*. Just as a speaker conveys his meaning to a great extent by his tone of voice, so does a writer convey meaning by tone. You have heard a friend say, "It's a wonderful day," because the air was brisk and the sun was shining and it was Saturday, and you have heard him say the same thing when rain was pouring down and he had had a flat tire on the way to his Monday-morning class. You knew that one remark was sincere, however, and that the other was not; the words were identical, but the tone of voice was different. In the same way, a writer's words may mean exactly what they say or the opposite. Detecting a writer's tone in order to understand his meaning is, however, harder than detecting that of your friend: you cannot hear the writer's voice or see his gestures.

Basic questions to be answered in identifying tone are these: Who is the speaker? Who is the audience? The speaker in a piece of writing is not necessarily the writer. In the novel *Catcher in the Rye,* for example, the main speaker is a seventeen-year-old boy, not a man in his thirties. In *Romeo and Juliet,* two young lovers are speaking, along with many other characters, not one of whom speaks like the author, an English actor-playwright who left his wife and children to enter show business. You must try to learn as much as possible about the speaker, the person whom the author selects to tell a story. Next, who is the audience? What is its age? Education? Social and economic background? You can answer this series of questions by asking yourself what sort of people would be likely to listen to what the speaker is saying and what sort he would probably know.

Once the characteristics of speaker and audience have been established, everything that follows must be appropriate and consistent if the writer is doing a good job. The author must use words his speaker would use if the reader is to take his writing seriously. If the speaker is an adolescent, he does not talk about either lollipops or caviar. If he is an insurance salesman, he does not discuss astrophysics or the flowers of spring. The formality of the speaker's language, the amount of slang, the length of his sentences, the proportion of exact description to philosophical discussion, all make up tone. So do the author's use of connotation, stereotypes, symbols, and anything else which is part of writing.

Let us be more specific. Here are a few familiar phrases, each of which has a distinct tone. "The forecast for tomorrow is partly cloudy with moderate temperatures" is factual and flat. "They lived happily ever after" is a fairy-tale formula, incredible to persons who take monthly magazine quizzes entitled "Are you a satisfactory mate?" "Fourscore and seven years ago" has an old-fashioned dignity. "THIMK" is mocking. "But I *want* to . . . " is whiny, petulant, and childish. Would the same person say all these things or does each require its own speaker and audience?

Now let us give you two passages to compare. In the first, the speaker is a wealthy Bostonian, born in 1866, who is writing a letter to his son. They are characters in John P. Marquand's novel *The Late George Apley*, published in 1937.

> I should like to give you one specific example of what I mean. As you know, for a number of years I have been making a collection of Chinese bronzes. I have tried to inform myself fully about these things, and I have spent much time with many wily Oriental dealers. I have not done this because I particularly like these bronzes. As a matter of fact, I think many of my best ones are overdecorated and look inappropriate in the Hillcrest library. I have made this collection out of duty rather than out of predilection, from the conviction that everyone in a certain position owes it to the community to collect something. In this way industries are stimulated and scholars are given definite occupations. In the end the public will be the gainer. I had perceived that our Art Museum was short of Chinese bronzes and I started my collection at your Uncle William's suggestion. They will, of course, be left by my will to the Museum, just as your Uncle William proposes to leave his own very extensive collection of Chinese ceramics. No one in our position should consider himself alone, but first he should consider his duty to the community.

Is the tone clear and consistent? What is the tone? Does the speaker like Orientals? Industry? Scholars? How intimate are he and his son? Does the author respect the speaker?

The following portion of a single sentence from William Faulkner's short story "The Bear" is supposed to reflect the thoughts of a ten-year-old boy.

> . . . the doomed wilderness whose edges were being constantly and punily gnawed at by men with axes and plows who feared it because it was wilderness, men myriad and nameless even to one another in the land where the old bear had earned a name, through which ran not even a mortal animal but an anachronism, indomitable and invincible, out of an old dead time, a phantom, epitome and apotheosis of the old wild life at which the puny humans swarmed and hacked in a fury of abhorrence and fear, like pygmies about the ankles of a drowsing elephant: the old bear solitary, indomitable and alone, widowered, childless, and absolved of mortality—old Priam reft of his old wife and having outlived all his sons.

Do you know any ten-year-olds who think like this? Does the author want to be taken seriously? Can you take him seriously?

For practice, compare the tone of the following pairs of publications and note the elements that give each publication its special characteristics.

1. *Vogue* and *True Confessions*
2. *Reader's Digest* and *The New Yorker*

3. *Playboy* and *Sports Illustrated*
4. *The New York Times* and an underground newspaper
5. this textbook and a social science textbook

For each publication, identify the age, education, and social and economic background of the audience. How does the tone of each periodical appeal to its audience?

40 *Pyramus and Thisbe*

Edith Hamilton

1   Once upon a time the deep red berries of the mulberry tree were white as snow. The change in color came about strangely and sadly. The death of two young lovers was the cause.

2   Pyramus and Thisbe, he the most beautiful youth and she the love-liest maiden of all the East, lived in Babylon, the city of Queen Semiramis, in houses so close together that one wall was common to both. Growing up thus side by side they learned to love each other. They longed to marry, but their parents forbade. Love, however, cannot be forbidden. The more that flame is covered up, the hotter it burns. Also love can always find a way. It was impossible that these two whose hearts were on fire should be kept apart.

3   In the wall both houses shared there was a little chink. No one before had noticed it, but there is nothing a lover does not notice. Our two young people discovered it and through it they were able to whisper sweetly back and forth, Thisbe on one side, Pyramus on the other. The hateful wall that separated them had become their means of reaching each other. "But for you we could touch, kiss," they would say. "But at least you let us speak together. You give a passage for loving words to reach loving ears. We are not ungrateful." So they would talk, and as night came on and they must part, each would press on the wall kisses that could not go through to the lips on the other side.

4   Every morning when the dawn had put out the stars, and the sun's rays had dried the hoarfrost on the grass, they would steal to the crack and, standing there, now utter words of burning love and now lament their hard fate, but always in softest whispers. Finally a day came when they could endure no longer. They decided that that very night they would try to slip away and steal out through the city into the open country where at last they could be together in freedom. They agreed to meet at a well-known place, the Tomb of Ninus, under a tree there, a tall mulberry full of snow-white berries, near which a cool spring bubbled up. The plan pleased them and it seemed to them the day would never end.

5   At last the sun sank into the sea and night arose. In the darkness Thisbe crept out and made her way in all secrecy to the tomb. Pyramus had not come; still she waited for him, her love making her bold. But of a sudden she saw by the light of the moon a lioness. The fierce beast had made a kill; her jaws were bloody and she was coming to slake her thirst in the spring. She was still far enough away for Thisbe to escape, but as she fled she dropped her cloak. The lioness came upon it on her way back to her lair and she mouthed it and tore it before disappearing into the woods. That is what Pyramus saw when he appeared a few minutes later. Before him lay the bloodstained shreds of the cloak and clear in the dust were the tracks of the lioness. The conclusion was inevitable. He never doubted that he knew all. Thisbe was dead. He had let his love, a tender maiden, come alone to a place full of danger, and not been there first to protect her. "It is I who killed you," he said. He lifted up from the trampled dust what was left of the cloak and kissing it again and again carried it to the mulberry tree. "Now," he said, "you shall drink my blood too." He drew his sword and plunged it into his side. The blood spurted up over the berries and dyed them a dark red.

6   Thisbe, although terrified of the lioness, was still more afraid to fail her lover. She ventured to go back to the tree of the tryst, the mulberry with the shining white fruit. She could not find it. A tree was there, but not one gleam of white was on the branches. As she stared at it, something moved on the ground beneath. She started back shuddering. But in a moment, peering through the shadows, she saw what was there. It was Pyramus, bathed in blood and dying. She flew to him and threw her arms around him. She kissed his cold lips and begged him to look at her, to speak to her. "It is I, your Thisbe, your dearest," she cried to him. At the sound of her name he opened his heavy eyes for one look. Then death closed them.

7   She saw his sword fallen from his hand and beside it her cloak stained and torn. She understood all. "Your own hand killed you," she said, "and your love for me. I too can be brave. I too can love. Only death would have had the power to separate us. It shall not have that power now." She plunged into her heart the sword that was still wet with his life's blood.

8   The gods were pitiful at the end, and the lovers' parents too. The deep red fruit of the mulberry is the everlasting memorial of these true lovers, and one urn holds the ashes of the two whom not even death could part.

UNDERSTANDING THE SELECTION

1. Carefully describe the speaker, not the author. How old is he? How well educated? Does he approve of the young lovers? What does he think of love—is it important or comical or sham? Does he approve of suicide?

2. Carefully describe the audience to whom the story is told. Are its members young or old? How well educated are they?

3. What do the connotations of "Once upon a time" suggest about speaker and audience? Of "our two young people" (paragraph 3)?

4. What is the tone of the story?

5. Why would you not expect to find this story printed in *True Romance?* In *Seventeen?* In *Time* magazine?

6. If you were going to make this story into a movie, whom would you cast as Pyramus and Thisbe?

7. Why do you think their parents forbade Pyramus and Thisbe to marry?

8. Why does Pyramus say, "It is I who killed you"?

9. What metaphor is used for love in paragraph 2?

10. What is the difference in meaning of the two "but's" in paragraph 3?

11. Although this story is an old myth, first told by Ovid, a Roman poet who lived in the time of Christ, it has something in common with modern scientific research. What?

12. What, then, is one purpose in telling myths?

41   Once in a Saintly Passion

James Thomson

Once in a saintly passion
  I cried with desperate grief,
"O Lord, my heart is black with guile,
  Of sinners I am chief."
Then stooped my guardian angel
  And whispered from behind,
"Vanity, my little man,
  You're nothing of the kind."

UNDERSTANDING THE SELECTION

1. How does the speaker feel toward himself?

2. How does his guardian angel feel toward him?

3. Is the guardian angel right in accusing the speaker of vanity? What exactly is vanity?

4. What is the tone of the first four lines? Of the second four lines? Of the whole poem?

42   The Certificate

Avram Davidson

1   The winter sunrise was still two hours away when Dr. Roger Freeman came to stand in front of the great door. By good fortune—incredibly good fortune—he had not been questioned in his furtive progress from the dormitory. If he had been stopped, or if his answer had been either disbelieved or judged inadequate, he might have been sent back to the dorm for punishment. The punishment would have been over, of course, in time for him to go to work at ten in the morning, but a man could suffer through several thousand eternities of Hell in those few hours. And no more than a low muffled groaning and a subdued convulsive movement of the body to show what was going on. You were able to sleep through it—if it was happening to someone else.

2   The great door was set well in from the street, and the cutting edge of the wind was broken by it.

3   Freeman was grateful for that. It was two years ago that he'd applied for a new overcoat, and the one he still had was ragged even then. Perhaps—if this was not to be his year for escape—in another year he would get the coat. He crowded into a corner and tried not to think of the cold.

4   After a little while another man joined him, then another, then a woman, then a couple. By sunrise there was a long line. They were all willing to risk it, risk punishment for being out before work, or for being late to work. Some merely wanted clothes. Some wanted permission to visit relatives in another locale. You could wait years for either. Or, you could wait years and not get either. And some, like Freeman, hoped against hope for a chance at escape.

5   Dr. Freeman stared at the door. The design was as intricate as it was incomprehensible. No doubt it made sense to the Hedderans. If you could understand it you might gain some understanding of the nature of their distant home. If you cared. It was fifty years since they had arrived, and men still knew almost nothing about them.

6   They were here. They would never go away. That was enough.

7   The man behind Dr. Freeman collapsed. No one paid any attention to him. After a moment there was a high, brief, humming. The man twitched, opened his eyes. He got to his feet.

8   And then the door opened.

9   *"Proceed in the order,"* the voice directed—a thick, flat Hedderan voice; harsh, yet glutinous. No one tried to push ahead, the lesson had been too well learned. Dr. Freeman got on the third escalator, rode down two levels. There had been a time when you rode *up*—but that was before the Hedderans came. They didn't like tall buildings—at least it seemed so. They'd never explained—that, or anything else. What they did not like they simply destroyed.

10   Dr. Freeman looked behind him as he approached the office. There must have been at least a dozen people behind him. They looked at him wolfishly. So few certificates were granted, and he was first in line. He looked away. He'd stayed awake all night in order to *be* the first. No one had the right to resent him. And the next man in line was young. What did he expect . . . ?

11   The door opened, the voice said, *"Proceed one at a single time."*

Fifty years, and the Hedderans still hadn't mastered the language. They didn't have to, of course. Roger Freeman entered the office, took the application form from the slot in the wall-machine found in every office, sat down at the table. When was the last time he had sat in a chair? No matter.

12   The form was in Hedderan, of course. The voice said, *"Name."* The voice said, *"Number."*

13   He wrote it down, Roger Freeman . . . 655-673-60-60-2. Idly he glanced at the cluster of Hedderan characters. If one could take the application form away, with Hedderan questions and English answers, perhaps— if there was time—a key could be found for translating. But it was impossible to take it away. If you spoiled it, you were out. You could apply only once a year. And if you *did* find out how to read their language, what then? Freeman's brother Bob had talked of rebellion—but that was years ago . . . and he didn't like to think what had happened to Bob. And besides, he hadn't *time*—he had to be at work by ten.

14   From ten in the morning until ten at night (the Hedderans had their own ways of reckoning time) he worked at a machine, pulling hard on levers. Some he had to bend down to reach, some he had to mount steps to reach. Up and down, up and down. He didn't know what the machine did, or even how it worked. And he no longer cared. He no longer cared about anything— except a new overcoat (or, at least, a *newer* one, not worn so thin), and his chances of escape.

15   *Age. Occupation. Previous Occupation.* Previous to the arrival of the Hedderans, that was. Fifty years ago. He had been a physician. An obsolete skill. Inside of every man nowadays there was a piece of . . . something . . . presumably it communicated with a machine somewhere deep in the Hedderan quarters. If you broke a bone or bled or even if you just fainted (as the young man behind him in line had), you were set right almost in the second. No one was ill for long—even worn-out organs were regenerated. Too few men had been left alive and, the Hedderans needed those who were left too much to let them sicken or die.

16   At last the long form was filled out. The harsh voice said, *"Now at once to Office Ten, Level Four."*

17   Dr. Freeman hastily obeyed. When they said 'at once,' they meant just that. The punishment might come like a single whiplash—or it might go on and on. You never knew. Maybe the Hedderans knew. But they never told. The man next behind the outer door scuttled in as Freeman left. The others waited. Not more than three could expect to be processed before it would be time to return to work.

18   Office Ten, Level Four, asked him the same questions, but in a different order. He was then directed to Office Five, Level Seventeen. Here his two forms were fed into a machine, returned with markings stamped on them in Hedderan.

19   *"Office Eight, Level Two,"* the voice said. There, he fed his applications into the slot. After a moment they came back—unmarked.

20   *"Name Roger Freeman. Number 655-673-60-60-2. You have a single time application outstanding. Unpermitted two. You will cancel this one. Or you will cancel that one."*

21   Frantically he searched his mind. What application did he have outstanding? When was this rule made? The overcoat! If he went ahead with this new application and it was refused, he'd have to wait till next year to reinstate the one for the coat. And then more years of waiting . . . It was cold, the dormitory was ill-heated, he had no blanket. His present coat was very worn. Services for humans were minimal.

22   But he *had* to proceed with this new application. He was first in line. . . .

23   *"Speak,"* the thick, flat voice directed. *"Answer. Speak. Now."*

24   Gobbling his words in haste, Freeman said, "I cancel the one outstanding."

25   *"Insert forms."*

26   He did. Waited.

27   *"Proceed to Office Ten, Level Four."*

28   That was the second place he'd been to. A mistake? No matter, he had to go. Once again he entered. And waited.

29   A grunting noise caught his eye. He looked up, started, cowered. A Hedderan, his baffle-screen turned off, was gazing at him. The blank, grey, faceted eyes in the huge head, and the body, like a deformed foetus . . . then the baffle-screen went on again. Freeman shuddered. One rarely saw them. It had been years.

30   A piece of paper slid from the machine. He took it up, waiting for the command to proceed—where? Unless it could be accomplished before ten, there was no chance of escape for him this year. None whatever. He stared dully at the strange characters. The cold indifferent voice said, *"Name Roger Freeman. Number 655-673-60-60-2. Declared surplus. Application for death certificate is granted. Proceed for certificate to Office One, Level Five. At once."*

31   Tears rolled down Dr. Freeman's cheeks. "At last," he sobbed, joyfully. "At last . . . "

32   And then he hastily left. He had achieved his escape after all—but only if he got there before ten o'clock.

UNDERSTANDING THE SELECTION

1. Judging from their names, what kind of people would you expect Roger Freeman and the Hedderans to be? In other words, discuss the connotations of their names.

2. How has the coming of the Hedderans changed relationships among

human beings? How does the dialogue reflect this? How does the tone of the story reflect this?

3. Where do you think the Hedderans come from? In what year does the story take place?

4. Why is Dr. Freeman's profession—medicine—an "obsolete skill"?

5. Reread paragraph 7. What caused the humming? Why did the man get up after he heard it?

6. Dr. Freeman chooses death instead of life. What are his reasons? Would you make the same choice? In the story men can live indefinitely. Would you like to?

7. Is this story aptly titled? Why or why not?

43   *I Heard a Fly Buzz*

Emily Dickinson

I heard a Fly buzz—when I died—
The Stillness in the Room
Was like the Stillness in the Air—
Between the Heaves of Storm—

The Eyes around—had wrung them dry—   5
And Breaths were gathering firm
For that last Onset—when the King
Be witnessed—in the Room—

I willed my Keepsakes—Signed away
What portion of me be   10
Assignable—and then it was
There interposed a Fly—

With Blue—uncertain stumbling Buzz—
Between the light—and me—
And then the Windows failed—and then   15
I could not see to see—

UNDERSTANDING THE SELECTION

1. In the introduction to this section on tone, we cautioned you that a writer may choose to have someone else speak for him, that the speaker in a story or poem need not be the writer. It should be obvious to you that the speaker in this poem is not the poet Emily Dickinson. Why? Describe the speaker as fully as you can. What elements of the poem did you use to determine the speaker's characteristics?

2. Although this is not a particularly symbolic poem, some of the details in it are symbols. What are they? Who, for example, is "the King" being awaited in the room?

3. What would you say was the tone of this poem? What is the speaker's attitude toward death? To whom is the speaker talking? What is his attitude toward his audience?

4. Why do you think Miss Dickinson wrote this poem? What was she talking about when she set this particular scene?

Irony

One device many writers use that requires special consideration is *irony*. It is the device used by writers who are struck by the blindness, complacency, stupidity, folly—and yet humanness—of mankind. These authors see a discrepancy between what a man thinks himself to be and what he really is. Or they note a discrepancy between what a man really is and what others see him to be. Or they say one thing but mean something quite different.

Real life is full of ironic events. For example, we often read in the newspaper of a trusted bank employee embezzling hundreds of thousands of dollars and going off to Rio to live in luxury. It is ironic that he was also a vestryman of the First Baptist Church and the leader of a Boy Scout troop. Or it is ironic when an actor famous for his tough he-man roles on the screen is arrested for parading through Pershing Square dressed in women's clothes. This form of irony—in which a character is not what he seems to be —is especially useful to writers for creating suspense.

A classic example of this type of irony is the Greek myth of Oedipus. Oedipus, King of Thebes, believes that it is his duty to find and punish the long-undiscovered murderer of the former king, Laius. What he does not realize is that he himself is the guilty one, for in his youth he arrogantly killed Laius—whom he regarded as an insignificant old man—on a lonely country road. Nor does he realize that Laius was also his father, from whom he had been sent away as a child. Oedipus is a mighty, noble king, but he is also a murderer. The irony of his situation—the discrepancy between his nobility and his baseness—is eventually revealed.

Irony also exists in the way that fate deals with individuals or society. It is ironic that Martin Luther King, Jr., who dedicated his life to nonviolence, died by violence. It is equally ironic that we have spent centuries learning how to prevent infants' deaths—and now we must learn how to prevent infants' births. The story of Oedipus also illustrates irony of fate, for in killing Laius he was fulfilling a prophecy—a fate—that he had hoped to avoid. He had been told by a fortune-teller that he would murder his own father, and in order to avoid that fate, he had fled from the home of his parents, vowing never to return. What he did not know was that his "parents" were only foster-parents. It was fate that placed him on the same road as Laius, his real father, and provoked him into raising his staff and striking the death blow. The entire land of Thebes suffered for years as a result of this irony of fate.

A third kind of irony resides in the discrepancy between what some-one says and what he means. The student who gets a flat tire on the free-way in the pouring rain, arrives in class halfway through an exam, and then exclaims, "Oh, wow! What a beautiful morning!" has expressed himself ironically. As you might expect, much of the humor or bite in literature de-rives from ironic expression like this.

Irony is used in so many forms, we cannot discuss them all here. What all irony has in common, though, is discrepancy of some sort: in tone, in situation, in behavior of a character. When you read you must be espe-cially alert to signs of irony or you will often miss the writer's point altogether.

44 Your Little Hands

Samuel Hoffenstein

Your little hands,
Your little feet,
Your little mouth—
Oh, God, how sweet!

Your little nose,   5
Your little ears,
Your eyes, that shed
Such little tears!

Your little voice,
So soft and kind;   10
Your little soul,
Your little mind!

UNDERSTANDING THE SELECTION

1. What does the girl look like?

2. What are "little tears"? Does the girl cry often? What sorts of things make her cry?

3. Are little hands, feet, and voices attractive? Are little souls and minds attractive?

4. What do you expect the connotations of *little* to be throughout the poem? What are they in lines 11 and 12?

5. Why is the poem ironic?

45   *Onward, Christian Soldiers*
Sabine Baring-Gould

Onward, Christian soldiers, marching as to war,
With the cross of Jesus going on before:
Christ the Royal Master leads against the foe;
Forward into battle, see his banners go.
Onward, Christian soldiers, marching as to war,
With the cross of Jesus going on before.

UNDERSTANDING THE SELECTION

1. What basic metaphor is used in this hymn? Do you consider it a good metaphor?
2. Work through the selection, showing what things are being compared in every place where the basic metaphor is used.
3. Does the writer perceive some discrepancy between the two parts of his metaphor? Do *you* find some discrepancy between them?
4. Did the author of these lyrics intend them to be ironic? Are they in fact ironic?

46   *A Fighting Christian Gospel*
Art Hoppe

1   In these days of wars and riots, with neighbors arming themselves against neighbors, good Christians naturally turn to The Bible for comfort.
2   Undoubtedly, good Christians can find the greatest comfort these days in that little known Book of The Bible, "The Gospel According to St. Pontius."
3   There is nothing to make a man feel more comfortable these days, good Christians agree, than going out, buying a gun, stocking up on ammunition and curling up with St. Pontius. Chapter and verse follow.

4   And seeing the multitudes, he went up into a mountain: and when his disciples came unto him, he taught them, saying,

5   Blessed are the proud in spirit, for no man shall dare trifle with them.
6   Blessed are the self-righteous, for their aim shall not waver.
7   Blessed are the well-to-do, for they shall be thrice-armed and with better weapons.
8   Blessed are the peacemakers, particularly the Colt .44.

9   And I say unto you, whosoever shall smite thee on the right cheek, counter with a left hook.

10   Ye have heard that it hath been said, thou shalt love thy neighbor and hate thine enemy. But I say unto you, How do you know you can trust thy neighbor?

11   And it came to pass that when he had ended his Sermon on the Mount and was come down from the mountain, great multitudes followed him. And he organized them into companies and battalions and regiments, saying unto them,

12   Render unto God that which is God's. And, having done that, render Caesar's soldiers wherever you catch them.

13   After this manner therefore pray ye: Our Father which art in heaven, Hallowed be thy name. Give us this day revenge upon our enemies. Forgive us our tactical errors and lead us not into ambushes, but deliver us an encouraging body count.

14   Strengthen our arms so that we may smite the enemy hip and thigh and bless our swords so that they may drink deep of his blood in the righteousness of our cause. For ours will be this kingdom, and the power, and the glory, forever. Amen.

15   And, lo, his prayers were granted and he became a great General, slaughtering the enemy by the thousands and destroying their cities and laying waste to the countryside.

16   And he grew rich in years and honors: Founder of the Judea First Committee, Executive Secretary of the Aramaic Citizens Councils, and Honorary Commander of the Nazareth Minutemen.

17   And on his death bed he called his Disciples unto him, saying, Go ye forth to all nations, teaching them that they shalt not kill, except on orders of a superior officer, in self defense or to get even.

18   And then he spake prophecy, saying, And they who shall follow in this path shall be known as Good Christians, even unto the end of the world. Amen.

19   And, lo, so it came to pass.

UNDERSTANDING THE SELECTION

1. Between what two things is the discrepancy that Art Hoppe writes about?

2. Hoppe refers to many Biblical passages in his article. Find the original passages in the first three Gospels and compare them with his version. Are his references allusions?

3. Irony is most often a humorous device. Do you find this selection funny? Was it intended to be?

4. Is Hoppe criticizing the Bible? People who profess to be Christians? Society in general? Or what?

5. What is the difference in the tone of "Onward Christian Soldiers" (Selection 45) and "A Fighting Christian Gospel"?

6. Using Hoppe's technique of showing discrepancy between things as we say they are and as they really are, try writing a paragraph in which you criticize some institution in our society.

47 The Cask of Amontillado

Edgar Allan Poe

1   The thousand injuries of Fortunato I had borne as I best could; but when he ventured upon insult, I vowed revenge. You, who so well know the nature of my soul, will not suppose, however, that I gave utterance to a threat. *At length* I would be avenged; this was a point definitively settled— but the very definitiveness with which it was resolved, precluded the idea of risk. I must not only punish, but punish with impunity. A wrong is unredressed when retribution overtakes its redresser. It is equally unredressed when the avenger fails to make himself felt as such to him who has done the wrong.

2   It must be understood, that neither by word nor deed had I given Fortunato cause to doubt my good-will. I continued, as was my wont, to smile in his face, and he did not perceive that my smile *now* was at the thought of his immolation.

3   He had a weak point—this Fortunato—although in other regards he was a man to be respected and even feared. He prided himself on his connoisseurship in wine. Few Italians have the true virtuoso spirit. For the most part their enthusiasm is adopted to suit the time and opportunity— to practise imposture upon the British and Austrian *millionnaires.* In painting and gemmary Fortunato, like his countrymen, was a quack—but in the matter of old wines he was sincere. In this respect I did not differ from him materially: I was skilful in the Italian vintages myself, and bought largely whenever I could.

4   It was about dusk, one evening during the supreme madness of the carnival season, that I encountered my friend. He accosted me with excessive warmth, for he had been drinking much. The man wore motley. He had on a tight-fitting parti-striped dress, and his head was surmounted by the conical cap and bells. I was so pleased to see him, that I thought I should never have done wringing his hand.

5   I said to him: "My dear Fortunato, you are luckily met. How remarkably well you are looking today! But I have received a pipe of what passes
for Amontillado, and I have my doubts."
6   "How?" said he. "Amontillado? A pipe? Impossible! And in the middle of the carnival!"
7   "I have my doubts," I replied; "and I was silly enough to pay the full
Amontillado price without consulting you in the matter. You were not to
be found, and I was fearful of losing a bargain."
8   "Amontillado!"
9   "I have my doubts."
10   "Amontillado!"
11   "And I must satisfy them."
12   "Amontillado!"
13   "As you are engaged, I am on my way to Luchesi. If anyone has a
critical turn, it is he. He will tell me—"
14   "Luchesi cannot tell Amontillado from Sherry."
15   "And yet some fools will have it that his taste is a match for your
own."
16   "Come, let us go."
17   "Whither?"
18   "To your vaults."
19   "My friend, no; I will not impose upon your good nature. I perceive
you have an engagement. Luchesi—"
20   "I have no engagement; come."
21   "My friend, no. It is not the engagement, but the severe cold with
which I perceive you are afflicted. The vaults are insufferably damp. They
are encrusted with niter."
22   "Let us go, nevertheless. The cold is merely nothing. Amontillado!
You have been imposed upon; and as for Luchesi, he cannot distinguish
sherry from Amontillado."
23   Thus speaking, Fortunato possessed himself of my arm. Putting on
a mask of black silk, and drawing a *roquelaure* closely about my person,
I suffered him to hurry me to my palazzo.
24   There were no attendants at home; they had absconded to make
merry in honor of the time. I had told them that I should not return until
the morning, and had given them explicit orders not to stir from the house.
These orders were sufficient, I well knew, to insure their immediate disappearance, one and all, as soon as my back was turned.
25   I took from their sconces two flambeaux, and giving one to Fortunato,
bowed him through several suites of rooms to the archway that led into
the vaults. I passed down a long and winding staircase, requesting him to
be cautious as he followed. We came at length to the foot of the descent,

and stood together on the damp ground of the catacombs of the Montresors.

26   The gait of my friend was unsteady, and the bells upon his cap jingled as he strode.

27   "The pipe," said he.

28   "It is farther on," said I; "but observe the white webwork which gleams from these cavern walls."

29   He turned towards me, and looked into my eyes with two filmy orbs that distilled the rheum of intoxication.

30   "Niter?" he asked, at length.

31   "Niter," I replied. "How long have you had that cough?"

32   "Ugh! ugh! ugh!—ugh! ugh! ugh!—ugh! ugh! ugh!—ugh! ugh! ugh!—ugh! ugh! ugh!"

33   My poor friend found it impossible to reply for many minutes.

34   "It is nothing," he said, at last.

35   "Come," I said, with decision, "we will go back; your health is precious. You are rich, respected, admired, beloved; you are happy, as once I was. You are a man to be missed. For me it is no matter. We will go back; you will be ill, and I cannot be responsible. Besides, there is Luchesi—"

36   "Enough," he said; "the cough is a mere nothing: it will not kill me. I shall not die of a cough."

37   "True—true," I replied; "and, indeed, I had no intention of alarming you unnecessarily—but you should use all proper caution. A draught of this Medoc will defend us from the damps."

38   Here I knocked off the neck of a bottle which I drew from a long row of its fellows that lay upon the mould.

39   "Drink," I said, presenting him the wine.

40   He raised it to his lips with a leer. He paused and nodded to me familiarly, while his bells jingled.

41   "I drink," he said, "to the buried that repose around us."

42   "And I to your long life."

43   He again took my arm, and we proceeded.

44   "These vaults," he said, "are extensive."

45   "The Montresors," I replied, "were a great and numerous family."

46   "I forget your arms."

47   "A huge human foot d'or, in a field azure; the foot crushes a serpent rampant whose fangs are imbedded in the heel."

48   "And the motto?"

49   *"Nemo me impune lacessit."*

50   "Good!" he said.

51   The wine sparkled in his eyes and the bells jingled. My own fancy grew warm with the Medoc. We had passed through walls of piled bones,

with casks and puncheons intermingling, into the inmost recesses of the catacombs. I paused again, and this time I made bold to seize Fortunato by an arm above the elbow.

52   "The niter!" I said; "see, it increases. It hangs like moss upon the vaults. We are below the river's bed. The drops of moisture trickle among the bones. Come, we will go back ere it is too late. Your cough—"

53   "It is nothing," he said; "let us go on. But first, another draught of the Medoc."

54   I broke and reached him a flagon of De Grâve. He emptied it at a breath. His eyes flashed with a fierce light. He laughed and threw the bottle upward with a gesticulation I did not understand.

55   I looked at him in surprise. He repeated the movement—a grotesque one.

56   "You do not comprehend?" he said.

57   "Not I," I replied.

58   "Then you are not of the brotherhood."

59   "How?"

60   "You are not of the masons."

61   "Yes, yes," I said; "yes, yes."

62   "You? Impossible! A mason?"

63   "A mason," I replied.

64   "A sign," he said.

65   "It is this." I answered, producing a trowel from beneath the folds of my *roquelaure.*

66   "You jest," he exclaimed, recoiling a few paces. "But let us proceed to the Amontillado."

67   "Be it so," I said, replacing the tool beneath the cloak, and again offering him my arm. He leaned upon it heavily. We continued our route in search of the Amontillado. We passed through a range of low arches, descended, passed on, and descending again, arrived at a deep crypt, in which the foulness of the air caused our flambeaux rather to glow than flame.

68   At the most remote end of the crypt there appeared another less spacious. Its walls had been lined with human remains, piled to the vault overhead, in the fashion of the great catacombs of Paris. Three sides of this interior crypt were still ornamented in this manner. From the fourth the bones had been thrown down, and lay promiscuously upon the earth, forming at one point a mound of some size. Within the wall thus exposed by the displacing of the bones, we perceived a still interior recess, in depth about four feet, in width three, in height six or seven. It seemed to have been constructed for no especial use within itself, but formed merely the interval between two of the colossal supports of the roof of the catacombs, and was backed by one of their circumscribing walls of solid granite.

69   It was in vain that Fortunato, uplifting his dull torch, endeavored to pry into the depths of the recess. Its termination the feeble light did not enable us to see.

70   "Proceed," I said; "herein is the Amontillado. As for Luchesi—"

71   "He is an ignoramus," interrupted my friend, as he stepped unsteadily forward, while I followed immediately at his heels. In an instant he had reached the extremity of the niche, and finding his progress arrested by the rock, stood stupidly bewildered. A moment more and I had fettered him to the granite. In its surface were two iron staples, distant from each other about two feet, horizontally. From one of these depended a short chain, from the other a padlock. Throwing the links about his waist, it was but the work of a few seconds to secure it. He was too much astounded to resist. Withdrawing the key I stepped back from the recess.

72   "Pass your hand," I said, "over the wall; you cannot help feeling the niter. Indeed it is *very* damp. Once more let me *implore* you to return. No? Then I must positively leave you. But I must first render you all the little attentions in my power."

73   "The Amontillado!" ejaculated my friend, not yet recovered from his astonishment.

74   "True," I replied; "the Amontillado."

75   As I said these words I busied myself among the pile of bones of which I have before spoken. Throwing them aside, I soon uncovered a quantity of building stone and mortar. With these materials and with the aid of my trowel, I began vigorously to wall up the entrance of the niche.

76   I had scarcely laid the first tier of the masonry when I discovered that the intoxication of Fortunato had in a great measure worn off. The earliest indication I had of this was a low moaning cry from the depth of the recess. It was *not* the cry of a drunken man. There was then a long and obstinate silence. I laid the second tier, and the third, and the fourth; and then I heard the furious vibrations of the chain. The noise lasted for several minutes, during which, that I might hearken to it with the more satisfaction, I ceased my labors and sat down upon the bones. When at last the clanking subsided, I resumed the trowel, and finished without interruption the fifth, the sixth, and the seventh tier. The wall was now nearly upon a level with my breast. I again paused, and holding the flambeaux over the masonwork, threw a few feeble rays upon the figure within.

77   A succession of loud and shrill screams, bursting suddenly from the throat of the chained form, seemed to thrust me violently back. For a brief moment I hesitated—I trembled. Unsheathing my rapier, I began to grope with it about the recess; but the thought of an instant reassured me. I placed my hand upon the solid fabric of the catacombs, and felt satisfied. I reapproached the wall. I replied to the yells of him who clamored. I re-echoed—I aided—I surpassed them in volume and in strength. I did this, and the clamorer grew still.

78   It was now midnight, and my task was drawing to a close. I had completed the eighth, the ninth, and the tenth tier. I had finished a portion of the last and the eleventh; there remained but a single stone to be fitted and plastered in. I struggled with its weight; I placed it partially in its destined position. But now there came from out the niche a low laugh that erected the hairs upon my head. It was succeeded by a sad voice, which I had difficulty in recognizing as that of the noble Fortunato. The voice said—

79   "Ha! ha! ha!—he! he! he!—a very good joke indeed—an excellent jest. We will have many a rich laugh about it at the palazzo—he! he! he!—over our wine—he! he! he!"

80   "The Amontillado!" I said.

81   "He! he! he!—he! he! he!—yes, the Amontillado. But is it not getting late? Will not they be awaiting us at the palazzo, the Lady Fortunato and the rest? Let us be gone."

82   "Yes," I said, "let us be gone."

83   *"For the love of God, Montresor!"*

84   "Yes," I said, "for the love of God!"

85   But to these words I hearkened in vain for a reply. I grew impatient. I called aloud:

86   "Fortunato!"

87   No answer, I called again:

88   "Fortunato!"

89   No answer still. I thrust a torch through the remaining aperture and let it fall within. There came forth in return only a jingling of the bells. My heart grew sick—on account of the dampness of the catacombs. I hastened to make an end of my labor. I forced the last stone into its position; I plastered it up. Against the new masonry I re-erected the old rampart of bones. For the half of a century no mortal has disturbed them. *In pace requiescat!*

UNDERSTANDING THE SELECTION

1. Here are definitions for the foreign words that Edgar Allan Poe uses in "The Cask of Amontillado":

amontillado: a rare, dry, pale, Spanish sherry wine
roquelaure (paragraph 23): a knee-length cloak buttoned in front
flambeaux (paragraph 25): torches
Nemo me impune lacessit (paragraph 49): "No one attacks me with impunity"
In pace requiescat (paragraph 89): "May he rest in peace"

2. Discuss the setting of the story. Where does the story take place? When? Try to determine the century, the season of the year, the time of

day. Why did Poe choose this particular setting for his story? What are the connotations of the setting?

3. Discuss the irony in Fortunato's name and in his carnival costume.

4. Montresor's name means "my treasure" in French. Discuss connotation in his name. Is his name also ironic? Discuss Montresor generally. What is his nationality, for instance? Is it important?

5. What do you think were the "thousand injuries of Fortunato" which Montresor had to bear? What do most people think of Fortunato? What does he think of himself? What does he think of Montresor? Is Montresor justified in calling him insulting? What do *you* think of Fortunato?

6. What is Montresor's idea of a satisfactory revenge? Do you think it is desirable to get revenge when you feel you have been wronged? If so, is your idea of satisfactory revenge like Montresor's or different? If it is different, explain how it differs.

7. Find at least five ironic speeches in the story—speeches where the speaker means one thing and the listener or reader understands something quite different.

8. To whom is Montresor telling the story? Do you think he has ever told it before? Why does he decide to tell it now? Many critics feel that Montresor is confessing his crime to a priest. Do you agree? What evidence can you find in the story that indicates that he is or that he isn't confessing guiltily?

9. Select a jury from amongst your classmates and conduct a trial of Montresor. As prosecuting attorney, would you ask for the death penalty for Montresor? Why or why not?

10. Select two students to act out the final scene in the story. Begin where Montresor says "Proceed" (paragraph 70). In what tone does Montresor speak here? Is it consistent with the tone of the rest of his "confession"?

48 *Sic Transit*
David McEnery

Photograph by David McEnery.

UNDERSTANDING THE SELECTION

1. We have said that irony occurs when there is a discrepancy of some sort in a situation. What discrepancy makes this picture ironic? Does the discrepancy make the picture funny?

2. The title of this photograph—"Sic Transit"—is also ironic. It is actually an allusion to a Latin phrase, *Sic transit gloria mundi*—"Thus passes the glory of the world." By quoting only part of the original phrase, the writer who titled the picture was able to evoke certain connotations to express his feeling about the man carrying the sign. What discrepancy do you discern between the meaning of the original phrase and the sound of *sic transit?*

Comment

Thus far we have asked you to study some of the things that go into writing: connotation, metaphor, allusion, symbol, tone, irony. Now we want you to study what comes out of writing: *comment.* "What does the author mean?" is another way of asking, "What comment does he make about himself or other people or the world?" This *comment* is what he *means.*

Each element—that is, each action or character or word—which the author uses in his writing is there because in some way it helps to make his comment clear. If he wishes to comment that our lives can be upset by unexpected and threatening events, he may use a little girl and a spider to illustrate his comment, as in "Little Miss Muffet." The symbol of the girl expresses unprotected innocence clearly and succinctly, and what could be more threatening than an oversized spider? Or the author can go on to add that when our lives are upset, we can adjust ourselves to the event and even assume that we are better off, as in "The Pobble Who Has No Toes," in which the Pobble symbolizes any man who is somehow grotesque and different. If he wishes to comment that the earth is beautiful, he uses words with beautiful connotations, as in Fukuyabu Kiyowara's "Because River-fog." These elements support, illustrate, and are consistent with the final comment an author makes.

In rare instances, an author makes no comment. The quality which makes a certain book memorable, however, is the annoying or pleasing or jarring insight of the writer's comment about man and his situation. Many critics call this comment the *theme* of a work; we prefer our term because we consider it a more accurate label for the end product of writing. Any thoughtful writer has some comment to make, and if you can detect what his comment is, you will know what he means.

49 On Flunking a Nice Boy out of School

John Ciardi

I wish I could teach you how ugly
decency and humility can be when they are not
the election of a contained mind but only
the defenses of an incompetent. Were you taught
meekness as a weapon? Or did you discover,   5
by chance maybe, that it worked on mother
and was generally a good thing—
at least when all else failed—to get you over

the worst of what was coming? Is that why you bring
these sheep-faces to Tuesday?   10

They won't do.

It's three months' work I want, and I'd sooner have it
from the brassiest lumpkin in pimpledom, but have it,
than all these martyred repentances from you.

UNDERSTANDING THE SELECTION

1. Who is the speaker in this poem?
2. Who is the "you" he is addressing?
3. The poet uses two words concerned with conflict in this poem: *defenses* and *weapon.* What is the conflict he is talking about? How can meekness be a weapon?
4. Ciardi says, ". . . it worked on mother and was generally a good thing" (lines 6 and 7). What is "it"? Whose mother is he referring to? The speaker's? The mother of "you"? Both? Neither?
5. How can students bring "sheep-faces to Tuesday"?
6. Describe the "brassiest lumpkin in pimpledom." What are the connotations of these words?
7. What does *martyred* mean in the last line?
8. How does the poet use irony?
9. How would the speaker react to Annabel and Midge (Selection 6)? To Tommy Grimes (Selection 32)? To the wastrel (Selection 36)?
10. What comment does the author make?

50 Snakes

T. H. White

1   The snakes are about again. Last year I used to go out with Hughesdon to catch them, and then turn them loose in the sitting-room. At one time I had about a dozen. There are four in the room just now.
2   Grass snakes are fascinating pets. It is impossible to impose upon them, or to steal their affections, or to degrade either party in any way. They are always inevitably themselves, and with a separate silurian beauty. The plates of the jaw are fixed in an antediluvian irony. They move with silence, unless in crackling grass or with a scaly rustle over a wooden floor, pouring themselves over obstacles and round them. They are inquisitive. They live loose in the room, except that I lock them up at nights so that

the maids can clean in the mornings without being frightened. The big open fireplace is full of moss and ferns, and there is an aquarium full of water in which they can soak themselves if they wish. But mostly they prefer to lie under the hot pipes of the radiator, or to burrow inside the sofa. We had to perform a Caesarian operation on the sofa last year, to get out a big male.

3   It is nice to come into the room and look quickly round it, to see what they are doing. Perhaps there is one behind Aldous Huxley on the bookshelves, and it is always worth moving the left-hand settle away from the wall. One of them has a passion for this place and generally falls out. Another meditates all day in the aquarium, and the fourth lives in the moss.

4   Or it is nice to be working in the arm-chair, and to look up suddenly at an imagined sound. A female is pouring from behind the sofa. As the floor is of polished wood she gets a poor grip of it (she prefers the sheepskin hearth-rug) and elects to decant herself along the angle between wall and floor. Here she can press sideways as well as downwards, and gets a better grip.

5   She saw our movement as we looked up, and now stops dead, her head raised in curiosity. Her perfect forked tongue flickers blackly out of its specially armoured hole (like the hole for the starting handle in a motor, but constructed so as to close itself when not in use) and waves itself like lightning in our direction. It is what she feels with in front of her, her testing antennae, and this is her mark of interrogation. An emphatic movement: she can't reach us, but she is thinking Who or What? And so the tongue comes out. We sit quite still.

6   The tongue comes out two or three times (its touch on the hand is as delicate as the touch of a butterfly) and flickers in the air. It is a beautiful movement, with more down in it than up. It can be faintly reproduced by waggling the bent forefinger quickly in a vertical plane. Then she goes on with her pour, satisfied, towards her objective in the moss. We sit as still as a mouse.

7   I try to handle these creatures as little as possible. I do not want to steal them from themselves by making them pets. The exchange of hearts would degrade both of us. It is only that they are nice. Nice to see the strange wild things loose, living their ancient unpredictable lives with such grace. They are more ancient than the mammoth, and infinitely more beautiful. They are dry, cool and strong. The fitting and variation of the plates, the lovely colouring, the movement, their few thoughts: one could meditate upon them like a jeweller for months.

8   It is exciting to catch them. You go to a good wood, and look for snaky places in it. It is difficult to define these. There has to be undergrowth, but not overgrowth: a sunny patch, a glade or tiny clearing in the trees: perhaps long grass and a bit of moss, but not too wet. You go into it and there is a rustle. You can see nothing, but dive straight at the sound. You see just a few inches of the back, deceptively fluid for catching hold of, as it flashes from side to side. You must pounce on it at once, for there is no time to think, holding it down or grabbing it by head or tail or anywhere. There is no time to select. This is always exciting to me, because I frighten myself by thinking that it might be an adder. As a matter of fact, there are very few adders in the Shire, and in any case they move differently. An adder would strike back at you, I suppose, but a grass snake does not. It pretends to strike, with mouth wide open and the most formidable-looking fangs; but it stops its head within a millimetre of the threatened spot, a piece of bluff merely.

9   When you have grabbed your snake, you pick it up. Instantly it curls round your hand and arm, hissing and lunging at you with the almost obtuse angle of its jaw; exuding a white fluid from its vent, which has a metallic stink like acetylene. Take no notice of it at all. Like an efficient governess with a refractory child, you speak sharply to the smelly creature and hold it firmly. You take hold of its tail, unwind it, roll it in a ball (it is wriggling so much that it generally helps in this), tie it up in your handkerchief, put it in your trouser pocket and look for another.

10   When you loose it in your sitting-room it rushes off along the floor, swishing frantically but making little progress on the polished wood, and conceals itself in the darkest corner. At night, when you come to lock it up, it makes a fuss. It produces the smell again, and the hiss. In the morning it is the same. Next night perhaps the smell is omitted, or fainter. In a few days there is only a dim hiss, a kind of grumble. This goes as well, until there is only a gently protesting undulation as it is lifted off the ground.

11   I remember particularly two of last year's snakes. One was a baby male (the yellow markings are brighter in the male) only about eight inches long. He was a confiding snake, and I once took him to church in my pocket, to make him a Christian and to comfort me during the sermon. I hope it was not an undue interference with his life: I never carried him about like that again, he seemed to like the warmth of my pocket, and I believe he did not change his creed.

12   Talking of Christians, I never christened the snakes. To have called them names would have been ridiculous, as it is with cars. A snake cannot have a name. If it had to be addressed I suppose it would be addressed by its generic title: Snake.

13   The other one, I regret to say, was nearly a pet. She was a well-grown female with a scar on her neck. I suppose this had been done to her by man. It was the scar that first attracted me to her, or rather made me take special notice of her, because she was easy to distinguish. I soon found that when the time came for putting her to bed she did not undulate. She never troubled

to conceal herself at bed-time, nor to slide away from me when I approached. She would crawl right up to me, and pour over my feet while I was working. There was no horrible affection or prostration; only she was not afraid of me. She went over my feet because they were in a direct line with the place she was making for. She trusted or at least was indifferent.

14   It was a temptation. One coldish afternoon she was sitting in my chair when I wanted to read. I picked her up and put her in my lap. She was not particularly comfortable, and began to go away. I held her gently by the tail. She decided that it was not worth a scene, and stayed. I put my free hand over her, and she curled up beneath it, the head sticking out between two fingers and the tongue flickering every now and then, when a thought of curiosity entered her slow, free mind.

15   After that I used sometimes to sit with my two hands cupped, and she would curl between them on cold days. My hands were warm, that was all.

16   It was not quite all. I am afraid a hideous tinge of possession is creeping into this account. When other people came into the room she used to hiss. I would be dozing with her tight, dry coils between my palms, and there would be a hiss. The door would have opened and somebody would have come in. Or again, if I showed her to people she would hiss at them. If they tried to catch her, she would pour away. But when I gave her to them she was quiet.

17   I think I succeeded in keeping my distance. At any rate, she had a love affair with one of the males. I remember finding them coiled together on the corner table: a double rope-coil of snake which looked like a single one, except that it had two heads. I did not realise that this was an affair of the heart, at the time.

18   Later on she began to look ill. She was lumpy and flaccid. I became worried about the commissariat. Snakes rarely eat—seldom more than once a fortnight—but when they do eat they are particular. The staple food is a live frog, swallowed alive and whole. Anybody who has ever kept snakes will know how difficult it is to find a frog. The whole of the Shire seems to be populated by toads: one can scarcely move without treading on a toad: but toads disagree with snakes. They exude something from the skin.

19   I had been short of frogs lately, and (as I merely kept them loose in the aquarium so that the snakes could help themselves when they wanted) did not know when she had last had a meal. I thought I was starving her and became agitated. I spent hours looking for frogs, and found one eventually, but she wouldn't touch it. I tried a gold-fish, but that was no good either. She got worse. I was afraid she was poisoned, or melancholic from her unnatural surroundings.

20   Then came the proud day. I got back at half-past twelve, and looked for her on the hearth-rug, but she was not there. She was in the aquarium, sunlit from the french windows. Not only she. I went closer and looked. There were twenty-eight eggs.

21   Poor old lady, she was in a dreadful state. Quite apathetic and power-less, she could scarcely lift her head. Her body had fallen in on itself, leav-ing two ridges, as if she were quite a slim snake dressed in clothes too big for her. When I picked her up she hung limp, as if she were actually dead; but her tongue flickered. I didn't know what to do.

22   I got a gold-fish bowl and half-filled it with fresh grass clippings. I put her in it, with the frog, and tied paper over the top as if it were a jam jar. I made holes in the paper and took it out on to the lawn, in the full glare of the summer sun. Snakes are woken up by heat, and the bowl would con-centrate the sun's beams. It was all I could think of or do, before I went in to lunch.

23   I came back in half an hour. The bowl was warm with moisture, the grass clippings were browning, the frog was gone; and inside was Matilda (she positively deserved a name) as fit as a flea and twice as frisky.

24   The scarred snake may have been a good mistress, but she was a bad mother. If she had known anything about maternity, she would not have laid her eggs in the aquarium. It seems that water is one of the things that is fatal to the eggs of grass snakes. I picked them out, and put them in another gold-fish bowl, this time full of grass clippings that were already rotten. Then I left them in the sun. They only went mouldy.

25   She was completely tame, and the inevitable happened. The time came for me to go away for two months, so I gave her her liberty. I took her out into the fountain court (next time it shall be into the deepest and most unpopulated forest) and put her on the ground in the strong July sun-light. She was delighted by it, and pleased to go. I watched her to-froing away, till she slipped into the angle of a flowerbed, and then went resolutely indoors. There were plenty of other things in the future besides grass snakes.

26   That night I went down to the lake to bathe, and stepped over a dead snake in the moonlight. I guessed before I looked for the scar. I had kept my distance successfully, so that there were no regrets at parting, but I had destroyed a natural balance. She had lost her bitter fear of man: a thing which it is not wise to lose.

27   I feel some difficulty in putting this properly. Some bloody-minded human being had come across her on a path, and gone for her with a stick. She was harmless, useless dead, very beautiful, easy prey. He slaughtered her with a stick, and grass snakes are not easy to kill. It is easy to maim them, to bash them on the head until the bones are pulp. The lower jaw no longer articulates with the upper one, but lies sideways under the crushed skull,

shewing the beautiful colours of its unprotected inner side. The whole reserved face suddenly looks pitiful, because it has been spoilt and ravaged.
The black tongue makes a feeble flicker still.

28   These things had been done, to a creature which was offering confidence, with wanton savagery. Why? Why the waste of beauty and the
degradation to the murderer himself? He was not creating a beauty by destroying this one. He cannot even have considered himself clever.

UNDERSTANDING THE SELECTION

1. Why does White feel that both he and the snakes would be degraded
if he made pets of them? Is it degrading to make a pet of a dog? A cat? A
bird? A turtle?

2. Is it sacrilegious to take a snake to church? Why does White say, "I
hope it was not an undue interference with his life" (paragraph 11)? What
does this suggest about White himself and his attitudes toward people?

3. Why is it ridiculous for snakes to have names? Why does White finally
christen his snake?

4. Why does White say *"horrible* affection" (paragraph 13) and *"hideous*
tinge of possession" (paragraph 16)? Is possessiveness toward pets bad?
Toward people? Is possessiveness a usual part of love?

5. What does "Poor old lady" (paragraph 21) reveal about White's feelings toward Matilda?

6. Have you a stereotype of snakes? Does Matilda fit it?

7. White says, after he found Matilda dead, "I had kept my distance successfully, so that there were no regrets at parting" (paragraph 26). Do you
believe him? Why or why not?

8. Why do you think Matilda was killed? Is man instinctively afraid of
snakes?

9. "She had lost her bitter fear of man: a thing which it is not wise to lose"
(paragraph 26). Why ought animals to fear man? Ought man also to fear
man?

10. What does White imply in the last three paragraphs about the nature of
man?

11. What is the tone of the selection? What specific elements create the
tone? Note that White begins by talking about "I." In paragraphs 5 and 6 he
uses "we." He goes back to "I" in paragraph 7 but shifts to "one" in the
final sentence. The next paragraph contains both "you" and "I," while paragraphs 9 and 10 have "you" only. From paragraph 11 on, White writes "I."
What is the reason for these shifts? How do they affect the tone?

12. Discuss irony in the selection.

13. What comment does the selection make?

51 *from Black Like Me*

John Howard Griffin

1   By dark I was away from the beach area and out in the country. Strangely, I began getting rides. Men would pass you in daylight but pick you up after dark.

2   I must have had a dozen rides that evening. They blear into a nightmare, the one scarcely distinguishable from the other.

3   It quickly became obvious why they picked me up. All but two picked me up the way they would pick up a pornographic photograph or book—except that this was verbal pornography. With a Negro, they assumed they need give no semblance of self-respect or respectability. The visual element entered into it. In a car at night visibility is reduced. A man will reveal himself in the dark, which gives an illusion of anonymity, more than he will in the bright light. Some were shamelessly open, some shamelessly subtle. All showed morbid curiosity about the sexual life of the Negro, and all had, at base, the same stereotyped image of the Negro as an inexhaustible sex-machine with oversized genitals and a vast store of experiences, immensely varied. They appear to think that the Negro has done all of those "special" things they themselves have never dared to do. They carried the conversation into the depths of depravity. I note these things because it is harrowing to see decent-looking men and boys assume that because a man is black they need show him none of the reticences they would, out of respect, show the most derelict white man. I note them, too, because they differed completely from the "bull sessions" men customarily have among themselves. These latter, no matter how frank, have generally a robust tone that says: "We are men, this is an enjoyable thing to do and to discuss, but it will never impugn the basic respect we give one another; it will never distort our humanity." In this, the atmosphere, no matter how coarse, has a verve and an essential joviality that casts out morbidity. It implies respect for the persons involved. But all that I could see here were men shorn of respect either for themselves or their companion.

4   In my grogginess and exhaustion, these conversations became ghoulish. Each time one of them let me out of his car, I hoped the next would spare me his pantings. I remained mute and pleaded my exhaustion and lack of sleep.

5   "I'm so tired, I just can't think," I would say.

6   Like men who had promised themselves pleasure, they would not be denied. It became a strange sort of hounding as they nudged my skull for my sexual reminiscences.

7   "Well, did you ever do such-and-such?"

8 "I don't know . . ." I moaned.

9 "What's the matter—haven't you got any manhood? My old man told me you wasn't really a man till you'd done such-and-such."

10 Or the older ones, hardened, cynical in their lechery. "Now, don't try to kid me. I wasn't born yesterday. You know you've done such-and-such, just like I have. Hell, it's good that way. Tell me, did you ever get a white woman?"

11 "Do you think I'm crazy?" I tacitly denied the racist's contention, for he would not hesitate to use it against the Negroes in his conversations around town: "Why, I had one of them admit to me just last night that he craves white women."

12 "I didn't ask if you was crazy," he said. "I asked if you ever had one— or ever really wanted one." Then, conniving, sweet-toned, "There's plenty white women would like to have a good buck Negro."

13 "A Negro'd be asking for the rope to get himself mixed up with white women."

14 "You're just telling me that, but I'll bet inside you think differently . . ."

15 "This is sure beautiful country through here. What's the main crop?"

16 "*Don't* you? You can tell me. Hell, I don't care."

17 "No sir," I sighed.

18 "You're lying in your teeth and you know it."

19 Silence. Soon after, almost abruptly he halted the car and said, "Okay, this is as far as I go." He spoke as though he resented my uncooperative attitude, my refusal to give him this strange verbal sexual pleasure.

20 I thanked him for the ride and stepped down onto the highway. He drove on in the same direction.

21 Soon another picked me up, a young man in his late twenties who spoke with an educated flair. His questions had the spurious elevation of a scholar seeking information, but the information he sought was entirely sexual, and presupposed that in the ghetto the Negro's life is one of marathon sex with many different partners, open to the view of all: in a word, that marital fidelity and sex as love's goal of union with the beloved object were exclusively the white man's property. Though he pretended to be above such ideas as racial superiority and spoke with genuine warmth, the entire context of his talk reeked of preconceived ideas to the contrary.

22 "I understand Negroes are much more broad-minded about such things," he said warmly.

23 "I don't know."

24 "I understand you make more of an art—or maybe *hobby* out of your sex than we do."

25 "I doubt it."

26   "Well, you people don't seem to have the inhibitions we have. We're all basically puritans. I understand Negroes do a lot more things—different kinds of sex—than we do. Oh, don't get me wrong. I admire your attitude, think it's basically healthier than ours. You don't get so damned many *conflicts.* Negroes don't have much neuroses, do they? I mean you people have a more realistic tradition about sex—you're not so sheltered from it as we are."

27   I know that what he really meant was that Negroes grew up seeing it from infancy. He had read the same stories, the same reports of social workers about parents sharing a room with children, the father coming home drunk and forcing the mother onto the bed in full view of the young ones. I felt like laughing in his face when I thought of the Negro families I had known already as a Negro: the men on the streets, in the ghettos, the housewives and their great concern that their children "grow up right."

28   "You people regard sex as a *total* experience—and that's how it should be. Anything that makes you feel good is morally all right for you. Isn't that the main difference?"

29   "I don't think there's any difference, " I said cautiously, not wanting to test the possibility of his wrath at having a Negro disagree with him.

30   "You *don't?*" His voice betrayed excitement and eagerness; gave no hint of offense.

31   "Our ministers preach sin and hell just as much as yours," I said. "We've got the same puritanical background as you. We worry just as much as white people about our children losing their virginity or being perverted. We've got the same miserable little worries and problems over our sexual effectiveness, the same guilts that you have.

32   He appeared astonished and delighted, not at what I said but at the fact that I could say it. His whole attitude of enthusiasm practically shouted, "Why, you talk *intelligently!*" He was so obtuse he did not realize the implied insult in his astonishment that a black man could do anything but say "yes sir" and mumble four-letter words.

33   Again, he asked questions scarcely different from those that white men would ask themselves; especially scholars who would discuss cultural differences on a detached plane. Yet here the tone was subtly conniving. He went through the motions of courteous research, but he could not hide his real preoccupation. He asked about the size of Negro genitalia and the details of Negro sex life. Only the language differed from the previous inquirers—the substance was the same. The difference was that here I could disagree with him without risking a flood of abuse or petulance. He quoted Kinsey and others. It became apparent he was one of those young men who possess an impressive store of facts, but no truths. This again would have no significance and would be unworthy of note except for one thing:

I have talked with such men many times as a white and they never show the glow of prurience he revealed. The significance lay in the fact that my blackness and his concepts of what my blackness implied allowed him to expose himself in this manner. He saw the Negro as a different species. He saw me as something akin to an animal in that he felt no need to maintain his sense of human dignity, though certainly he would have denied this.

UNDERSTANDING THE SELECTION

1. In 1959 John Howard Griffin, a white journalist, acted upon a plan he had had in mind for some time—he turned himself into a Negro. With the help of a dermatologist he darkened his skin and for most of the month of November he traveled through the South as a black man. *Black Like Me* records his experiences. Its contents first appeared in *Sepia* magazine in March, 1960, and generated national and international interest. A major consequence for Griffin was that he, his wife and children, and his parents, all of whom lived in Texas, were so vilified and threatened that his parents sold everything and moved out of the country, and Griffin with his own family moved away.

The selection printed here is dated November 19, about midway through the period Griffin was black. He was traveling from Biloxi, Mississippi, to Mobile, Alabama.

2. Central to the selection is the white man's stereotype of the black man. Do you know people who share this stereotype?

3. Griffin observes that men do at night what they will not do during the day. Can you cite experiences of your own that bear out this observation?

4. What does Griffin mean when he says, in paragraph 33, ". . . he was one of those young men who possess an impressive store of facts, but no truths"? What is the difference between fact and truth?

5. What is the tone of the selection? Discuss all the ironies you see in this article.

6. What comment does the selection make?

52   *Soccer Game*

David Seymour ("Chim")

Photograph by David Seymour ("Chim"). © Magnum Photos, Inc.

UNDERSTANDING THE SELECTION

1. Discuss irony in this picture.

2. Compare this photograph with "Ring-around-a-rosy" (Selection 12). What things in both are similar? What things are dissimilar? Which is the "better" photograph? Why? Which do you like better? Why? Which one do you think you will remember longer? Why?

3. What comment is the photographer making?

4. This picture was taken in Italy in 1949. What else can you deduce about the time and place it was taken? Is the setting important for understanding the photographer's comment or is the comment independent of time and place?

53 The Three Fat Women of Antibes

W. Somerset Maugham

1   One was called Mrs. Richman and she was a widow. The second
was called Mrs. Sutcliffe; she was American and she had divorced two husbands. The third was called Miss Hickson and she was a spinster. They were
all in the comfortable forties and they were all well off. Mrs. Sutcliffe had
the odd first name of Arrow. When she was young and slender she had
liked it well enough. It suited her and the jests it occasioned though too
often repeated were very flattering; she was not disinclined to believe that
it suited her character too: it suggested directness, speed and purpose.
She liked it less now that her delicate features had grown muzzy with fat,
that her arms and shoulders were so substantial and her hips so massive.
It was increasingly difficult to find dresses to make her look as she liked
to look. The jests her name gave rise to now were made behind her back
and she very well knew that they were far from obliging. But she was by
no means resigned to middle age. She still wore blue to bring out the colour
of her eyes and, with the help of art, her fair hair had kept its lustre. What
she liked about Beatrice Richman and Frances Hickson was that they were
both so much fatter than she, it made her look quite slim; they were both
of them older and much inclined to treat her as a little young thing. It was
not disagreeable. They were good-natured women and they chaffed her
pleasantly about her beaux; they had both given up the thought of that kind
of nonsense, indeed Miss Hickson had never given it a moment's consideration, but they were sympathetic to her flirtations. It was understood
that one of these days Arrow would make a third man happy.
2   "Only you mustn't get any heavier, darling," said Mrs. Richman.
3   "And for goodness' sake make certain of his bridge," said Miss Hickson.
4   They saw for her a man of about fifty, but well-preserved and of distinguished carriage, an admiral on the retired list and a good golfer, or a
widower without encumbrances, but in any case with a substantial income.
Arrow listened to them amiably, and kept to herself that fact that this was
not at all her idea. It was true that she would have liked to marry again, but
her fancy turned to a dark slim Italian with flashing eyes and a sonorous
title or to a Spanish don of noble lineage; and not a day more than thirty.
There were times when, looking at herself in her mirror, she was certain
she did not look any more than that herself.
5   They were great friends, Miss Hickson, Mrs. Richman and Arrow
Sutcliffe. It was their fat that had brought them together and bridge that

had cemented their alliance. They had met first at Carlsbad, where they were staying at the same hotel and were treated by the same doctor who used them with the same ruthlessness. Beatrice Richman was enormous. She was a handsome woman, with fine eyes, rouged cheeks and painted lips. She was very well content to be a widow with a handsome fortune. She adored her food. She liked bread and butter, cream, potatoes and suet puddings, and for eleven months of the year ate pretty well everything she had a mind to, and for one month went to Carlsbad to reduce. But every year she grew fatter. She upbraided the doctor, but got no sympathy from him. He pointed out to her various plain and simple facts.

6   "But if I'm never to eat a thing I like, life isn't worth living," she expostulated.

7   He shrugged his disapproving shoulders. Afterwards she told Miss Hickson that she was beginning to suspect he wasn't so clever as she had thought. Miss Hickson gave a great guffaw. She was that sort of woman. She had a deep bass voice, a large flat sallow face from which twinkled little bright eyes; she walked with a slouch, her hands in her pockets, and when she could do so without exciting attention smoked a long cigar. She dressed as like a man as she could.

8   "What the deuce should I look like in frills and furbelows?" she said. "When you're as fat as I am you may just as well be comfortable."

9   She wore tweeds and heavy boots and whenever she could went about bareheaded. But she was as strong as an ox and boasted that few men could drive a longer ball than she. She was plain of speech, and she could swear more variously than a stevedore. Though her name was Frances she preferred to be called Frank. Masterful, but with tact, it was her jovial strength of character that held the three together. They drank their waters together, had their baths at the same hour, they took their strenuous walks together, pounded about the tennis court with a professional to make them run, and ate at the same table their sparse and regulated meals. Nothing impaired their good humour but the scales, and when one or other of them weighed as much on one day as she had the day before neither Frank's coarse jokes, the bonhomie of Beatrice nor Arrow's pretty kittenish ways sufficed to dispel the gloom. Then drastic measures were resorted to, the culprit went to bed for twenty-four hours and nothing passed her lips but the doctor's famous vegetable soup which tasted like hot water in which a cabbage had been well rinsed.

10   Never were three women greater friends. They would have been independent of anyone else if they had not needed a fourth at bridge. They were fierce, enthusiastic players and the moment the day's cure was over they sat down at the bridge table. Arrow, feminine as she was, played the best game of the three, a hard, brilliant game, in which she showed no mercy

and never conceded a point or failed to take advantage of a mistake. Beatrice was solid and reliable. Frank was dashing; she was a great theorist, and had all the authorities at the tip of her tongue. They had long arguments over the rival systems. They bombarded one another with Culbertson and Sims. It was obvious that not one of them ever played a card without fifteen good reasons, but it was also obvious from the subsequent conversation that there were fifteen equally good reasons why she should not have played it. Life would have been perfect, even with the prospect of twenty-four hours of that filthy soup when the doctor's rotten (Beatrice) bloody (Frank) lousy (Arrow) scales pretended one hadn't lost an ounce in two days, if only there had not been this constant difficulty of finding someone to play with them who was in their class.

11   It was for this reason that on the occasion with which this narrative deals Frank invited Lena Finch to come and stay with them at Antibes. They were spending some weeks there on Frank's suggestion. It seemed absurd to her, with her common sense, that immediately the cure was over Beatrice who always lost twenty pounds should by giving way to her ungovernable appetite put it all on again. Beatrice was weak. She needed a person of strong will to watch her diet. She proposed then that on leaving Carlsbad they should take a house at Antibes, where they could get plenty of exercise—everyone knew that nothing slimmed you like swimming—and as far as possible could go on with the cure. With a cook of their own they could at least avoid things that were obviously fattening. There was no reason why they should not all lose several pounds more. It seemed a very good idea. Beatrice knew what was good for her, and she could resist temptation well enough if temptation was not put right under her nose. Besides, she liked gambling, and a flutter at the Casino two or three times a week would pass the time very pleasantly. Arrow adored Antibes, and she would be looking her best after a month at Carlsbad. She could just pick and choose among the young Italians, the passionate Spaniards, the gallant Frenchmen, and the long-limbed English who sauntered about all day in bathing trunks and gay-coloured dressing-gowns. The plan worked very well. They had a grand time. Two days a week they ate nothing but hard-boiled eggs and raw tomatoes and they mounted the scales every morning with light hearts. Arrow got down to eleven stone and felt just like a girl; Beatrice and Frank by standing in a certain way just avoided the thirteen. The machine they had bought registered kilogrammes, and they got extraordinarily clever at translating these in the twinkling of an eye to pounds and ounces.

12   But the fourth at bridge continued to be the difficulty. This person played like a fool, the other was so slow that it drove you frantic, one was quarrelsome, another was a bad loser, a third was next door to a crook. It was strange how hard it was to find exactly the player you wanted.

13   One morning when they were sitting in pyjamas on the terrace over-looking the sea, drinking their tea (without milk or sugar) and eating a rusk prepared by Dr. Hudebert and guaranteed not to be fattening, Frank looked up from her letters.

14   "Lena Finch is coming down to the Riviera," she said.

15   "Who's she?" asked Arrow.

16   "She married a cousin of mine. He died a couple of months ago and she's just recovering from a nervous breakdown. What about asking her to come here for a fortnight?"

17   "Does she play bridge?" asked Beatrice.

18   "You bet your life she does," boomed Frank in her deep voice. "And a damned good game too. We should be absolutely independent of out-siders."

19   "How old is she?" asked Arrow.

20   "Same age as I am."

21   "That sounds all right."

22   It was settled. Frank, with her usual decisiveness, stalked out as soon as she had finished her breakfast to send a wire, and three days later Lena Finch arrived. Frank met her at the station. She was in deep but not obtrusive mourning for the recent death of her husband. Frank had not seen her for two years. She kissed her warmly and took a good look at her.

23   "You're very thin, darling," she said.

24   Lena smiled bravely.

25   "I've been through a good deal lately. I've lost a lot of weight."

26   Frank sighed, but whether from sympathy with her cousin's sad loss, or from envy, was not obvious.

27   Lena was not, however, unduly depressed, and after a quick bath was quite ready to accompany Frank to Eden Roc. Frank introduced the stranger to her two friends and they sat down in what was known as the Monkey House. It was an enclosure covered with glass overlooking the sea, with a bar at the back, and it was crowded with chattering people in bathing costumes, pyjamas or dressing-gowns, who were seated at the tables having drinks. Beatrice's soft heart went out to the lorn window, and Arrow, seeing that she was pale, quite ordinary to look at and probably forty-eight, was prepared to like her very much. A waiter approached them.

28   "What will you have, Lena dear?" Frank asked.

29   "Oh, I don't know, what you all have, a dry Martini or a White Lady."

30   Arrow and Beatrice gave her a quick look. Everyone knows how fattening cocktails are.

31   "I daresay you're tired after your journey," said Frank kindly.

32   She ordered a dry Martini for Lena and a mixed lemon and orange juice for herself and her two friends.

33   "We find alcohol isn't very good in all this heat," she explained.

34   "Oh, it never affects me at all," Lena answered airily. "I like cocktails."

35   Arrow went very slightly pale under her rouge (neither she nor Beatrice ever wet their faces when they bathed and they thought it absurd of Frank, a woman of her size, to pretend she liked diving) but she said nothing. The conversation was gay and easy, they all said the obvious things with gusto, and presently they strolled back to the villa for luncheon.

36   In each napkin were two little antifat rusks. Lena gave a bright smile as she put them by the side of her plate.

37   "May I have some bread?" she asked.

38   The grossest indecency would not have fallen on the ears of those three women with such a shock. Not one of them had eaten bread for ten years. Even Beatrice, greedy as she was, drew the line there. Frank, the good hostess, recovered herself first.

39   "Of course, darling," she said and turning to the butler asked him to bring some.

40   "And some butter," said Lena in that pleasant easy way of hers.

41   There was a moment's embarrassed silence.

42   "I don't know if there's any in the house," said Frank, "but I'll enquire. There may be some in the kitchen."

43   "I adore bread and butter, don't you?" said Lena, turning to Beatrice.

44   Beatrice gave a sickly smile and an evasive reply. The butler brought a long crisp roll of French bread. Lena slit it in two and plastered it with the butter which was miraculously produced. A grilled sole was served.

45   "We eat very simply here," said Frank. "I hope you won't mind."

46   "Oh, no, I like my food very plain," said Lena as she took some butter and spread it over her fish. "As long as I can have bread and butter and potatoes and cream I'm quite happy."

47   The three friends exchanged a glance. Frank's great sallow face sagged a little and she looked with distaste at the dry, insipid sole on her plate. Beatrice came to the rescue.

48   "It's such a bore, we can't get cream here," she said. "It's one of the things one has to do without on the Riviera."

49   "What a pity," said Lena.

50   The rest of the luncheon consisted of lamb cutlets, with the fat carefully removed so that Beatrice should not be led astray, and spinach boiled in water, with stewed pears to end up with. Lena tasted her pears and gave the butler a look of enquiry. That resourceful man understood her at once and though powdered sugar had never been served at that table before handed her without a moment's hesitation a bowl of it. She helped herself liberally. The other three pretended not to notice. Coffee was served and Lena took three lumps of sugar in hers.

51   "You have a very sweet tooth," said Arrow in a tone which she struggled to keep friendly.

52   "We think saccharine so much more sweetening," said Frank, as she put a tiny tablet of it into her coffee.

53   "Disgusting stuff," said Lena.

54   Beatrice's mouth drooped at the corners, and she gave the lump sugar a yearning look.

55   "Beatrice," boomed Frank sternly.

56   Beatrice stifled a sigh, and reached for the saccharine.

57   Frank was relieved when they could sit down to the bridge table. It was plain to her that Arrow and Beatrice were upset. She wanted them to like Lena and she was anxious that Lena should enjoy her fortnight with them. For the first rubber Arrow cut with the newcomer.

58   "Do you play Vanderbilt or Culbertson?" she asked her.

59   "I have no conventions," Lena answered in a happy-go-lucky way, "I play by the light of nature."

60   "I play strict Culbertson," said Arrow acidly.

61   The three fat women braced themselves to the fray. No conventions indeed! They'd learn her. When it came to bridge even Frank's family feeling was forgotten and she settled down with the same determination as the others to trim the stranger in their midst. But the light of nature served Lena very well. She had a natural gift for the game and great experience. She played with imagination, quickly, boldly, and with assurance. The other players were in too high a class not to realise very soon that Lena knew what she was about, and since they were all thoroughly good-natured, generous women, they were gradually mollified. This was real bridge. They all enjoyed themselves. Arrow and Beatrice began to feel more kindly towards Lena, and Frank, noticing this, heaved a fat sigh of relief. It was going to be a success.

62   After a couple of hours they parted, Frank and Beatrice to have a round of golf, and Arrow to take a brisk walk with a young Prince Roccamare whose acquaintance she had lately made. He was very sweet and young and good-looking. Lena said she would rest.

63   They met again just before dinner.

64   "I hope you've been all right, Lena dear," said Frank. "I was rather conscience-stricken at leaving you with nothing to do all this time."

65   "Oh, don't apologise. I had a lovely sleep and then I went down to

Juan and had a cocktail. And d'you know what I discovered? You'll be so pleased. I found a dear little tea-shop where they've got the most beautiful thick fresh cream. I've ordered half a pint to be sent every day. I thought it would be my little contribution to the household."

66   Her eyes were shining. She was evidently expecting them to be delighted.

67   "How very kind of you," said Frank, with a look that sought to quell the indignation that she saw on the faces of her two friends. "But we never eat cream. In this climate it makes one so bilious."

68   "I shall have to eat it all myself then," said Lena cheerfully.

69   "Don't you ever think of your figure?" Arrow asked with icy deliberation.

70   "The doctor said I must eat."

71   "Did he say you must eat bread and butter and potatoes and cream?"

72   "Yes. That's what I thought you meant when you said you had simple food."

73   "You'll get simply enormous," said Beatrice.

74   Lena laughed gaily.

75   "No, I shan't. You see, nothing ever makes me fat. I've always eaten everything I wanted to and it's never had the slightest effect on me."

76   The stony silence that followed this speech was only broken by the entrance of the butler.

77   *"Mademoiselle est servie,"* he announced.

78   They talked the matter over late that night, after Lena had gone to bed, in Frank's room. During the evening they had been furiously cheerful, and they had chaffed one another with a friendliness that would have taken in the keenest observer. But now they dropped the mask. Beatrice was sullen, Arrow was spiteful and Frank was unmanned.

79   "It's not very nice for me to sit there and see her eat all the things I particularly like," said Beatrice plaintively.

80   "It's not very nice for any of us," Frank snapped back.

81   "You should never have asked her here," said Arrow.

82   "How was I to know?" cried Frank.

83   "I can't help thinking that if she really cared for her husband she would hardly eat so much," said Beatrice. "He's only been buried two months. I mean, I think you ought to show some respect for the dead."

84   "Why can't she eat the same as we do?" asked Arrow viciously. "She's a guest."

85   "Well, you heard what she said. The doctor told her she must eat."

86   "Then she ought to go to a sanatorium."

87   "It's more than flesh and blood can stand, Frank," moaned Beatrice.

88   "If I can stand it you can stand it."

89   "She's your cousin, she's not our cousin," said Arrow. "I'm not going to sit there for fourteen days and watch that woman make a hog of herself."

90   "It's so vulgar to attach all this importance to food," Frank boomed, and her voice was deeper than ever. "After all the only thing that counts really is spirit."

91   "Are you calling *me* vulgar, Frank?" asked Arrow with flashing eyes.

92   "No, of course she isn't," interrupted Beatrice.

93   "I wouldn't put it past you to go down in the kitchen when we're all in bed and have a good square meal on the sly."

94   Frank sprang to her feet.

95   "How dare you say that, Arrow! I'd never ask anybody to do what I'm not prepared to do myself. Have you known me all these years and do you think me capable of such a mean thing?"

96   "How is it you never take off any weight then?"

97   Frank gave a gasp and burst into a flood of tears.

98   "What a cruel thing to say! I've lost pounds and pounds."

99   She wept like a child. Her vast body shook and great tears splashed on her mountainous bosom.

100   "Darling, I didn't mean it," cried Arrow.

101   She threw herself on her knees and enveloped what she could of Frank in her own plump arms. She wept and the mascara ran down her cheeks.

102   "D'you mean to say I don't look thinner?" Frank sobbed. "After all I've gone through."

103   "Yes, dear, of course you do," cried Arrow through her tears. "Everybody's noticed it."

104   Beatrice, though naturally of a placid disposition, began to cry gently. It was very pathetic. Indeed, it would have been a hard heart that failed to be moved by the sight of Frank, that lion-hearted woman, crying her eyes out. Presently, however, they dried their tears and had a little brandy and water, which every doctor had told them was the least fattening thing they could drink, and then they felt much better. They decided that Lena should have the nourishing food that had been ordered her and they made a solemn resolution not to let it disturb their equanimity. She was certainly a first-rate bridge player and after all it was only for a fortnight. They would do whatever they could to make her stay enjoyable. They kissed one another warmly and separated for the night feeling strangely uplifted. Nothing should interfere with the wonderful friendship that had brought so much happiness into their three lives.

105   But human nature is weak. You must not ask too much of it. They ate grilled fish while Lena ate macaroni sizzling with cheese and butter; they ate grilled cutlets and boiled spinach while Lena ate *pâté de foie gras;*

twice a week they ate hard-boiled eggs and raw tomatoes, while Lena ate peas swimming in cream and potatoes cooked in all sorts of delicious ways. The chef was a good chef and he leapt at the opportunity afforded him to send up one dish more rich, tasty and succulent than the other.

106   "Poor Jim," sighed Lena, thinking of her husband, "he loved French cooking."

107   The butler disclosed the fact that he could make half a dozen kinds of cocktail and Lena informed them that the doctor had recommended her to drink burgundy at luncheon and champagne at dinner. The three fat women persevered. They were gay, chatty and even hilarious (such is the natural gift that women have for deception) but Beatrice grew limp and forlorn, and Arrow's tender blue eyes acquired a steely glint. Frank's deep voice grew more raucous. It was when they played bridge that the strain showed itself. They had always been fond of talking over their hands, but their discussions had been friendly. Now a distinct bitterness crept in and sometimes one pointed out a mistake to another with quite unnecessary frankness. Discussion turned to argument and argument to altercation. Sometimes the session ended in angry silence. Once Frank accused Arrow of deliberately letting her down. Two or three times Beatrice, the softest of the three, was reduced to tears. On another occasion Arrow flung down her cards and swept out of the room in a pet. Their tempers were getting frayed. Lena was the peacemaker.

108   "I think it's such a pity to quarrel over bridge," she said. "After all, it's only a game."

109   It was all very well for her. She had had a square meal and half a bottle of champagne. Besides, she had phenomenal luck. She was winning all their money. The score was put down in a book after each session, and hers mounted up day after day with unfailing regularity. Was there no justice in the world? They began to hate one another. And though they hated her too they could not resist confiding in her. Each of them went to her separately and told her how detestable the others were. Arrow said she was sure it was bad for her to see so much of women so much older than herself. She had a good mind to sacrifice her share of the lease and go to Venice for the rest of the summer. Frank told Lena that with her masculine mind it was too much to expect that she could be satisfied with anyone so frivolous as Arrow and so frankly stupid as Beatrice.

110   "I must have intellectual conversation," she boomed. "When you have a brain like mine you've got to consort with your intellectual equals."

111   Beatrice only wanted peace and quiet.

112   "Really I hate women," she said. "They're so unreliable; they're so malicious."

113   By the time Lena's fortnight drew to its close the three fat women were barely on speaking terms. They kept up appearances before Lena, but when she was not there made no pretences. They had got past quarrelling. They ignored one another, and when this was not possible treated each other with icy politeness.

114   Lena was going to stay with friends on the Italian Riviera and Frank saw her off by the same train as that by which she had arrived. She was taking away with her a lot of their money.

115   "I don't know how to thank you," she said, as she got into the carriage. "I've had a wonderful visit."

116   If there was one thing that Frank Hickson prided herself on more than on being a match for any man it was that she was a gentlewoman, and her reply was perfect in its combination of majesty and graciousness.

117   "We've all enjoyed having you here, Lena," she said. "It's been a real treat."

118   But when she turned away from the departing train she heaved such a vast sigh of relief that the platform shook beneath her. She flung back her massive shoulders and strode home to the villa.

119   "Ouf!" she roared at intervals. "Ouf!"

120   She changed into her one-piece bathing-suit, put on her espadrilles and a man's dressing-gown (no nonsense about it) and went to Eden Roc. There was still time for a bathe before luncheon. She passed through the Monkey House, looking about her to say good morning to anyone she knew, for she felt on a sudden at peace with mankind, and then stopped dead still. She could not believe her eyes. Beatrice was sitting at one of the tables, by herself; she wore the pyjamas she had bought at Molyneux's a day or two before, she had a string of pearls round her neck, and Frank's quick eyes saw that she had just had her hair waved; her cheeks, her eyes, her lips were made up. Fat, nay vast, as she was, none could deny that she was an extremely handsome woman. But what was she doing? With the slouching gait of the Neanderthal man which was Frank's characteristic walk she went up to Beatrice. In her black bathing-dress Frank looked like the huge cetacean which the Japanese catch in the Torres Straits and which the vulgar call a sea-cow.

121   "Beatrice, what are you doing?" she cried in her deep voice.

122   It was like the roll of thunder in the distant mountains. Beatrice looked at her coolly.

123   "Eating," she answered.

124   "Damn it, I can see you're eating."

125   In front of Beatrice was a plate of *croissants* and a plate of butter, a pot of strawberry jam, coffee and a jug of cream. Beatrice was spreading butter thick on the delicious hot bread, covering this with jam, and then pouring the thick cream over all.

126   "You'll kill yourself," said Frank.

127   "I don't care," mumbled Beatrice with her mouth full.

128   "You'll put on pounds and pounds."

129   "Go to hell!"

130   She actually laughed in Frank's face. My God, how good those *croissants* smelt!

131   "I'm disappointed in you, Beatrice. I thought you had more character."

132   "It's your fault. That blasted woman. You would have her down. For a fortnight I've watched her gorge like a hog. It's more than flesh and blood can stand. I'm going to have one square meal if I bust."

133   The tears welled up to Frank's eyes. Suddenly she felt very weak and womanly. She would have liked a strong man to take her on his knee and pet her and cuddle her and call her little baby names. Speechless she sank down on a chair by Beatrice's side. A waiter came up. With a pathetic gesture she waved towards the coffee and *croissants.*

134   "I'll have the same," she sighed.

135   She listlessly reached out her hand to take a roll, but Beatrice snatched away the plate.

136   "No, you don't," she said. "You wait till you get your own."

137   Frank called her a name which ladies seldom apply to one another in affection. In a moment the waiter brought her *croissants,* butter, jam and coffee.

138   "Where's the cream, you fool?" she roared like a lioness at bay.

139   She began to eat. She ate gluttonously. The place was beginning to fill up with bathers coming to enjoy a cocktail or two after having done their duty by the sun and the sea. Presently Arrow strolled along with Prince Roccamare. She had on a beautiful silk wrap which she held tightly round her with one hand in order to look as slim as possible and she bore her head high so that he should not see her double chin. She was laughing gaily. She felt like a girl. He had just told her (in Italian) that her eyes made the blue of the Mediterranean look like pea-soup. He left her to go into the men's room to brush his sleek black hair and they arranged to meet in five minutes for a drink. Arrow walked on to the women's room to put a little more rouge on her cheeks and a little more red on her lips. On her way she caught sight of Frank and Beatrice. She stopped. She could hardly believe her eyes.

140   "My God!" she cried. "You beasts. You hogs." She seized a chair. "Waiter."

141   Her appointment went clean out of her head. In the twinkling of an eye the waiter was at her side.

142   "Bring me what these ladies are having," she ordered.

143   Frank lifted her great heavy head from her plate.

144   "Bring me some *pâté de foie gras,"* she boomed.

145   "Frank!" cried Beatrice.

146   "Shut up."

147   "All right. I'll have some too."

148   The coffee was brought and the hot rolls and cream and the *pâté de foie gras* and they set to. They spread the cream on the *pâté* and they ate it. They devoured great spoonfuls of jam. They crunched the delicious crisp bread voluptuously. What was love to Arrow then? Let the Prince keep his palace in Rome and his castle in the Apennines. They did not speak. What they were about was much too serious. They ate with solemn, ec-static fervour.

149   "I haven't eaten potatoes for twenty-five years," said Frank in a far-off brooding tone.

150   "Waiter," cried Beatrice, "bring fried potatoes for three."

151   *"Très bien, Madame."*

152   The potatoes were brought. Not all the perfumes of Arabia smelt so sweet. They ate them with their fingers.

153   "Bring me a dry Martini," said Arrow.

154   "You can't have a dry Martini in the middle of a meal, Arrow," said Frank.

155   "Can't I? You wait and see."

156   "All right then. Bring me a double dry Martini," said Frank.

157   "Bring three double dry Martinis," said Beatrice.

158   They were brought and drunk at a gulp.The women looked at one another and sighed. The misunderstandings of the last fortnight dissolved and the sincere affection each had for the other welled up again in their hearts. They could hardly believe that they had ever contemplated the pos-sibility of severing a friendship that had brought them so much solid satis-faction. They finished the potatoes.

159   "I wonder if they've got any chocolate éclairs," said Beatrice.

160   "Of course they have."

161   And of course they had. Frank thrust one whole into her huge mouth, swallowed it and seized another, but before she ate it she looked at the other two and plunged a vindictive dagger into the heart of the monstrous Lena.

162   "You can say what you like, but the truth is she played a damned rotten game of bridge, really."

163   "Lousy," agreed Arrow.

164   But Beatrice suddenly thought she would like a meringue.

UNDERSTANDING THE SELECTION

1. Find out where Carlsbad and Antibes are. Is the setting of this story important, or could it be set equally well in Hollywood and Las Vegas? What connotations have Carlsbad and Antibes?

2. A "stone" (paragraph 11) is a British measure of weight. How much is it?

3. What reasons do the three women give against Lena's eating as she does? What is the real reason they object to her meals? Is this an example of irony?

4. As the three fat women begin to hate one another, each tells Lena how detestable the others are. What reason does each give? Do you find it believable that three friends would act this way? Explain.

5. What comment does the story make? Do you believe that Maugham's insights into human nature are accurate? Cite experiences of your own to support your answer.

6. Although this is a funny story, you cannot say that Maugham's tone is necessarily humorous. What is the tone of the tale? In what way is the tone related to Maugham's comment?

7. Compare Arrow, Beatrice, and Frank with Annabel and Midge ("The Standard of Living," Selection 6). What similarities do you see in all of these women? Would you say that "The Three Fat Women of Antibes" and "The Standard of Living" make similar comments on human behavior?

54   No Daughter of Mine
Charles Philbrick

The littlest person I have ever loved
And the briefest, so maybe the best I have loved
Has long lain scattered of liver and lights and fine eyes
Once bright with questions of me, but soon tired
Of the handful of hours they had already known,   5
Blue eyes that drew their lids to let me know
To let her go.
            That body wrongly light
Is now many years of me gone to some earth,
With no stone, as we wished it, and nothing for name.

Unfathered by nothing: no daughter of mine.   10

UNDERSTANDING THE SELECTION

1. In this poem, a father writes of the death of his daughter, as we learn from the title. How old do you think she was when she died? How long ago did she die?

2. Why does he call his daughter "maybe the best I have loved" (line 2)?

3. Are the connotations of "liver and lights and fine eyes" (line 3) appro-

priate to the poem? Are they consistent with each other? What, by the way, are *lights?*

4. In line 7 the poet mentions *light.* What does the word mean here?

5. How did the daughter feel about dying?

6. How does the father feel about her death? Is he reconciled? Angry? Grieving? What is the tone of the poem?

7. Why does the daughter have "no stone . . . and nothing for name"?

8. What comment does the poet make about mortality and loss?

what do you think
of what
the author says?

We have suggested ways to answer the questions "What does the author say?" and "What does the author mean?" Now we are ready to suggest ways to answer the question "What do you think of what the author says?"

First, a warning. What you think of what the author says is not necessarily the same as whether or not you like what he says. What you like or dislike is up to you. You may prefer the Smothers Brothers to *The Brothers Karamazov,* but you cannot go on to say, "Because I prefer the Smothers Brothers, their material is better." Like whichever of the following selections you please, and do not be so meek that you think you should like them all merely because they are included in a textbook, but think about all of them.

Thinking about what a writer says implies judging his work. You may judge his writing to be good—wise, perceptive, and hence entertaining —or bad—ridiculous, illogical, and hence dull. Or, most probably, you will decide that it is partly good and partly bad.

How do you start thinking about and judging writing? We have already given you a number of questions as guides. Here is a list of them.

1. What kind of order does the writer use to arrange his material?
2. What kinds of connotation does he use? Are his connotations consistent?
3. Are his metaphors fresh and vivid or stale and tired?
4. Do his allusions clarify or muddy his comment?
5. If he uses symbols, are they clear and do they enhance his comment, or are they scattered about like a child's toys for you to fall over?
6. Does he use stereotypes? If so, does he seem to know that he is using them?
7. Is the tone consistent with the comment?
8. Is the comment worth making?

There are other questions that we have hinted at but have not expressed. Here is an additional list.

9. If the writer presents facts, are they accurate?
10. Does he use only some of the available facts in order to influence you?
11. Do the people you know behave as he claims people do? If not, is he an inaccurate observer or is your circle of acquaintances limited to a few types? Or is he being ironic?
12. What sort of prejudices has he? Are they the same as yours? Can you or he give better reasons for your prejudices?
13. What assumptions does he make about the universe and man? Has life a meaning or not? Is man good or bad? Do you make the same assumptions he does?
14. Do you think the writer's comment will mean as much 100 years from now as it does today?

In the following section four groups of selections commenting on problems which confront us all are collected for you to compare. Be sure you know exactly what each writer says and exactly what he means. Then compare the comment each makes and judge which selection in each group makes its comment most effectively.

In going through this section, you will discover that we have asked no questions to help you understand the last group of selections. Throughout the book we have tried to encourage you to ask questions about what you read and to find answers in the works themselves. Starting with the selections in Group 4 of this section, you are on your own.

Group 1:
warfare

55 *Little Miss Muffet*
Paul Dehn

Little Miss Muffet
Crouched on a tuffet,
   Collecting her shell-shocked wits.
There dropped (from a glider)
An H-bomb beside her—
   Which frightened Miss Muffet to *bits*.

56 *War in Tampa*
The National Advisory Commission on Civil Disorders

1   On Sunday, June 11, 1967, Tampa, Florida, sweltered in the 94-degree heat. A humid wind ruffled the bay, where thousands of persons watched the hydroplane races. Since early morning the Police Department's Selective Enforcement Unit, designed as a riot control squad, had been employed to keep order at the races.

2   At 5:30 P.M., a block from the waterfront, a photo supply warehouse was broken into. Forty-five minutes later two police officers spotted three Negro youths as they walked near the State Building. When the youths caught sight of the officers, they ducked into an alley. The officers gave chase. As they ran, the suspects left a trail of photographic equipment scattered from yellow paper bags they were carrying.

3 The officers transmitted a general broadcast over the police radio. As other officers arrived on the scene, a chase began through and around the streets, houses, and alleys of the neighborhood. When Negro residents of the area adjacent to the Central Park Village Housing Project became aware of the chase, they began to participate. Some attemped to help the officers in locating the suspects.

4 R. C. Oates, one of 17 Negroes on the 511-man Tampa police force, spotted 19-year-old Martin Chambers, bare to the waist, wriggling away beneath one of the houses. Oates called for Chambers to surrender. Ignoring him, Chambers emerged running from beneath the house. A white officer, J. L. Calvert, took up the pursuit.

5 Pursuing Calvert, in turn, were three young Negroes, all spectators. Behind one of the houses a high cyclone fence created a two-foot wide alley twenty-five feet in length.

6 As Chambers darted along the fence, Officer Calvert rounded the corner of the house. Calvert yelled to him to halt. Chambers ignored him. Calvert pointed his .38 revolver and fired. The slug entered the back of Chambers and passed completely through his body. Raising his hands over his head, he clutched at the cyclone fence.

7 When the three youths running behind Officer Calvert came upon the scene, they assumed Chambers had been shot standing in the position in which they saw him. Rumor quickly spread through the neighborhood that a white police officer had shot a Negro youth who had had his hands over his head and was trying to surrender.

8 The ambulance that had been summoned became lost on the way. The gathering crowd viewing the bloody, critically injured youth grew increasingly belligerent.

9 Finally, Officer Oates loaded Chambers into his car and drove him to the hospital. The youth died shortly thereafter.

10 As officers were leaving the scene, a thunderstorm broke. Beneath the pelting rain, the spectators scattered. When an officer went back to check the area he found no one on the streets.

11 A few minutes after 7:00 P.M., the Selective Enforcement Unit, tired and sun-parched, reported in from the races. A half hour later a report was received that 500 persons were gathering. A police car was sent into the area to check the report. The officers could find no one. The men of the Selective Enforcement Unit were told to go home.

12 The men in the scout car had not, however, penetrated into the Central Park Village Housing complex where, as the rain ended, hundreds of persons poured from the apartments. At least half were teenagers and young adults. As they began to mill about and discuss the shooting, old grievances, both real and imagined, were resurrected: discriminatory practices of local stores, advantages taken by white men of Negro girls, the kicking in the face of a Negro boy by a white man as the Negro lay handcuffed on the ground, blackballing of two Negro high schools by the athletic conference.

13   Although officials prided themselves on supposedly good race relations and relative acceptance by whites of integration of schools and facilities, Negroes, composing almost 20 percent of the population, had had no one of their own race to represent them in positions of policy or power, nor to appeal to for redress of grievances.

14   There was no Negro on the city council; none on the school board: none in the fire department; none of high rank on the police force. Six of every 10 houses inhabited by Negroes were unsound. Many were shacks with broken window panes, gas leaks, and rat holes in the walls. Rents averaged $50 to $60 a month. Such recreational facilities as did exist lacked equipment and supervisors. Young toughs intimidated the children who tried to use them.

15   The majority of Negro children never reached the eighth grade. In the high schools, only 3 to 4 percent of Negro seniors attained the minimum passing score on the State's college entrance examination, one-tenth the percentage of white students.

16   A difference of at least three-and-a-half years in educational attainment separated the average Negro and white. Fifty-five percent of the Negro men in Tampa were working in unskilled jobs. More than half of the families had incomes of less than $3,000 a year. The result was that 40 percent of the Negro children lived in broken homes, and the city's crime rate ranked in the top 25 percent in the nation.

17   About a month before, police-community relations had been severely strained by the actions of a pair of white officers who were subsequently transferred to another beat.

18   When Officer Oates returned to the area he attempted to convince the crowd to disperse by announcing that a complete investigation would be made into the shooting. He seemd to be making headway when a young woman came running down the street screaming that the police had killed her brother. Her hysteria galvanized the crowd. Rock throwing began. Police cars driving into the area were stoned. The police, relying on a previous experience when, after withdrawal of their units, the crowd had dispersed, decided to send no more patrol cars into the vicinity.

19   This time the maneuver did not work. From nearby bars and tawdry night spots patrons joined the throng. A window was smashed. Haphazard looting began. As fluid bands of rioters moved down the Central Avenue

business district, stores whose proprietors were particularly disliked were singled out. A grocery store, a liquor store, a restaurant were hit. The first fire was set.

20   Because of the dismissal of the Selective Enforcement Unit and the lack of accurate intelligence information, the police department was slow to react. Although Sheriff Malcolm Beard of Hillsborough County was in contact with the Department throughout the evening, it was not until after 11:00 P.M. that a request for deputies was made to him.

21   At 11:30 P.M. a recall order, issued earlier by the police department, began to bring officers back into the area. By this time, the streets in the vicinity of the housing project were lighted by the flames of burning buildings.

22   Falling power lines whipped sparks about the skirmish line of officers as they moved down the street. The popping noise of what sounded to the officers like gunshots came from the direction of the housing project.

23   The officers did not return the fire. Police announced from a sound car that anyone caught armed would be shot. The firing ceased. Then, and throughout the succeeding two days, law enforcement officers refrained from the use of firearms. No officer or civilian suffered a gunshot wound during the riot.

24   Driving along the expressway, a young white couple, Mr. and Mrs. C. D., were startled by the fires. Deciding to investigate, they took the off-ramp into the midst of the riot. The car was swarmed over. Its windows were shattered. C. D. was dragged into the street.

25   As he emerged from a bar in which he had spent the evening, 19-year old J. C., a Negro fruit-picker from Arkansas, was as surprised by the riot as Mr. and Mrs. C. D. Rushing toward the station wagon in which the young woman was trapped, he interposed himself between her and the mob. Although rocks and beer cans smashed the windows, she was able to drive off. J. C. pushed through to where the white man lay. With the hoots and jeers of rioting youths ringing in his ears, J. C. helped him, also, to escape.

26   By 1:00 A.M., police officers and sheriff's deputies had surrounded an area several blocks square. Firemen began to extinguish the flames which, by this time, had spread to several other establishments from the three stores in which they had, originally, been set. No resistance was met. Control was soon re-established.

27   Governor Claude Kirk flew to Tampa. Since the chief of police was absent, and since the Governor regarded the sheriff as his "direct arm," Sheriff Beard was placed in charge of the combined forces of the police and sheriff's departments.

28   For the next 12 hours the situation remained quiet but tense. By afternoon of Monday, June 12, the sheriff's and police forces both had been
fully committed. The men were tired. There were none in reserve.

29   As a precaution, the Sheriff requested that a National Guard con-
tingent be made available.

30   Late in the afternoon Governor Kirk met with the residents at a school
in the Central Park Village area. It was a tense meeting. Most speakers,
whether white or Negro, were booed and hissed. The meeting broke up
without concrete results. Nevertheless, the Governor believed it had enabled
the residents to let off steam.

31   That evening, as National Guard troops began to supplant local forces
in maintaining a perimeter and establishing roving patrols, anti-poverty
workers went from door to door, urging citizens to stay off the streets.

32   A reported attempt by Black Muslims to incite further violence failed.
Although there were scattered reports of trouble from several areas of the
city, and a few fires were set—largely in vacant buildings—there were no
major incidents. Several youths with a cache of Molotov cocktails were
arrested. They were white.

33   All the next day false reports poured into Police Headquarters. Everyday scenes took on menacing tones. Twenty Negro men, bared to the waist
and carrying clubs were reported to be gathering. They turned out to be
construction workers.

34   Mayor Nuccio met with residents. At their suggestion that the man
most likely to carry weight with the youngsters was Coach Jim Williams,
he placed a call to Tallahassee, where Williams was attending a coaching
clinic.

35   An impressive-looking man with graying hair, Williams arrived in Tampa almost 48 hours after the shooting of Martin Chambers. Together with
another coach he went to an eatery called The Greek Stand, behind which
he found a number of youngsters fashioning an arsenal of bottles, bricks,
and Molotov cocktails. As in the crowds that were once more beginning
to gather, the principal complaint was the presence of the National Guard,
which, the residents asserted, gave them a feeling of being hemmed in.
Williams decided to attempt to negotiate the removal of the National Guard
if the people would agree to keep the peace and to disperse.

36   When Sheriff Beard arrived at a meeting called for the College Hill
Elementary School, Robert Gilder of the NAACP was speaking to leaders
of the Negro youth. Some were college students who had been unable to
get summer jobs. One was a Vietnam veteran who had been turned down
for a position as a swimming pool lifeguard. The youths believed that discrimination had played a part in their failure to find jobs.

37   The suggestion was made to Sheriff Beard that the National Guard be pulled out of the Negro areas, and that these young men, as well as others, be given the opportunity to keep order. The idea, which was encouraged by James Hammond, Director of the Commission of Community Relations, made sense to the Sheriff. He decided to take a chance on the Youth Patrol.

38   In another part of the city, West Tampa, two Negro community leaders, Dr. James O. Brookins and attorney Delano S. Stewart, were advised by acquaintances that, unless the intensive patrolling of Negro neighborhoods ceased, people planned to set fires in industrial districts that evening. Like Coach Williams, Dr. Brookins and Stewart contacted neighborhood youths, and invited Sheriff Beard to a meeting. The concept of the Youth Patrol was expanded. Participants were identified first by phosphorescent arm bands, and later by white hats.

39   During the next 24 hours 126 youths, some of whom had participated in the riot, were recruited into the patrol. Many were high school dropouts.

40   On Wednesday, the inquiry into the death of Martin Chambers was concluded. With the verdict that Officer Calvert had fired the shot justifiably and in the line of duty, apprehension rose that trouble would erupt again. The leaders of the Youth Patrol were called in. The Sheriff explained the law to them, and pointed out that the verdict was in conformance with the law. Despite the fact that the verdict was not to their liking, the White Hats continued to keep order.

UNDERSTANDING THE SELECTION

1. After the extensive and horrifying riots in American cities during July 1968, President Johnson appointed the National Advisory Commission on Civil Disorders and charged the members with providing answers to three questions: What happened? Why did it happen? What can be done to prevent it from happening again? This selection recounts what happened in Tampa, Florida, during one of the earliest, least destructive of the summer's riots.

2. Is this material arranged primarily in time or in space?

3. How much use does the selection make of connotation, metaphor, allusion, symbol, and irony? How specific is the writing? What is the tone of the writing? Why do you think this particular tone was selected?

4. What event touched off the riot? Who was to blame for the riot? Or was nobody to blame?

5. What were the underlying causes of the riot?

6. Did the city and state officials act responsibly during the riot? Did the police act responsibly? Did the black community act responsibly?

7. How should cities protect themselves against future riots?

8. Are riots ever justified?

9. In their summary of the report, the commission members claim that "White racism is essentially responsible for the explosive mixture which has been accumulating in our cities since the end of World War II." Do you agree with their opinion?

10. In their preface, the members of the commission ask two questions: "How can we as a people end the resort to violence while we build a better society?" And, "How can the nation realize the promise of a single society— one nation indivisible—which yet remains unfulfilled?" How would you answer those questions?

11. This selection deals with the problems of a racial minority. What other kinds of minorities encounter discrimination in the United States? Consider age, sex, religion, politics, education, income, and so forth.

12. Discuss the comment made in this selection.

57   *The Death of The Ball Turret Gunner*

Randall Jarell

From my mother's sleep I fell into the State
And I hunched in its belly till my wet fur froze.
Six miles from earth, loosed from its dream of life,
I woke to black flak and the nightmare fighters.
When I died they washed me out of the turret with a hose.

UNDERSTANDING THE SELECTION

1. Who and where is the speaker? How old is he? What do you think he did before he became a gunner?

2. Rephrase the first three lines of the poem. Try to make clear what the author means by his metaphors: *sleep, fell, belly, fur, woke.*

3. Why is *State* capitalized? What are the speaker's attitudes toward the State?

4. What is the tone of the poem?

5. What comment does the poem make?

58   *War*

Joseph Langland

When my young brother was killed
By a mute and dusty shell in the thorny brush
Crowning the boulders of the Villa Verde Trail
On the island of Luzon,

I laid my whole dry body down,   5
Dropping my face like a stone in a green park
On the east banks of the Rhine;

On an airstrip skirting the Seine
His sergeant brother sat like a stick in his barracks
While cracks of fading sunlight   10
Caged the dusty air;

In the rocky rolling hills west of the Mississippi
His father and mother sat in a simple Norwegian parlor
With a photograph smiling between them on the table
And their hands fallen into their laps   15
Like sticks and dust;

And still other brothers and sisters,
Linking their arms together,
Walked down the dusty road where once he ran
And into the deep green valley   20
To sit on the stony banks of the stream he loved
And let the murmuring waters
Wash over their blood-hot feet with a springing crown of tears.

UNDERSTANDING THE SELECTION

1. Do stanzas 2 through 5 occur simultaneously, or do they occur in sequence?
2. What do sticks, stones, and dust symbolize?
3. What is "a springing crown of tears" (line 23)? Exactly what does it describe?
4. Is "War" an appropriate title? Does the poet give an accurate picture of war?
5. What comment does the poet make?

59 from Glances at History

Samuel Clemens

1   In a speech which he made more than five hundred years ago, and which has come down to us intact, he said:

2   We, free citizens of the Great Republic, feel an honest pride in her greatness, her strength, her just and gentle government, her wide liber-

ties, her honored name, her stainless history, her unsmirched flag, her hands clean from oppression of the weak and from malicious conquest, her hospitable door that stands open to the hunted and the persecuted of all nations; we are proud of the judicious respect in which she is held by the monarchies which hem her in on every side, and proudest of all of that lofty patriotism which we inherited from our fathers, which we have kept pure, and which won our liberties in the beginning and has preserved them unto this day. While that patriotism endures the Republic is safe, her greatness is secure, and against them the powers of the earth cannot prevail.

3   I pray you to pause and consider. Against our traditions we are now entering upon an unjust and trivial war, a war against a helpless people, and for a base object—robbery. At first our citizens spoke out against this thing, by an impulse natural to their training. Today they have turned, and their voice is the other way. What caused the change? Merely a politician's trick—a highsounding phrase, a blood-stirring phrase which turned their uncritical heads: *Our Country, right or wrong!* An empty phrase, a silly phrase. It was shouted by every newspaper, it was thundered from the pulpit, the Superintendent of Public Instruction placarded it in every schoolhouse in the land, the War Department inscribed it upon the flag. And every man who failed to shout it or who was silent, was proclaimed a traitor—none but those others were patriots. To be a patriot, one had to say, and keep on saying, "Our Country, right or wrong," and urge on the little war. Have you not perceived that that phrase is an insult to the nation?

4   For in a republic, who *is* "the Country"? Is it the Government which is for the moment in the saddle? Why, the Government is merely a *servant*—merely a temporary servant; it cannot be its prerogative to determine what is right and what is wrong, and decide who is a patriot and who isn't. Its function is to obey orders, not originate them. Who, then, is "the Country"? Is it the newspaper? is it the pulpit? is it the school superintendent? Why, these are mere parts of the country, not the whole of it; they have not command, they have only their little share in the command. They are but one in the thousand; it is in the thousand that command is lodged; *they* must determine what is right and what is wrong; they must decide who is a patriot and who isn't.

5   Who are the thousand—that is to say, who are "the Country"? In a monarchy, the king and his family are the country; in a republic it is the common voice of the people. Each of you, for himself, by himself and on his own responsibility, must speak. And it is a solemn and weighty responsibility, and not lightly to be flung aside at the bullying of pulpit, press, government, or the empty catch-phrases of politicians. Each must for himself alone decide what is right and what is wrong, and which course is patriotic and which isn't. You cannot shirk this and be a man. To decide it against your convictions is to be an unqualified and inexcusable traitor, both to yourself and to your country, let man label you as they may. If you alone of all the nation shall decide one way, and that way be the right way according to your convictions of the right, you have done your duty by yourself and by your country—hold up your head! You have nothing to be ashamed of.

6   Only when a republic's *life* is in danger should a man uphold his government when it is in the wrong. There is no other time.

7   This Republic's life is not in peril. The nation has sold its honor for a phrase. It has swung itself loose from its safe anchorage and is drifting, its helm is in pirate hands. The stupid phrase needed help, and it got another one: "Even if the war be wrong we are in it and must fight it out: *we cannot retire from it without dishonor.*" Why, not even a burglar could have said it better. We cannot withdraw from this sordid raid because to grant peace to those little people upon their terms—independence—would dishonor us. You have flung away Adam's phrase—you should take it up and examine it again. He said, *"An inglorious peace is better than a dishonorable war."*

8   You have planted a seed, and it will grow.

UNDERSTANDING THE SELECTION

1. This piece was found in this fragmentary form among the papers of Samuel Clemens after his death in 1910. Clemens wrote it as if it were a speech, but he did not identify the speaker, who is a creation of his imagination. What can you deduce about the speaker? Consider his age, education, social status. What can you deduce about his audience?

2. How much use does the writer make of connotation, metaphor, symbol, stereotype, irony?

3. What is the tone of the selection?

4. What comment does the writer make?

5. Can a nation remain strong and cohesive if each man decides for himself what is right and what is wrong and which course is patriotic and which is not (paragraph 4)? Or is it wiser to permit such decisions to be made by the nation as a whole? What are the dangers if each individual decides for himself? What are they if "the nation" decides for everyone?

6. Clemens quotes a famous phrase in this selection, "Our country, right or wrong." Check in a book of quotations for the history of this phrase and its variations. Has everyone using it meant the same thing? Is it a good motto for a nation?

7. In our introduction to Part 3, we suggested that one way to judge a piece of writing was to ask, "Will it mean as much a hundred years from now as it does today?" This selection was written sometime before 1910. What

recent historical events suggest that this selection is of enduring value?

8. The authors of the selections in this group wrote as a result of an expansionist war in the late nineteenth century (Clemens), World War II (Dehn, Jarrell, and Langland), and the undeclared urban wars of the 1960s. Have they anything in common in their attitudes toward war? Which selection makes war most vivid to you? Or are the selections using war only as a background while they comment on something else? Can you think of writings (or films) about war which show it quite differently from the way these selections view it?

9. Which of these selections do you think is the best piece of writing? Why? Give specific reasons for your answer, not just a vague "I like it." You may want to refer to the list of questions on page 188.

60   *No Room . . .*
Werner Bischof

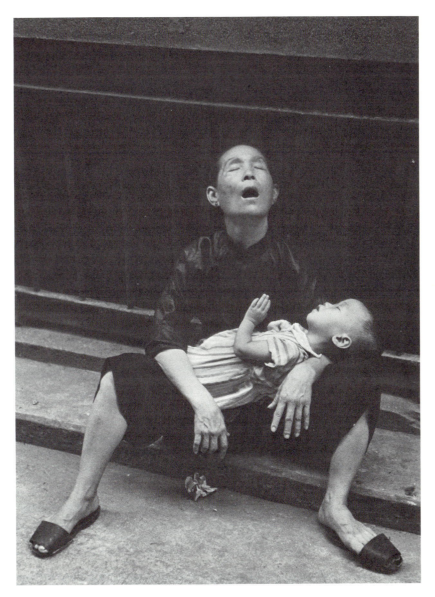

Photograph by Werner Bischof. © Magnum Photos, Inc.

UNDERSTANDING THE SELECTION

1. This mother and child, refugees from Shanghai, were photographed in Hong Kong in 1952.

2. Originally the picture had no title. Why do you think we titled it "No Room . . ."? What allusion are we making? Do you think the title is appropriate or not? Would you prefer some other title, and if you would, what title would you choose?

3. What do you think the mother will do next? How do you think she will manage to exist? Does this photograph say something about your world as well as the refugee mother's world? See if you can find out how many people currently are refugees throughout the world. Or is it impossible to ferret out such information? How important do you think such statistics are? How important do you think this photograph is?

4. Selections 35, 36, and 37 dealt with mothers. Does this mother share certain qualities with the others or does she seem wholly different? Explain.

5. Specifically what comment is the photographer making? Does he make it effectively? Will the photograph be as effective in a hundred years as it is now?

Group 2:
honor

61 Falstaff on Honor
William Shakespeare

1   *Fal.* I would 'twere bedtime, Hal, and all well.
2   *Prince.* Why, thou owest God a death. [*Exit.*]

3   *Fal.* 'Tis not due yet. I would be loath to pay him before his day. What need I be so forward with him that calls not on me? Well, 'tis no matter; honour pricks me on. Yea, but how if honour prick me off when I come on? How then? Can honour set to a leg? No. Or an arm? No. Or take away the grief of a wound? No. Honour hath no skill in surgery then? No. What is honour? A word. What is that word honour? Air. A trim reckoning! Who hath it? He that died a Wednesday. Doth he feel it? No. Doth he hear it? No. 'Tis insensible then? Yea, to the dead. But will it not live with the living? No. Why? Detraction will not suffer it. Therefore I'll none of it. Honour is a mere scutcheon—and so ends my catechism. *Exit.*

UNDERSTANDING THE SELECTION

1. This passage comes from *King Henry the Fourth, Part I,* one of Shakespeare's historical plays. It occurs at the end of act 5, scene 1. The two characters are Prince Hal, who has been shown as a playboy heir to the throne, an intimate of commoners and rogues; and Sir John Falstaff, his closest associate, a grossly fat man, given to lying, gluttony, and sloth. A rebellion against King Henry IV, Hal's father, has started, and the two are about to go into battle, a battle in which Hal kills his chief rival and reveals a princely nature, while Falstaff plays dead to escape being killed.
2. What are the meanings of these phrases in paragraph 3: "forward"? "a trim reckoning"? "Detraction will not suffer it"? "a mere scutcheon"?
3. What use does Shakespeare make of connotation, metaphor, symbol, and irony? What is the tone of the speech?
4. Falstaff is one of the most famous characters in dramatic literature, and this speech is perhaps his best known. What can you infer about Falstaff's character from it?
5. What does Falstaff mean by honor (note the British spelling *honour* in the text)? Be very precise and specific in your answer. Is his definition the

same as yours? If not, give your own definition, making it as specific as possible.

6. Clearly Falstaff does not believe honor is worth dying for. Do you believe it is? Is anything worth dying for? If you believe so, what would you die for?

7. Falstaff also believes that honor does not live on after death, as he says in "Detraction will not suffer it." What reason does he give for this loss of reputation? Do you believe he is correct in his judgment of human nature? Cite examples to support your own position.

62 *Unexpected Rewards of Virtue*
Fred J. Cook

1   On March 10, 1961, Douglas William Johnson, a fifty-year-old Negro janitor in Los Angeles, a man who had felt the pinch of poverty, drove to an apartment house under construction to see if he could get the job of cleaning up the debris. With him was his wife, Helen, thirty-eight. The superintendent whom he had to see about the debris-cleaning chore wasn't at the site, and so Johnson climbed back into his station wagon and started home. He had driven only a short distance when he happened to see, . . . in the street in front of his car, a bulky canvas bag. Thinking it might contain something useful, Johnson stopped, picked it up and tossed it into the back of the station wagon.

2   As he got behind the wheel and drove off, his wife, possessed by curiosity, turned around and began to examine the bag. It was sealed, but it bore a tag. The tag said that the bag contained $240,000 in $10 and $20 bills.

3   "Do you know what you've picked up?" Mrs. Johnson asked her husband. "There's $240,000 in that bag!"

4   "No!" he said—and started to shake all over.

5   Explaining his reaction later, Johnson told reporters: "I was knocked off my feet. I never dreamed I'd have my hands on anything like that."

6   Here certainly was king-sized temptation. Bills of relatively small denominations are not easily traced, and Johnson—the part-time maintenance man, father of three sons—had $240,000 worth of those bills at his finger tips. What to do?

7   "I thought if I kept that money I'd never be able to look my three kids in the face again," Johnson explained, using the simplistic imagery of a bygone age when man had stature and was supposed to be responsible for his acts.

8   So Johnson acted according to the dictates of pure and simple honesty. As soon as he reached home, he telephoned a friend, a former Chicago policeman, to find out whom he should notify about the money; the friend advised him to call the FBI. He did. In minutes, four FBI agents were at his door, recovering the money bag that had fallen from the rear of a passing Brinks truck. The truck had traveled for some distance before the $240,000 loss was discovered, and scores of police and FBI agents had begun to search along the truck's route when Johnson telephoned that he had the missing money.

9   Brinks paid Johnson a $10,000 reward for his honesty, but this wasn't the end of the story. A little more than a month later, on April 21, 1961, the press of the nation recorded the sad and revealing sequel. Johnson's life had been made utterly miserable; the strictly honest deed that should have made him the most admired of men had made him instead the most despised, ridiculed and harassed.

10   Crackpots wrote obscene letters to him, neighbors ridiculed him, fellow workers needled him, schoolmates taunted his sons. The universal theme was that Johnson had proven himself to be the world's greatest boob by returning that $240,000 once he had it in his hands. The taunts became too much for his oldest son, Richard, sixteen, who finally ran away from home, returning after a few days, hungry and disillusioned. "The kids kept saying things to me," he explained. "All the time, they were saying my father was dumb, and a fool and stupid. . . . I just couldn't stand it."

11   Johnson himself said it was "nice" that Brinks had give him a $10,000 reward, but he added:

12   "I can't leave the house to get work without someone throws it all up to me and calls me a fool. Can't be on the job without someone says, 'Why you need work? You had $240,000.' And now it's hurting my boys.

13   "I wish I'd never seen any of it. I wish we'd let that money sit in the street and rot. I wish we'd thrown it down a sewer or burned it.

14   "That money? It's not worth anything. It has made me a poor man."

15   This tragedy of the honest man, pilloried on the unfaith of a dishonest age, inspired novelist Nelson Algren to write Douglas Johnson a letter bitterly satirizing the reverse morality by which we live. This is the letter:

> 16   It is one thing to get caught doing something crooked, but the man who snitched on himself for doing something innocent, as you did in returning $240,000 in small bills to the Brinks Express Co., makes me wonder not only whether you are worthy of the name of an American, but even whether you can call yourself an honest janitor.
> 17   Where were *you* when millions of Americans felt their blood pound with pride in Charles Van Doren, replying to reporters who asked him if he intended to give the money back, "No"—IN THUNDER!
> 18   Where were *you* when James C. Hagerty advised us on television that the moral of the U-2 incident was "Don't get caught"?
> 19   I regret, for your sake as well as my own, that in this crisis you did not think along the same lines as Mr. Ike Williams, former lightweight cham-

pion of the world, thinks now. When congratulated recently by Mr. Estes Kefauver on having turned down a hundred-thousand-dollar bribe in return for throwing a fight and offered the hope, by Senator Kefauver, that in time he would be glad he resisted the temptation, Mr. Williams replied that he would regret turning it down the rest of his life.

20   I believe you have not only deprived yourself of a contented existence by returning money that belonged to you as much as to anybody else in the free world, but have struck at the very foundation of our society.

21   For shame, Mr. Johnson, for shame.

22   For shame, indeed. In a monied society, Douglas Johnson had committed the cardinal sin; acting on honest impulse, he had returned a fortune that he might have kept. In . . . his harrowing experience . . . one finds a barometer that accurately gauges the shabbiness of our ethical standards.

UNDERSTANDING THE SELECTION

1. What kind of organization, space or time, does the author use in this selection?

2. Are the speaker and the writer the same person?

3. How much education has Johnson? How do you know?

4. Why was Johnson so viciously attacked for returning the money? Do you think he should have kept it?

5. The most difficult part of this essay to read is Nelson Algren's letter, which refers to several persons and incidents that you may not recognize. Algren himself is a contemporary novelist and essayist.

Charles Van Doren (paragraph 17) was a college instructor in 1957 when he won about thirty times his yearly salary as a player in a television quiz game. Later he and other contestants in various quiz shows were accused of having been given the answers beforehand by producers and their aides. The ensuing investigation into television ethics was begun by a New York grand jury and continued by a congressional subcommittee. Many persons felt that taking money under the circumstances was perfectly moral since no one was hurt. Others contended that an industry and an audience which regarded honesty as unimportant proved that the nation had already been severely damaged.

Shortly after the congressional inquiries into television, the U-2 incident occurred. On May 1, 1960, an American U-2 reconnaissance plane was shot down over the U.S.S.R. The administration at first denied and then admitted that the pilot (who was imprisoned by Soviet authorities and later exchanged for a Soviet spy) had been taking photographs of Soviet territory and that such flights had been a practice for about four years. The nation was disturbed because a branch of the government was spying in time of peace and because that fact was at first denied. James C. Hagerty, who said, "Don't get caught," was press secretary to President Dwight D. Eisenhower at the time of the incident.

The late Estes Kefauver, Senator from Tennessee, conducted several hearings into crime which touched on gambling and bribery.

6. What is the tone of the fifth paragraph of Algren's letter? What is the comment of the paragraph?

7. If you were overcharged in a supermarket, what would you do? If you were given too much change, what would you do? What would you tell your child to do?

8. This selection makes many references to honesty. Do you believe that honesty is a virtue? Are you honest? Are your friends? Your parents? You might consider the following questions:

Have you ever cheated on an exam?
Have you ever made a long-distance call on a friend's phone and not paid for it?
Have you ever taken an ashtray or a spoon or a towel from a restaurant or a motel?
Have you ever lied to your parents? To your date? To your best friend?

9. What is the relationship between honesty and honor? Or is there no relationship?

10. In his final phrase, Cook refers to "the shabbiness of our ethical standards." Do you agree that our standards are shabby? Or is Cook applying old-fashioned standards to a society that has adopted a new code of ethics?

63   A Funeral Oration

David Wright

Composed at thirty, my funeral oration: Here lies
David John Murray Wright, 6'2", myopic blue eyes;
Hair grey (very distinguished looking, so I am told);
Shabbily dressed as a rule: susceptible to cold;
Acquainted with what are known as the normal vices;   5
Perpetually short of cash; useless in a crisis;
Preferring cats, hated dogs; drank (when he could) too much;
Was deaf as a tombstone; and extremely hard to touch.

> Academic achievements: B.A., Oxon (2nd class);
> Poetic: the publication of one volume of verse,   10
> Which in his thirtieth year attained him no fame at all
> Except among intractable poets, and a small
> Lunatic fringe congregating in Soho pubs.
> He could roll himself cigarettes from discarded stubs,
> Assume the first position of Yoga; sail, row, swim;   15
> And though deaf, in church appear to be joining a hymn.
> Often arrested for being without a permit,
> Starved on his talents as much as he dined on his wit,
> Born in a dominion to which he hoped not to go back
> Since predisposed to imagine white possibly black: 20
> His life, like his times, was appalling; his conduct odd;
> He hoped to write one good line; died believing in God.

UNDERSTANDING THE SELECTION

1. David Wright, the poet, was born in South Africa but now lives in London. *Oxon* (line 9) is the abbreviation for Oxford University in England. *Soho* (line 13) is the bohemian section of London where many artists and entertainers live and work. ". . . born in a dominion" (line 19) refers to Wright's South African homeland.

2. How is this poem organized, in time or in space?

3. How much use does Wright make of connotation, metaphor, symbol? How much use of them do you expect to find in a poem? What is the tone of this poem? Do you consider it "poetic"?

4. Do you think that the poet gives an honest appraisal of himself? Is a clear insight into one's own nature a useful quality, or are people happier if they do not see themselves clearly? *Can* people see themselves as they really are, or is the human situation basically ironic?

5. Why do you suppose we have included this selection in a group of readings on honor?

6. Try writing a funeral oration for yourself.

64 *The Artist*

Guy de Maupassant

1   "Bah! Monsieur," the old mountebank said to me; "it is a matter of exercise and habit, that is all! Of course one requires to be a little gifted that way and not to be butter-fingered, but what is chiefly necessary is patience and daily practice for long, long years."

2   His modesty surprised me all the more, because of all performers who are generally infatuated with their own skill he was the most wonderfully clever one I had met. Certainly I had frequently seen him, for everybody had seen him in some circus or other, or even in traveling shows, performing the trick that consists of putting a man or woman with extended arms against a wooden target and in throwing knives between their fingers and round their heads from a distance. There is nothing very extraordinary in it, after all, when one knows *the tricks of the trade* and that the knives are not the least sharp and stick into the wood at some distance from the flesh. It is the rapidity of the throws, the glitter of the blades and the curve which the handles make toward their living object which give an air of danger to an exhibition that has become commonplace and only requires very middling skill.

3   But here there was no trick and no deception and no dust thrown into the eyes. It was done in good earnest and in all sincerity. The knives were as sharp as razors, and the old mountebank planted them close to the flesh, exactly in the angle between the fingers. He surrounded the head with a perfect halo of knives and the neck with a collar from which nobody could have extricated himself without cutting his carotid artery; while, to increase the difficulty, the old fellow went through the performance without seeing, his whole face being covered with a close mask of thick oilcloth.

4   Naturally, like other great artists, he was not understood by the crowd, who confounded him with vulgar tricksters, and his mask only appeared to them a trick the more, and a very common trick into the bargain.

5   "He must think us very stupid," they said. "How could he possibly aim without having his eyes open?"

6   And they thought there must be imperceptible holes in the oilcloth, a sort of latticework concealed in the material. It was useless for him to allow the public to examine the mask for themselves before the exhibition began. It was all very well that they could not discover any trick, but they were only all the more convinced that they were being tricked. Did not the people know that they ought to be tricked?

7   I had recognized a great artist in the old mountebank, and I was quite sure that he was altogether incapable of any trickery. I had told him so while expressing my admiration to him, and he had been touched by my open admiration and above all by the justice I had done him. Thus we became good friends, and he explained to me, very modestly, the real trick which the crowd does not understand, the eternal trick contained in these simple words: "To be gifted by nature and to practice every day for long, long years."

8   He had been especially struck by the certainty which I expressed that any trickery must become impossible to him. "Yes," he said to me, "quite impossible! Impossible to a degree which you cannot imagine. If I were to tell you! But where would be the use?"

9   His face clouded over, and his eyes filled with tears. I did not venture to force myself into his confidence. My looks, however, were not so discreet as my silence and begged him to speak, so he responded to their mute appeal.

10   "After all," he said, "why should I not tell you about it? You will understand me." And he added, with a look of sudden ferocity: "She understood it, at any rate!"

11   "Who?" I asked.

12   "My strumpet of a wife," he replied. "Ah! monsieur, what an abominable creature she was—if you only knew! Yes, she understood it too well, too well, and that is why I hate her so; even more on that account than for having deceived me. For that is a natural fault, is it not, and may be pardoned? But the other thing was a crime, a horrible crime."

13   The woman who stood against the wooden target every night with her arms stretched out and her fingers extended, and whom the old mountebank fitted with gloves and with a halo formed of his knives, which were as sharp as razors and which he planted close to her, was his wife. She might have been a woman of forty and must have been fairly pretty, but with a perverse prettiness; she had an impudent mouth, a mouth that was at the same time sensual and bad, with the lower lip too thick for the thin, dry upper lip.

14   I had several times noticed that every time he planted a knife in the board she uttered a laugh, so low as scarcely to be heard, but which was very significant when one heard it, for it was a hard and very mocking laugh. I had always attributed that sort of reply to an artifice which the occasion required. It was intended, I thought, to accentuate the danger she incurred and the contempt that she felt for it, thanks to the sureness of the thrower's hands, and so I was very much surprised when the mountebank said to me:

15   "Have you observed her laugh, I say? Her evil laugh which makes fun of me and her cowardly laugh which defies me? Yes, cowardly, because she knows that nothing can happen to her, nothing, in spite of all she deserves, in spite of all that I ought to do to her, in spite of all that I *want* to do to her."

16   "What do you want to do?"

17   "Confound it! Cannot you guess? I want to kill her."

18   "To kill her, because she has—"

19   "Because she has deceived me? No, no, not that, I tell you again. I have forgiven her for that a long time ago, and I am too much accustomed to it! But the worst of it is that the first time I forgave her, when I told her

that all the same I might someday have my revenge by cutting her throat, if I chose, without seeming to do it on purpose, as it if were an accident, mere awkwardness—"

20   "Oh! So you said that to her?"

21   "Of course I did, and I meant it. I thought I might be able to do it, for you see I had the perfect right to do so. It was so simple, so easy, so tempting! Just think! A mistake of less than half an inch, and her skin would be cut at the neck where the jugular vein is, and the jugular would be severed. My knives cut very well! And when once the jugular is cut—good-by. The blood would spurt out, and one, two, three red jets, and all would be over; she would be dead, and I should have had my revenge!"

22   "That is true, certainly, horribly true!"

23   "And without any risk to me, eh? An accident, that is all; bad luck, one of those mistakes which happen every day in our business. What could they accuse me of? Whoever would think of accusing me even? Homicide through imprudence, that would be all! They would even pity me rather than accuse me. 'My wife! My poor wife!' I should say, sobbing. 'My wife, who is so necessary to me, who is half the breadwinner, who takes part in my performance!' You must acknowledge that I should be pitied!"

24   "Certainly, there is not the least doubt about that."

25   "And you must allow that such a revenge would be a very nice revenge, the best possible revenge which I could have with assured impunity."

26   "Evidently that is so."

27   "Very well! But when I told her so, as I have told you, and more forcibly still, threatening her, as I was mad with rage and ready to do the deed that I had dreamed of on the spot, what do you think she said?"

28   "That you were a good fellow and would certainly not have the atrocious courage to—"

29   "Tut! tut! tut! I am not such a good fellow as you think. I am not frightened of blood, and that I have proved already, though it would be useless to tell you how and where. But I had no necessity to prove it to her, for she knows that I am capable of a good many things, even of crime; especially of one crime."

30   "And she was not frightened?"

31   "No. She merely replied that I could not do what I said; you understand. That I could not do it!"

32   "Why not?"

33   "Ah! monsieur, so you do not understand? Why do you not? Have I not explained to you by what constant, long, daily practice I have learned to plant my knives without seeing what I am doing?"

34   "Yes; well, what then?"

35   "Well! Cannot you understand what she has understood with such terrible results, that now my hand would no longer obey me if I wished to make a mistake as I threw?"

36   "Is it possible?"

37   "Nothing is truer, I am sorry to say. For I really have wished to have the revenge which I have dreamed of and which I thought so easy. Exasperated by that bad woman's insolence and confidence in her own safety, I have several times made up my mind to kill her and have exerted all my energy and all my skill to make my knives fly aside when I threw them to make a border round her neck. I have tried with all my might to make them deviate half an inch, just enough to cut her throat. I wanted to, and I have never succeeded, never. And always the slut's horrible laugh makes fun of me, always, always."

38   And with a deluge of tears, with something like a roar of unsatiated and muzzled rage, he ground his teeth as he wound up: "She knows me, the jade; she is in the secret of my work, of my patience, of my trick, routine, whatever you may call it! She lives in my innermost being and sees into it more closely than you or than I do myself. She knows what a faultless machine I have become, the machine of which she makes fun, the machine which is too well wound up, the machine which cannot get out of order—and she knows that I *cannot* make a mistake."

UNDERSTANDING THE SELECTION

1. In this selection, the knife-thrower is called a *mountebank.* The word *mountebank* comes from Italian and literally means "one who mounts a bench" to attract an audience to trick them or sell them quack remedies. Do you think that label is appropriate for the knife-thrower?

2. Describe the mountebank as fully as you can—his age, appearance, education, and personality.

3. What events do you suppose happened in the past to cause the mountebank's remarks in paragraph 29? How do you think he proved that he was not afraid of blood? What one crime do you think he is especially capable of?

4. Why does the writer say, "Did not people know that they ought to be tricked"? (paragraph 6)

5. Compare the mountebank and Montresor ("The Cask of Amontillado," Selection 47). How does each feel about revenge? Which has the greater cause to seek revenge?

6. Why does the old mountebank not achieve his revenge? What prevents him from doing it since he almost certainly would not be accused of murder?

7. What does the story suggest about the nature of art? Is it correct to call the knife-thrower an artist?

8. Why is this selection included in this group of readings about honor?

65   The One Percenter

Rudy Janu

Photograph by Rudy Janu. From Nancy Palmer Agency.

UNDERSTANDING THE SELECTION

1. Is there connotation in this picture? If so, discuss its connotations.
2. Is there allusion? Symbol? Stereotype?
3. Arrange the following items in the order of their importance, with the most important first, as the One Percenter would arrange them, as Tommy Grimes (Selection 32) would arrange them, as Douglas Johnson (Selection 62) would, and as you would. Compare the lists you make. Which list seems to you most typical of American values?

      a. a college degree
      b. a new Harley-Davidson
      c. color television
      d. belief in God
      e. getting stoned
      f. a motorcycle run to Las Vegas
      g. a new Mannlicher
      h. installment buying
      i. a peace march
      j. marriage
      k. writing a poem or painting a picture
      l. a swinging Saturday night

4. Do you think the One Percenter has a sense of honor? If so, what do you think he considers honorable? Does he care about his reputation? Honesty? His friends? Doing his job well? Or what?

66 *from The Civil Rights Struggle*

Martin Luther King, Jr.

1   I feel compelled to comment briefly on the oft-heard charge that we who urge non-cooperation with evil in the form of civil disobedience are equally lawless.

2   Paradoxically, although the devotees of nonviolent action have embraced Thoreau's and Gandhi's civil disobedience on a scale dwarfing any past experience in American history, they do respect law. They feel a moral responsibility to obey just laws. But they recognize that there are also unjust laws.

3   From a purely moral point of view, an unjust law is one that is out of harmony with the moral law of the universe. More concretely, an unjust law is one in which the minority is compelled to observe a code that is not binding on the majority. An unjust law is one in which people are required to obey a code that they had no part in making because they were denied the right to vote.

4   In disobeying such unjust laws, we do so peacefully, openly and non-violently. Most important, we willingly accept the penalty, whatever it is. But in this way the public comes to reexamine the law in question. In Selma, over 3,000 Negroes from all walks of life went to jail, suffered brutality and discomfort, so that the nation could reexamine the voting registration laws—and find them woefully inadequate. We call it doing witness—you would call it testifying—with our bodies.

5   This distinguishes our position on civil disobedience from the "uncivil disobedience" or lawlessness of the segregationist. In the face of laws they consider unjust—(like Brown vs Board of Education) the racists seek to defy, evade and circumvent the law, and they are unwilling to accept the penalty. In the face of the law, they will shoot a Viola Liuzzo through an automobile window. In the face of the law they will club Rev. Reeb to death and seek to avoid the consequences. They will shoot a Jimmy Jackson. They flee from these crimes and flout the law; they are unwilling to accept the penalty. The end result of their defiance is anarchy and disrespect for the law.

6   We, on the other hand, believe that he who openly disobeys a law, a law that conscience tells him is unjust, and then willingly accepts the penalty, gives evidence thereby that he so respects that law that he belongs in jail until it is changed. Our appeal is to the conscience.

7   It is essential to understand our aim is to persuade. And we are ready to suffer when necessary and even risk our lives to become witnesses to the truth as we see it. . . .

8   As I have said so often, there are certain technical words within every academic discipline which soon become stereotypes and cliches. Every academic discipline has its technical nomenclature. Modern psychology has the word that is probably used more than any other word in psychology. It is the word "maladjusted." Certainly we all want to live the well adjusted life in order to avoid neurotic and schizophrenic personalities. But I must honestly say to you tonight, my friends, that there are some things in our nation and in our world of which I am proud to be maladjusted. I call upon all men of good will to be maladjusted until the good society is realized.

9   I must honestly say to you that I never intend to adjust myself to segregation and discrimination. I never intend to become adjusted to religious bigotry.

10   I never intend to adjust myself to madness of militarism and the self-defeating effects of physical violence. . . .

11   It may be that our world needs to form a new organization, the International Association for the Advancement of Creative Maladjustment. Men and women will be maladjusted, and will in the midst of the injustices of today cry out in words that echo across the countries, "Let Justice roll down like waters and righteousness, like a mighty stream."

12   They will be maladjusted as Abraham Lincoln was, who had the vision to see that this nation could not survive half slave and half free; as maladjusted as Thomas Jefferson, who in an age amazingly adjusted to slavery, could etch across the pages of history words lifted to cosmic proportions, "We hold these truths to be self evident, that all men are created equal, that they are endowed by their Creator with certain inalienable rights, and that among these are life, liberty and the pursuit of happiness."

13   They will be as maladjusted as Jesus of Nazareth, who could say to the men and women of his day, "Love your enemies, bless them that curse you, pray for them that despitefully use you."

14   Through such maladjustments we may be able to emerge from the bleak and desolate midnight of man's inhumanity to man into the bright and glittering daybreak of freedom and justice.

15   May I say in conclusion, that I have faith in America, and I still believe somehow that in spite of the difficulties of the moment we will solve this problem. We are developing a coalition of conscience, a grand alliance, which will one day bring an end to the evils that have clouded our days and transform dark years into a bright future.

16   Before the victory is won some more will have to go to jail; before the victory is won, some will have to get scarred up a bit; before the victory is won, some will be misunderstood and called bad names. Before the victory is won maybe somebody else will face physical death, but if physical death is the price that some must pay to free their children and their white brothers from a permanent death of the spirit, then nothing can be more redemptive.

17   I do not despair of the future. We as Negroes will win our freedom all over our country because the goal of America is freedom. Abused and scorned though we may be, our destiny is America's destiny. Before the Pilgrims landed at Plymouth we were here. Before the pen of Jefferson etched the majestic words of the Declaration of Independence across the pages of history, we were here. More than two centuries our foreparents labored in this country without wages. They made cotton king. They built the homes of their masters in the midst of the greatest suffering and humiliation. Yet out of an enduring vitality, they continued to grow and develop.

18   If the inexpressible cruelties of slavery could not stop us, the opposition we now face will surely fail. We will win our freedom because the sacred heritage of our country and the eternal will of God are embodied in our echoing demands.

19   This is our faith. With this faith we will be able to hew out of the mountain of despair the stone of hope. With this faith we will transform the jangling discords of our country into a beautiful symphony of brotherhood.

20   I close by quoting the words of an old Negro slave preacher who didn't quite have his grammar right, but who uttered words of great symbolic profundity and those words were uttered in the form of prayer:

21   "Lord, we ain't what we ought to be. We ain't what we want to be. We ain't what we are going to be. But thank God we ain't what we was."

UNDERSTANDING THE SELECTION

1. Martin Luther King, Jr., delivered the speech from which this selection is taken to the Bar Association of New York City in April, 1965. A man who had been many times arrested and jailed, he drew an audience so large for this address that thousands of lawyers had to be turned away. Three years later, on April 4, 1968, King was assassinated in Memphis, Tennessee.

2. In paragraph 2, King alludes to Thoreau and Gandhi. Who were these men? What were their views on civil disobedience?

3. King distinguishes very carefully between civil disobedience and what he calls "uncivil disobedience." Exactly what differences does he see between the two?

4. Compare his views on following one's conscience with those expressed by Samuel Clemens in "Glances at History" (Selection 59). Is there any significant difference between the two?

5. King suggests the formation of an International Association for the Advancement of Creative Maladjustment. Are there things to which you would rather be maladjusted than adjusted? Consider the following items: electronic music, television commercials, rapidly changing fashions, shopping centers, freeways, telephones, nylon, TV dinners, false teeth, miracle medications, parents, professional sports.

6. Discuss the uses of connotation, metaphor, allusion, stereotype, and irony in this selection.

7. The final paragraph is the prayer of an "old Negro slave preacher." Is the tone of this paragraph different from the tone of the rest of the selection? Is it an appropriate and effective finale? Why do you suppose King chose these words for his conclusion?

8. What do you think honor means to Martin Luther King? Compare his views with those of Falstaff (Selection 61), Douglas Johnson (Selection

62), the poet (Selection 63), the knife-thrower (Selection 64), the One Per-center (Selection 65). Whose views most closely approach your own?

9. Compare the comments made in each of the six selections in this section.

10. Write a composition about the most honorable person you know. Define *honor* very precisely and show exactly how the person you have selected fits your definition.

Group 3:
love

67 How Do I Love Thee?
Elizabeth Barrett Browning

How do I love thee? Let me count the ways.
I love thee to the depth and breadth and height
My soul can reach, when feeling out of sight
For the ends of Being and ideal Grace.
I love thee to the level of everyday's   5
Most quiet need, by sun and candle-light.
I love thee freely, as men strive for Right;
I love thee purely, as they turn from Praise.
I love thee with the passion put to use
In my old griefs, and with my childhood's faith.   10
I love thee with a love I seemed to lose
With my lost saints—I love thee with the breath,
Smiles, tears, of all my life!— and, if God choose,
I shall but love thee better after death.

UNDERSTANDING THE SELECTION

1. What are "the depth and breadth and height" a soul can reach?
2. How does a soul feel "out of sight"? What does it feel with?
3. What exactly are "the ends of Being and ideal Grace"?
4. What level is "the level of everyday's/Most quiet need"?
5. In your experience, do men "strive for Right"? Do they do so "freely"?
6. In your experience, do they "turn from Praise"? Do they do so "purely"?
7. Elizabeth Barrett wrote this poem to her future husband, Robert Browning. Is "the passion put to use/In my old griefs" an appropriate emotion to feel for one's husband? Does a mature woman feel the same way about her husband as she did about the pet kitten that was killed when she was a little girl?
8. She says, "I love thee . . . with my childhood's faith." Childhood faith is usually uncritical, adoring, awestruck, and distant. Are these qualities appropriate in married love?
9. The words *soul, Being, Grace, purely, faith, saints,* and *God* have similar connotations. How do these connotations affect the tone of the poem? How do they affect the comment?
10. Can you draw a picture of the poem or of any part of it?

11. Does Mrs. Browning intend to be taken seriously? Can you take her seriously?

12. Why do so many persons like this poem?

13. You may have found it difficult to answer some of these questions. Is that because you are a bad reader or because Mrs. Browning has written a bad poem?

68   *I Wish I Were Close*

Yamabe No Akahito

I wish I were close
To you as the wet skirt of
A salt girl to her body.
I think of you always.

(Translated by Kenneth Rexroth)

UNDERSTANDING THE SELECTION

1. What is a "salt girl"?
2. Can you draw a picture of the girl?
3. Does the poet intend to be taken seriously? Can you take him seriously?
4. Which poem is "better," this one or "How Do I Love Thee?" Why?

69   *Buick*

Karl Shapiro

As a sloop with a sweep of immaculate wing on her delicate
    spine
And a keel as steel as a root that holds in the sea as she leans,
Leaning and laughing, my warm-hearted beauty, you ride,
    you ride,
You tack on the curves with parabola speed and a kiss of
    goodbye,
Like a thoroughbred sloop, my new high-spirited spirit, my
    kiss.   5

As my foot suggests that you leap in the air with your hips
    of a girl,
My finger that praises your wheel and announces your
    voices of song,

Flouncing your skirts, you blueness of joy, you flirt of politeness,
You leap, you intelligence, essence of wheelness with silvery
nose,
And your platinum clocks of excitement stir like the hairs of
a fern.   *10*

But how alien you are from the booming belts of your birth
and the smoke
Where you turned on the stinging lathes of Detroit and
Lansing at night
And shrieked at the torch in your secret parts and the amor-
ous tests,
But now with your eyes that enter the future of roads you
forget;
You are all instinct with your phosphorous glow and your
streaking hair.   *15*

And now when we stop it is not as the bird from the shell
that I leave
Or the leathery pilot who steps from his bird with a sneer of
delight,
And not as the ignorant beast do you squat and watch me
depart,
But with exquisite breathing you smile, with satisfaction of
love,
And I touch you again as you tick in the silence and settle
in sleep.   *20*

UNDERSTANDING THE SELECTION

1. How does the speaker feel toward the car? How does the car feel toward the speaker? Does Shapiro imply that the speaker and the car are
engaged in a mutually passionate love affair or is it one-sided?

2. Do American men love their cars?

3. Is the poem an insult to women? A playful exaggeration? A satire?
What exactly is its tone?

4. Does the comparison of the car to a sloop in lines 1 through 5 help or
hinder the comparison of the car to a girl? How about the comparisons
of a bird leaving its shell in line 16 and a pilot leaving his plane in line 17?
Do these help or hinder the comparison of the car to a girl?

5. Is this a love poem?

70   *Is Love An Art?*

Erich Fromm

1   Is love an art? Then it requires knowledge and effort. Or is love a
pleasant sensation, which to experience is a matter of chance, something
one "falls into" if one is lucky? This little book is based on the former premise, while undoubtedly the majority of people today believe in the latter.

2   Not that people think that love is not important. They are starved
for it; they watch endless numbers of films about happy and unhappy love
stories, they listen to hundreds of trashy songs about love—yet hardly anyone thinks that there is anything that needs to be learned about love.

3   This peculiar attitude is based on several premises which either sing-
ly or combined tend to uphold it. Most people see the problem of love primarily as that of *being loved*, rather than that of *loving*, of one's capacity
to love. Hence the problem to them is how to be loved, how to be lovable.
In pursuit of this aim they follow several paths. One, which is especially
used by men, is to be successful, to be as powerful and rich as the social
margin of one's position permits. Another, used especially by women, is
to make oneself attractive, by cultivating one's body, dress, etc. Other ways
of making oneself attractive, used both by men and women, are to develop
pleasant manners, interesting conversation, to be helpful, modest, inof-
fensive. Many of the ways to make oneself lovable are the same as those
used to make oneself successful, "to win friends and influence people." As a
matter of fact, what most people in our culture mean by being lovable is
essentially a mixture between being popular and having sex appeal.

4   A second premise behind the attitude that there is nothing to be
learned about love is the assumption that the problem of love is the problem
of an *object*, not the problem of a *faculty*. People think that to *love* is simple, but that to find the right object to love—or to be loved by—is difficult.
This attitude has several reasons rooted in the development of modern society. One reason is the great change which occurred in the twentieth century with respect to the choice of a "love object." In the Victorian age, as in
many traditional cultures, love was mostly not a spontaneous personal experience which then might lead to marriage. On the contrary, marriage was
contracted by convention—either by the respective families, or by a marriage broker, or without the help of such intermediaries; it was concluded on
the basis of social considerations, and love was supposed to develop once
the marriage had been concluded. In the last few generations the concept of
romantic love has become almost universal in the Western world. In the
United States, while considerations of a conventional nature are not entirely

absent, to a vast extent people are in search of "romantic love," of the personal experience of love which then should lead to marriage. This new concept of freedom in love must have greatly enhanced the importance of the *object* as against the importance of the *function*.

5   Closely related to this factor is another feature characteristic of contemporary culture. Our whole culture is based on the appetite for buying, on the idea of a mutually favorable exchange. Modern man's happiness consists in the thrill of looking at the shop windows, and in buying all that he can afford to buy, either for cash or on installments. He (or she) looks at people in a similar way. For the man an attractive girl—and for the woman an attractive man—are the prizes they are after. "Attractive" usually means a nice package of qualities which are popular and sought after on the personality market. What specifically makes a person attractive depends on the fashion of the time, physically as well as mentally. During the twenties, a drinking and smoking girl, tough and sexy, was attractive; today the fashion demands more domesticity and coyness. At the end of the nineteenth and the beginning of this century, a man had to be aggressive and ambitious —today he has to be social and tolerant—in order to be an attractive "package." At any rate, the sense of falling in love develops usually only with regard to such human commodities as are within reach of one's own possibilities for exchange. I am out for a bargain; the object should be desirable from the standpoint of its social value, and at the same time should want me, considering my overt and hidden assets and potentialities. Two persons thus fall in love when they feel they have found the best object available on the market, considering the limitations of their own exchange values. Often, as in buying real estate, the hidden potentialities which can be developed play a considerable role in this bargain. In a culture in which the marketing orientation prevails, and in which material success is the outstanding value, there is little reason to be surprised that human love relations follow the same pattern of exchange which governs the commodity and the labor market.

6   The third error leading to the assumption that there is nothing to be learned about love lies in the confusion between the initial experience of *"falling"* in love, and the permanent state of *being* in love, or as we might better say, of "standing" in love. If two people who have been strangers, as all of us are, suddenly let the wall between them break down, and feel close, feel one, this moment of oneness is one of the most exhilarating, most exciting experiences in life. It is all the more wonderful and miraculous for persons who have been shut off, isolated, without love. This miracle of sudden intimacy is often facilitated if it is combined with, or initiated by, sexual

attraction ana consummation. However, this type of love is by its very nature not lasting. The two persons become well acquainted, their intimacy loses more and more its miraculous character, until their antagonism, their disappointments, their mutual boredom kill whatever is left of the initial excitement. Yet, in the beginning they do not know all this: in fact, they take the intensity of the infatuation, this being "crazy" about each other, for proof of the intensity of their love, while it may only prove the degree of their preceding loneliness.

7   This attitude—that nothing is easier than to love—has continued to be the prevalent idea about love in spite of the overwhelming evidence to the contrary. There is hardly any activity, any enterprise, which is started with such tremendous hopes and expectations, and yet, which fails so regularly, as love. If this were the case with any other activity, people would be eager to know the reasons for the failure, and to learn how one could do better—or they would give up the activity. Since the latter is impossible in the case of love, there seems to be only one adequate way to overcome the failure of love—to examine the reasons for this failure, and to proceed to study the meaning of love.

8   The first step to take is to become aware that *love is an art,* just as living is an art; if we want to learn how to love we must proceed in the same way we have to proceed if we want to learn any other art, say music, painting, carpentry, or the art of medicine or engineering.

9   What are the necessary steps in learning any art?

10   The process of learning an art can be divided conveniently into two parts: one, the mastery of the theory; the other, the mastery of the practice. If I want to learn the art of medicine, I must first know the facts about the human body, and about various diseases. When I have all this theoretical knowledge, I am by no means competent in the art of medicine. I shall become a master in this art only after a great deal of practice, until eventually the results of my theoretical knowledge and the results of my practice are blended into one—my intuition, the essence of the mastery of any art. But, aside from learning the theory and practice, there is a third factor necessary to becoming a master in any art—the mastery of the art must be a matter of ultimate concern; there must be nothing else in the world more important than the art. This holds true for music, for medicine, for carpentry—and for love. And, maybe, here lies the answer to the question of why people in our culture try so rarely to learn this art, in spite of their obvious failures: in spite of the deep-seated craving for love, almost everything else is considered to be more important than love: success, prestige, money, power—almost all our energy is used for the learning of how to achieve these aims, and almost none to learn the art of loving.

UNDERSTANDING THE SELECTION

1. Erich Fromm assumes that love is an art. What does he think are the requirements of an art? Would he consider cooking an art ("Haschich Fudge," Selection 7)? Detecting ("The Musgrave Ritual," Selection 11)? Black magic ("from *The Black Arts,*" Selection 31)? Nursing ("Quiet Night," Selection 38)? Dieting ("The Three Fat Women of Antibes," Selection 53)? Knife throwing ("The Artist," Selection 64)? What would he consider *not* an art?

2. Fromm organizes his material quite carefully. For example, he says three assumptions lead to the idea that there is nothing to be learned about love. Then he enumerates the steps necessary to learning an art. Does he use arrangement in time or space? Or both?

3. In paragraph 4, Fromm points out that marriage used to be considered a prelude to love whereas now we feel love should precede marriage. Do you think our present attitudes lead to happy marriages? Do you think it is possible for two people to be happily married for their entire lives? Do you know any such couples?

4. In paragraph 5 Fromm says that men and women shop for attractive "packages" in the opposite sex. He says today's fashion demands "more domesticity and coyness" of women, whereas a man must be "social and tolerant." He wrote this book in 1956. Do you agree with his opinion of what makes an attractive "package"? If not, what qualities do you think most people look for?

5. Fromm also says, in paragraph 10, that we consider success, prestige, money, and power more important than love, and that we use most of our energy learning how to achieve these aims. Do you agree with him? What do you spend most of your energy on? Is what you spend most of your energy on the thing you really consider most important?

6. What comment does Fromm make in this selection? Do you think it will be as important one hundred years from now as it is today?

71   *Lover's Hands*

Rudolf Dietrich

Photograph by Rudolf Dietrich.

UNDERSTANDING THE SELECTION

1. In this photograph the hands symbolize love. Are they an appropriate symbol for love? What other symbols for love can you suggest?

2. The hands in the picture are clasping the head of the beloved. Are lovers more apt to show possessiveness, as the clasp here suggests, or to show generosity? Would the hands be a better symbol if they were open and offering?

3. If you have a camera, take a picture which you believe catches the essence of love. If you have no camera, find a picture in a magazine which effectively portrays love.

4. Before you can do the above assignment, you will have to decide on a definition of love. Most of us have been brought up to believe that we will fall romantically in love with someone of the opposite sex, marry, and live happily ever after. We have also been taught that love precedes marriage and that marriage without love is improper; most of us have been taught that sexual relationships are justifiable only within marriage, and many of us have been taught that marriage endures until death. But in the last few years "nice" people have begun to equate love and sex and to suggest that they can properly be expressed outside marriage. Despite these new ideas, people in many parts of the world seem to assign no value to romantic love; parents arrange marriages without greatly considering the feelings of the young people involved.

Love, then, is not easily defined. Its meaning differs even within our own country and is influenced by the mores of our particular communities and backgrounds. To help you with your definition, we suggest you narrow it to an emotion shared by two people who might decide to get married; that is, do not attempt to define mother love, father love, love of country, or love of life. Write out your definition and bring it to class along with your picture. Be prepared to discuss both picture and definition with your classmates.

72 A Summer Tragedy

Arna Bontemps

1   Old Jeff Patton, the black share farmer, fumbled with his bow tie. His fingers trembled and the high stiff collar pinched his throat. A fellow loses his hand for such vanities after thirty or forty years of simple life. Once a year, or maybe twice if there's a wedding among his kinfolks, he may spruce up; but generally fancy clothes do nothing but adorn the wall of the big room and feed the moths. That had been Jeff Patton's experience. He had not worn his stiff-bosomed shirt more than a dozen times in all his married life. His swallow-tailed coat lay on the bed beside him, freshly brushed and pressed, but it was as full of holes as the overalls in which he worked on weekdays. The moths had used it badly. Jeff twisted his mouth into a hideous toothless grimace as he contended with the obstinate bow. He stamped his good foot and decided to give up the struggle.

2   "Jennie," he called.

3   "What's that, Jeff?" His wife's shrunken voice came out of the adjoining room like an echo. It was hardly bigger than a whisper.

4   "I reckon you'll have to he'p me wid this heah bow tie, baby," he said meekly. "Dog if I can hitch it up."

5   Her answer was not strong enough to reach him, but presently the old woman came to the door, feeling her way with a stick. She had a wasted, dead-leaf appearance. Her body, as scrawny and gnarled as a string bean, seemed less than nothing in the ocean of frayed and faded petticoats that surrounded her. These hung an inch or two above the tops of her heavy unlaced shoes and showed little grotesque piles where the stockings had fallen down from her negligible legs.

6   "You oughta could do a heap mo' wid a thing like that'n me—beingst as you got yo' good sight."

7   "Looks like I oughta could," he admitted. "But ma fingers is gone democrat on me. I get all mixed up in the looking glass an' can't tell wicha way to twist the devilish thing."

8   Jennie sat on the side of the bed and old Jeff Patton got down on one knee while she tied the bow knot. It was a slow and painful ordeal for each of them in this position. Jeff's bones cracked, his knee ached, and it was only after a half dozen attempts that Jennie worked a semblance of a bow into the tie.

9   "I got to dress maself now," the old woman whispered. "These is ma old shoes an' stockings, and I ain't so much as unwrapped ma dress."

10   "Well, don't worry 'bout me no mo', baby," Jeff said. "That 'bout finishes me. All I gotta do now is slip on that old coat 'n ves' an' I'll be fixed to leave."

11   Jennie disappeared again through the dim passage into the shed room. Being blind was no handicap to her in that black hole. Jeff heard the cane placed against the wall beside the door and knew that his wife was on easy ground. He put on his coat, took a battered top hat from the bedpost and hobbled to the front door. He was ready to travel. As soon as Jennie could get on her Sunday shoes and her old black silk dress, they would start.

12   Outside the tiny log house, the day was warm and mellow with sunshine. A host of wasps were humming with busy excitement in the trunk of a dead sycamore. Gray squirrels were searching through the grass for hickory nuts and blue jays were in the trees, hopping from branch to branch.

Pine woods stretched away to the left like a black sea. Among them were scattered scores of log houses like Jeff's, houses of black share farmers. Cows and pigs wandered freely among the trees. There was no danger of loss. Each farmer knew his own stock and knew his neighbor's as well as he knew his neighbor's children.

13   Down the slope to the right were the cultivated acres on which the colored folks worked. They extended to the river, more than two miles away, and they were today green with the unmade cotton crop. A tiny thread of a road, which passed directly in front of Jeff's place, ran through these green fields like a pencil mark.

14   Jeff, standing outside the door, with his absurd hat in his left hand, surveyed the wide scene tenderly. He had been forty-five years on these acres. He loved them with the unexplained affection that others have for the countries to which they belong.

15   The sun was hot on his head, his collar still pinched his throat, and the Sunday clothes were intolerably hot. Jeff transferred the hat to his right hand and began fanning with it. Suddenly the whisper that was Jennie's voice came out of the shed room.

16   "You can bring the car round front whilst you's waitin'," it said feebly. There was a tired pause; then it added, "I'll soon be fixed to go."

17   "A'right, baby," Jeff answered. "I'll get it in a minute."

18   But he didn't move. A thought struck him that made his mouth fall open. The mention of the car brought to his mind, with new intensity, the trip he and Jennie were about to take. Fear came into his eyes; excitement took his breath. Lord, Jesus!

19   "Jeff . . . O Jeff," the old woman's whisper called.

20   He awakened with a jolt. "Hunh, baby?"

21   "What you doin'?"

22   "Nuthin. Jes studyin'. I jes been turnin' things round'n round in ma mind."

23   "You could be gettin' the car," she said.

24   "Oh yes, right away, baby."

25   He started round to the shed, limping heavily on his bad leg. There were three frizzly chickens in the yard. All his other chickens had been killed or stolen recently. But the frizzly chickens had been saved somehow. That was fortunate indeed, for these curious creatures had a way of devouring "Poison" from the yard and in that way protecting against conjure and black luck and spells. But even the frizzly chickens seemed now to be in a stupor. Jeff thought they had some ailment; he expected all three of them to die shortly.

26   The shed in which the old T-model Ford stood was only a grass roof held up by four corner poles. It had been built by tremulous hands at a time when the little rattletrap car had been regarded as a peculiar treasure. And, miraculously, despite wind and downpour it still stood.

27   Jeff adjusted the crank and put his weight upon it. The engine came to life with a sputter and bang that rattled the old car from radiator to tail-light. Jeff hopped into the seat and put his foot on the accelerator. The sput-tering and banging increased. The rattling became more violent. That was good. It was good banging, good sputtering and rattling, and it meant that the aged car was still in running condition. She could be depended on for this trip.

28   Again Jeff's thought halted as if paralyzed. The suggestion of the trip fell into the machinery of his mind like a wrench. He felt dazed and weak. He swung the car out into the yard, made a half turn and drove around to the front door. When he took his hands off the wheel, he noticed that he was trembling violently. He cut off the motor and climbed to the ground to wait for Jennie.

29   A few minutes later she was at the window, her voice rattling against the pane like a broken shutter.

30   "I'm ready, Jeff."

31   He did not answer, but limped into the house and took her by the arm. He led her slowly through the big room, down the step and across the yard.

32   "You reckon I'd oughta lock the do'?" he asked softly.

33   They stopped and Jennie weighed the question. Finally she shook her head.

34   "Ne' mind the do'," she said. "I don't see no cause to lock up things."

35   "You right," Jeff agreed. "No cause to lock up."

36   Jeff opened the door and helped his wife into the car. A quick shud-der passed over him. Jesus! Again he trembled.

37   "How come you shaking so?" Jennie whispered.

38   "I don't know," he said.

39   "You mus' be scairt, Jeff."

40   "No, baby, I ain't scairt."

41   He slammed the door after her and went around to crank up again. The motor started easily. Jeff wished that it had not been so responsive. He would have liked a few more minutes in which to turn things around in his head. As it was, with Jennie chiding him about being afraid, he had to keep going. He swung the car into the little pencil-mark road and started off toward the river, driving very slowly, very cautiously.

42   Chugging across the green countryside, the small battered Ford seemed tiny indeed. Jeff felt a familiar excitement, a thrill, as they came down the first slope to the immense levels on which the cotton was grow-

ing. He could not help reflecting that the crops were good. He knew what that meant, too; he had made forty-five of them with his own hands. It was true that he had worn out nearly a dozen mules, but that was the fault of old man Stevenson, the owner of the land. Major Stevenson had the odd notion that one mule was all a share farmer needed to work a thirty-acre plot. It was an expensive notion, the way it killed mules from overwork, but the old man held to it. Jeff thought it killed a good many share farmers as well as mules, but he had no sympathy for them. He had always been strong, and he had been taught to have no patience with weakness in men. Women or children might be tolerated if they were puny, but a weak man was a curse. Of course, his own children—

43   Jeff's thought halted there. He and Jennie never mentioned their dead children any more. And naturally he did not wish to dwell upon them in his mind. Before he knew it, some remark would slip out of his mouth and that would make Jennie feel blue. Perhaps she would cry. A woman like Jennie could not easily throw off the grief that comes from losing five grown children within two years. Even Jeff was still staggered by the blow. His memory had not been much good recently. He frequently talked to himself. And, although he had kept it a secret, he knew that his courage had left him. He was terrified by the least unfamiliar sound at night. He was reluctant to venture far from home in the daytime. And that habit of trembling when he felt fearful was now far beyond his control. Sometimes he became afraid and trembled without knowing what had frightened him. The feeling would just come over him like a chill.

44   The car rattled slowly over the dusty road. Jennie sat erect and silent, with a little absurd hat pinned to her hair. Her useless eyes seemed very large, very white in their deep sockets. Suddenly Jeff heard her voice, and he inclined his head to catch the words.

45   "Is we passed Delia Moore's house yet?" she asked.

46   "Not yet," he said.

47   "You must be drivin' mighty slow, Jeff."

48   "We might just as well take our time, baby."

49   There was a pause. A little puff of steam was coming out of the radiator of the car. Heat wavered above the hood. Delia Moore's house was nearly half a mile away. After a moment Jennie spoke again.

50   "You ain't really scairt, is you, Jeff?"

51   "Nah, baby, I ain't scairt."

52   "You know how we agreed—we gotta keep on goin'."

53   Jewels of perspiration appeared on Jeff's forehead. His eyes rounded, blinked, became fixed on the road.

54   "I don't know," he said with a shiver. "I reckon it's the only thing to do."

55   "Hm."

56   A flock of guinea fowls, pecking in the road, were scattered by the passing car. Some of them took to their wings; others hid under bushes. A blue jay, swaying on a leafy twig, was annoying a roadside squirrel. Jeff held an even speed till he came near Delia's place. Then he slowed down noticeably.

57   Delia's house was really no house at all, but an abandoned store building converted into a dwelling. It sat near a crossroads, beneath a single black cedar tree. There Delia, a cattish old creature of Jennie's age, lived alone. She had been there more years than anybody could remember, and long ago had won the disfavor of such women as Jennie. For in her young days Delia had been gayer, yellower and saucier than seemed proper in those parts. Her ways with menfolks had been dark and suspicious. And the fact that she had had as many husbands as children did not help her reputation.

58   "Yonder's old Delia," Jeff said as they passed.

59   "What she doin'?"

60   "Jes sittin' in the do'," he said.

61   "She see us?"

62   "Hm," Jeff said. "Musta did."

63   That relieved Jennie. It strengthened her to know that her old enemy had seen her pass in her best clothes. That would give the old she-devil something to chew her gums and fret about, Jennie thought. Wouldn't she have a fit if she didn't find out? Old evil Delia! This would be just the thing for her. It would pay her back for being so evil. It would also pay her, Jennie thought, for the way she used to grin at Jeff—long ago when her teeth were good.

64   The road became smooth and red, and Jeff could tell by the smell of the air that they were nearing the river. He could see the rise where the road turned and ran along parallel to the stream. The car chugged on monotonously. After a long silent spell, Jennie leaned against Jeff and spoke.

65   "How many bale o' cotton you think we got standin'?" she said.

66   Jeff wrinkled his forehead as he calculated.

67   "'Bout twenty-five, I reckon."

68   "How many you make las' year?"

69   "Twenty-eight," he said. "How come you ask that?"

70   "I's jes thinkin'," Jennie said quietly.

71   "It don't make a speck o'difference though," Jeff reflected. "If we get much or if we get little, we still gonna be in debt to old man Stevenson when he gets through counting up agin us. It's took us a long time to learn that."

72   Jennie was not listening to these words. She had fallen into a trance-like meditation. Her lips twitched. She chewed her gums and rubbed her gnarled hands nervously. Suddenly she leaned forward, buried her face in the nervous hands and burst into tears. She cried aloud in a dry cracked voice that suggested the rattle of fodder on dead stalks. She cried aloud like a child, for she had never learned to suppress a genuine sob. Her slight old frame shook heavily and seemed hardly able to sustain such violent grief.

73   "What's the matter, baby?" Jeff asked awkwardly. "Why you cryin' like all that?"

74   "I's jes thinkin'," she said.

75   "So you the one what's scairt now, hunh?"

76   "I ain't scairt, Jeff. I's jes thinkin' 'bout leavin' eve'thing like this— eve'thing we been used to. It's right sad-like."

77   Jeff did not answer, and presently Jennie buried her face again and cried.

78   The sun was almost overhead. It beat down furiously on the dusty wagon-path road, on the parched roadside grass and the tiny battered car. Jeff's hands, gripping the wheel, became wet with perspiration; his forehead sparkled. Jeff's lips parted. His mouth shaped a hideous grimace. His face suggested the face of a man being burned. But the torture passed and his expression softened again.

79   "You mustn't cry, baby," he said to his wife. "We gotta be strong. We can't break down."

80   Jennie waited a few seconds, then said, "You reckon we oughta do it, Jeff? You reckon we oughta go 'head an' do it, really?"

81   Jeff's voice choked; his eyes blurred. He was terrified to hear Jennie say the thing that had been in his mind all morning. She had egged him on when he had wanted more than anything in the world to wait, to reconsider, to think things over a little longer. Now she was getting cold feet. Actually there was no need of thinking the question through again. It would only end in making the same painful decision once more. Jeff knew that. There was no need of fooling around longer.

82   "We jes as well to do like we planned," he said. "They ain't nothin' else for us now—it's the bes' thing."

83   Jeff thought of the handicaps, the near impossibility, of making another crop with his leg bothering him more and more each week. Then there was always the chance that he would have another stroke, like the one that had made him lame. Another one might kill him. The least it could do would be to leave him helpless. Jeff gasped—Lord, Jesus! He could not bear to think of being helpless, like a baby, on Jennie's hands. Frail, blind Jennie.

84   The little pounding motor of the car worked harder and harder. The puff of steam from the cracked radiator became larger. Jeff realized that they were climbing a little rise. A moment later the road turned abruptly and he looked down upon the face of the river.

85   "Jeff."
86   "Hunh?"
87   "Is that the water I hear?"
88   "Hm. Tha's it."
89   "Well, which way you goin' now?"
90   "Down this-a way," he said. "The road runs 'long 'side o' the water a lil piece."
91   She waited a while calmly. Then she said, "Drive faster."
92   "A'right, baby," Jeff said.
93   The water roared in the bed of the river. It was fifty or sixty feet below the level of the road. Between the road and the water there was a long smooth slope, sharply inclined. The slope was dry, the clay hardened by prolonged summer heat. The water below, roaring in a narrow channel, was noisy and wild.
94   "Jeff."
95   "Hunh?"
96   "How far you goin'?"
97   "Jes a lil piece down the road."
98   "You ain't scairt, is you, Jeff?"
99   "Nah, baby," he said trembling. "I ain't scairt."
100   "Remember how we planned it, Jeff. We gotta do it like we said. Brave-like."
101   "Hm."
102   Jeff's brain darkened. Things suddenly seemed unreal, like figures in a dream. Thoughts swam in his mind foolishly, hysterically, like little blind fish in a pool within a dense cave. They rushed, crossed one another, jostled, collided, retreated and rushed again. Jeff soon became dizzy. He shuddered violently and turned to his wife.
103   "Jennie, I can't do it. I can't." His voice broke pitifully.
104   She did not appear to be listening. All the grief had gone from her face. She sat erect, her unseeing eyes wide open, strained and frightful. Her glossy black skin had become dull. She seemed as thin, as sharp and bony, as a starved bird. Now, having suffered and endured the sadness of tearing herself away from beloved things, she showed no anguish. She was absorbed with her own thoughts, and she didn't even hear Jeff's voice shouting in her ear.
105   Jeff said nothing more. For an instant there was light in his cavernous brain. The great chamber was, for less than a second, peopled by characters he knew and loved. They were simple, healthy creatures, and they behaved in a manner that he could understand. They had quality. But since he had already taken leave of them long ago, the remembrance did not break his heart again. Young Jeff Patton was among them, the Jeff Patton of fifty

years ago who went down to New Orleans with a crowd of country boys to the Mardi Gras doings. The gay young crowd, boys with candy-striped shirts and rouged-brown girls in noisy silks, was like a picture in his head. Yet it did not make him sad. On that very trip Slim Burns had killed Joe Beasley—the crowd had been broken up. Since then Jeff Patton's world had been the Greenbriar Plantation. If there had been other Mardi Gras carnivals, he had not heard of them. Since then there had been no time; the years had fallen on him like waves. Now he was old, worn out. Another paralytic stroke (like the one he had already suffered) would put him on his back for keeps. In that condition, with a frail blind woman to look after him, he would be worse off than if he were dead.

106   Suddenly Jeff's hands became steady. He actually felt brave. He slowed down the motor of the car and carefully pulled off the road. Below, the water of the stream boomed, a soft thunder in the deep channel. Jeff ran the car onto the clay slope, pointed it directly toward the stream and put his foot heavily on the accelerator. The little car leaped furiously down the steep incline toward the water. The movement was nearly as swift and direct as a fall. The two old black folks, sitting quietly side by side, showed no excitement. In another instant the car hit the water and dropped immediately out of sight.

107   A little later it lodged in the mud of a shallow place. One wheel of the crushed and upturned little Ford became visible above the rushing water.

UNDERSTANDING THE SELECTION

1. Consider Arna Bontemps' writing in the light of Part 2 of this book. Which of the writing devices we have discussed—connotation, metaphor, allusion, symbol—does Bontemps seem most adept at? Would you consider this story "good writing"? Why or why not?

2. We have included this story in our section on "Love," although it might easily have been included in the preceding section on "Honor" or the following section on "Identity." Do you think this is a love story? Why or why not?

3. Throughout literary history, stories of lovers who commit suicide or die in each other's arms are legion. In this book, for instance, we have the myth of "Pyramus and Thisbe" (Selection 40); Shakespeare used the same idea in *Romeo and Juliet;* more recently we have seen *West Side Story* and the famous French film *Jules and Jim,* in which the lovers deliberately drive into a river as the characters do in this story. Would you say, then, that "A Summer Tragedy" is a stereotyped story? If you do not think so, what do you feel saves it from stereotype?

4. The title of this story is "A Summer Tragedy." The word "tragedy" im-

plies something beyond our control—and we speak of auto accidents and assassinations as tragic. Do you consider the events in this story to be tragic? Why did Bontemps title the story as he did?

5. Is this story, like *Romeo and Juliet* and "Pyramus and Thisbe," a story that will mean as much a hundred years from now as it does today? What comment do you think is made in this story? Is it one that has significance to only one time and place, or is it worthy of consideration by all men at all times?

6. Several kinds of love are presented in this group of selections. Try to define the love demonstrated or discussed in each selection. Or is each merely a different facet of the same emotion?

7. Which selection in this group best conveys to you a sense of love? Is it also the best written selection?

Group 4:
identity

73   Clay
James Joyce

The matron had given her leave to go out as soon as the women's tea was over and Maria looked forward to her evening out. The kitchen was spick and span: the cook said you could see yourself in the big copper boilers. The fire was nice and bright and on one of the side-tables were four very big barmbracks. These barmbracks seemed uncut; but if you went closer you would see that they had been cut into long thick even slices and were ready to be handed round at tea. Maria had cut them herself.

Maria was a very, very small person indeed but she had a very long nose and a very long chin. She talked a little through her nose, always soothingly: *Yes, my dear,* and *No, my dear.* She was always sent for when the women quarrelled over their tubs and always succeeded in making peace. One day the matron had said to her:

—Maria, you are a veritable peace-maker!

And the sub-matron and two of the Board ladies had heard the compliment. And Ginger Mooney was always saying what she wouldn't do to the dummy who had charge of the irons if it wasn't for Maria. Everyone was so fond of Maria.

The women would have their tea at six o'clock and she would be able to get away before seven. From Ballsbridge to the Pillar, twenty minutes; from the Pillar to Drumcondra, twenty minutes; and twenty minutes to buy the things. She would be there before eight. She took out her purse with the silver clasps and read again the words *A Present from Belfast.* She was very fond of that purse because Joe had brought it to her five years before when he and Alphy had gone to Belfast on a Whit-Monday trip. In the purse were two half-crowns and some coppers. She would have five shillings clear after paying tram fare. What a nice evening they would have, all the children singing! Only she hoped that Joe wouldn't come in drunk. He was so different when he took any drink.

Often he had wanted her to go and live with them; but she would have felt herself in the way (though Joe's wife was ever so nice with her) and she had become accustomed to the life of the laundry. Joe was a good fellow. She had nursed him and Alphy too; and Joe used often say:

—Mamma is mamma but Maria is my proper mother.

After the break-up at home the boys had got her that position in the *Dublin by Lamplight* laundry, and she liked it. She used to have such a bad opinion of Protestants but now she thought they were very nice people, a little quiet and serious, but still very nice people to live with. Then she had her plants in the conservatory and she liked looking after them. She had lovely ferns and wax-plants and, whenever anyone came to visit her, she always gave the visitor one or two slips from her conservatory. There was one thing she didn't like and that was the tracts on the walls; but the matron was such a nice person to deal with, so genteel.

When the cook told her everything was ready she went into the women's room and began to pull the big bell. In a few minutes the women began to come in by twos and threes, wiping their steaming hands in their petticoats and pulling down the sleeves of their blouses over their red steaming arms. They settled down before their huge mugs which the cook and the dummy filled up with hot tea, already mixed with milk and sugar in huge tin cans. Maria superintended the distribution of the barmbrack and saw that every woman got her four slices. There was a great deal of laughing and joking during the meal. Lizzie Fleming said Maria was sure to get the ring and, though Fleming had said that for so many Hallow Eves, Maria had to laugh and say she didn't want any ring or man either; and when she laughed her grey-green eyes sparkled with disappointed shyness and the tip of her nose nearly met the tip of her chin. Then Ginger Mooney lifted up her mug of tea and proposed Maria's health while all the other women clattered with their mugs on the table, and said she was sorry she hadn't a sup of porter to drink it in. And Maria laughed again till the tip of her nose nearly met the tip of her chin and till her minute body nearly shook itself asunder because she knew that Mooney meant well though, of course, she had the notions of a common woman.

But wasn't Maria glad when the women had finished their tea and the cook and the dummy had begun to clear away the tea-things! She went into her little bedroom and, remembering that the next morning was a mass morning, changed the hand of the alarm from seven to six. Then she took off her working skirt and her house-boots and laid her best skirt out on the bed and her tiny dress-boots beside the foot of the bed. She changed her blouse too and, as she stood before the mirror, she thought of how she used to dress for mass on Sunday morning when she was a young girl; and she looked with quaint affection at the diminutive body which she had so often adorned. In spite of its years she found it a nice tidy little body.

When she got outside the streets were shining with rain and she was glad of her old brown raincloak. The tram was full and she had to sit on the little stool at the end of the car, facing all the people, with her toes barely touching the floor. She arranged in her mind all she was going to do and thought how much better it was to be independent and to have your own money in your pocket. She hoped they would have a nice evening. She was sure they would but she could not help thinking what a pity it was Alphy and Joe were not speaking. They were always falling out now but when they were boys together they used to be the best of friends: but such was life.

She got out of her tram at the Pillar and ferreted her way quickly among the crowds. She went into Downes's cake-shop but the shop was so full of people that it was a long time before she could get herself attended to. She bought a dozen of mixed penny cakes, and at last came out of the shop laden with a big bag. Then she thought what else would she buy: she wanted to buy something really nice. They would be sure to have plenty of apples and nuts. It was hard to know what to buy and all she could think of was cake. She decided to buy some plumcake but Downes's plumcake had not enough almond icing on top of it so she went over to a shop in Henry Street. Here she was a long time in suiting herself and the stylish young lady behind the counter, who was evidently a little annoyed by her, asked her was it wedding-cake she wanted to buy. That made Maria blush and smile at the young lady; but the young lady took it all very seriously and finally cut a thick slice of plumcake, parcelled it up and said:

—Two-and-four, please.

She thought she would have to stand in the Drumcondra tram because none of the young men seemed to notice her but an elderly gentleman made room for her. He was a stout gentleman and he wore a brown hard hat; he had a square red face and a greyish moustache. Maria thought he was a colonel-looking gentleman and she reflected how much more polite he was than the young men who simply stared straight before them. The gentleman began to chat with her about Hallow Eve and the rainy weather. He supposed the bag was full of good things for the little ones and said it was only right that the youngsters should enjoy themselves while they were young. Maria agreed with him and favoured him with demure nods and hems. He was very nice with her, and when she was getting out at the Canal Bridge she thanked him and bowed, and he bowed to her and raised his hat and smiled agreeably; and while she was going up along the terrace, bending her tiny head under the rain, she thought how easy it was to know a gentleman even when he has a drop taken.

Everybody said: *O, here's Maria!* when she came to Joe's house. Joe was there, having come home from business, and all the children had their Sunday dresses on. There were two big girls in from next door and games were going on. Maria gave the bag of cakes to the eldest boy, Alphy, to divide and Mrs Donnelly said it was too good of her to bring such a big bag of cakes and made all the children say:

—Thanks, Maria.

But Maria said she had brought something special for papa and mamma, something they would be sure to like, and she began to look for her plumcake. She tried in Downes's bag and then in the pockets of her raincloak and then on the hall-stand but nowhere could she find it. Then she asked all the children had any of them eaten it—by mistake, of course— but the children all said no and looked as if they did not like to eat cakes if they were to be accused of stealing. Everybody had a solution for the mystery and Mrs Donnelly said it was plain that Maria had left it behind her in the tram. Maria, remembering how confused the gentleman with the greyish moustache had made her, coloured with shame and vexation and disappointment. At the thought of the failure of her little surprise and of the two and fourpence she had thrown away for nothing she nearly cried outright.

But Joe said it didn't matter and made her sit down by the fire. He was very nice with her. He told her all that went on in his office, repeating for her a smart answer which he had made to the manager. Maria did not understand why Joe laughed so much over the answer he had made but she said that the manager must have been a very overbearing person to deal with. Joe said he wasn't so bad when you knew how to take him, that he was a decent sort so long as you didn't rub him the wrong way. Mrs Donnelly played the piano for the children and they danced and sang. Then the two next-door girls handed round the nuts. Nobody could find the nut-crackers and Joe was nearly getting cross over it and asked how did they expect Maria to crack nuts without a nutcracker. But Maria said she didn't like nuts and that they weren't to bother about her. Then Joe asked would she take a bottle of stout and Mrs Donnelly said there was port wine too in the house if she would prefer that. Maria said she would rather they didn't ask her to take anything: but Joe insisted.

So Maria let him have his way and they sat by the fire talking over old times and Maria thought she would put in a good word for Alphy. But Joe cried that God might strike him stone dead if ever he spoke a word to his brother again and Maria said she was sorry she had mentioned the matter. Mrs Donnelly told her husband it was a great shame for him to speak that way of his own flesh and blood but Joe said that Alphy was no brother of his and there was nearly being a row on the head of it. But Joe said he would not lose his temper on account of the night it was and asked his wife to open some more stout. The two next-door girls had arranged some Hallow Eve games and soon everything was merry again. Maria was delighted to see the children so merry and Joe and his wife in such good spirits. The next-door girls put some saucers on the table and then led the children up to the table, blindfold. One got the prayer-book and the other three got the water; and when one of the next-door girls got the ring Mrs Donnelly shook her finger at the blushing girl as much as to say: *O, I know all about it!* They insisted then on blindfolding Maria and leading her up to the table to see what she would get; and, while they were putting on the bandage, Maria laughed and laughed again till the tip of her nose nearly met the tip of her chin.

They led her up to the table amid laughing and joking and she put her hand out in the air as she was told to do. She moved her hand about here and there in the air and descended on one of the saucers. She felt a soft wet substance with her fingers and was surprised that nobody spoke or took off her bandage. There was a pause for a few seconds; and then a great deal of scuffling and whispering. Somebody said something about the garden, and at last Mrs Donnelly said something very cross to one of the next-door girls and told her to throw it out at once: that was no play. Maria understood that it was wrong that time and so she had to do it over again: and this time she got the prayer-book.

After that Mrs Donnelly played Miss McCloud's Reel for the children and Joe made Maria take a glass of wine. Soon they were all quite merry again and Mrs Donnelly said Maria would enter a convent before the year was out because she had got the prayer-book. Maria had never seen Joe so nice to her as he was that night, so full of pleasant talk and reminiscences. She said they were all very good to her.

At last the children grew tired and sleepy and Joe asked Maria would she not sing some little song before she went, one of the old songs. Mrs Donnelly said *Do, please, Maria!* and so Maria had to get up and stand beside the piano. Mrs Donnelly bade the children be quiet and listen to Maria's song. Then she played the prelude and said *Now, Maria!* and Maria, blushing very much, began to sing in a tiny quavering voice. She sang *I Dreamt that I Dwelt,* and when she came to the second verse she sang again:

> I dreamt that I dwelt in marble halls
> With vassals and serfs at my side
> And of all who assembled within those walls
> That I was the hope and the pride.
> I had riches too great to count, could boast
> Of a high ancestral name,
> But I also dreamt, which pleased me most,
> That you loved me still the same.

But no one tried to show her her mistake; and when she had ended her song Joe was very much moved. He said that there was no time like the long ago and no music for him like poor old Balfe, whatever other people might say; and his eyes filled up so much with tears that he could not find what he was looking for and in the end he had to ask his wife to tell him where the corkscrew was.

74   No Images

Waring Cuney

She does not know
Her beauty,
She thinks her brown body
Has no glory.

If she could dance
Naked,
Under palm trees
And see her image in the river
She would know

But there are no palm trees
On the street,
And dishwater gives back no images.

75   The Crisis in Women's Identity

Betty Friedan

I discovered a strange thing, interviewing women of my own generation over the past ten years. When we were growing up, many of us could not see ourselves beyond the age of twenty-one. We had no image of our own future, of ourselves as women.

I remember the stillness of a spring afternoon on the Smith campus in 1942, when I came to a frightening dead end in my own vision of the future. A few days earlier, I had received a notice that I had won a graduate fellowship. During the congratulations, underneath my excitement, I felt a strange uneasiness; there was a question that I did not want to think about.

"Is this really what I want to be?" The question shut me off, cold and alone, from the girls talking and studying on the sunny hillside behind the college house. I though I was going to be a psychologist. But if I wasn't sure, what did I want to be? I felt the future closing in—and I could not see myself in it at all. I had no image of myself, stretching beyond college. I had come at seventeen from a Midwestern town, an unsure girl; the wide horizons of the world and the life of the mind had been opened to me. I had begun to know who I was and what I wanted to do. I could not go back now. I could not go home again, to the life of my mother and the women of our town, bound to home, bridge, shopping, children, husbands, charity, clothes. But now that the time had come to make my own future, to take the deciding step, I suddenly did not know what I wanted to be.

I took the fellowship, but the next spring, under the alien California sun of another campus, the question came again, and I could not put it out of my mind. I had won another fellowship that would have committed me to research for my doctorate, to a career as professional psychologist. "Is this really what I want to be?" The decision now truly terrified me. I lived in a terror of indecision for days, unable to think of anything else.

The question was not important, I told myself. No question was important to me that year but love. We walked in the Berkeley hills and a boy said: "Nothing can come of this, between us. I'll never win a fellowship like yours." Did I think I would be choosing, irrevocably, the cold loneliness of that afternoon if I went on? I gave up the fellowship, in relief. But for years afterward, I could not read a word of the science that once I had thought of as my future life's work; the reminder of its loss was too painful.

I never could explain, hardly knew myself, why I gave up this career. I lived in the present, working on newspapers with no particular plan. I married, had children, lived according to the feminine mystique as a suburban housewife. But still the question haunted me. I could sense no purpose in my life, I could find no peace, until I finally faced it and worked out my own answer.

I discovered, talking to Smith seniors in 1959, that the question is no less terrifying to girls today. Only they answer it now in a way that my generation found, after half a lifetime, not to be an answer at all. These girls, mostly seniors, were sitting in the living room of the college house, having coffee. It was not too different from such an evening when I was a senior, except that many more of the girls wore rings on their left hands. I asked the ones around me what they planned to be. The engaged ones spoke of weddings, apartments, getting a job as a secretary while husband finished school. The others, after a hostile silence, gave vague answers about this job or that, graduate study, but no one had any real plans. A blonde with a ponytail asked me the next day if I had believed the things they had said. "None of it was true," she told me. "We don't like to be asked what we want to do. None of us know. None of us even like to think about it. The ones who are going to be married right away are the lucky ones. They don't have to think about it."

But I noticed that night that many of the engaged girls, sitting silently around the fire while I asked the others about jobs, had also seemed angry about something. "They don't want to think about not going on," my ponytailed informant said. "They know they're not going to use their education. They'll be wives and mothers. You can say you're going to keep on reading and be interested in the community. But that's not the same. You won't really go on. It's a disappointment to know you're going to stop now, and not go on and use it."

In counterpoint, I heard the words of a woman, fifteen years after she left college, a doctor's wife, mother of three, who said over coffee in her New England kitchen:

> The tragedy was, nobody ever looked us in the eye and said you have to decide what you want to do with your life, besides being your husband's wife and children's mother. I never thought it through until I was thirty-six, and my husband was so busy with his practice that he couldn't entertain me every night. The three boys were in school all day. I kept on trying to have babies despite an Rh discrepancy. After two miscarriages, they said I must stop. I thought that my own growth and evolution were over. I always knew as a child that I was going to grow up and go to college, and then get married, and that's as far as a girl has to think. After that, your husband determines and fills your life. It wasn't until I got so lonely as the doctor's wife and kept screaming at the kids because they didn't fill my life that I realized I had to make my own life. I still had to decide what I wanted to be. I hadn't finished evolving at all. But it took me ten years to think it through.

The feminine mystique permits, even encourages, women to ignore the question of their identity. The mystique says they can answer the question "Who am I?" by saying "Tom's wife . . . Mary's mother." But I don't think the mystique would have such power over American women if they did not fear to face this terrifying blank which makes them unable to see themselves after twenty-one. The truth is—and how long it has been true, I'm not sure, but it was true in my generation and it is true of girls growing up today—an American woman no longer has a private image to tell her who she is, or can be, or wants to be.

The public image, in the magazines and television commercials, is designed to sell washing machines, cake mixes, deodorants, detergents, rejuvenating face creams, hair tints. But the power of that image, on which companies spend millions of dollars for television time and ad space, comes from this: American women no longer know who they are. They are sorely in need of a new image to help them find their identity. As the motivational researchers keep telling the advertisers, American women are so unsure of who they should be that they look to this glossy public image to decide every detail of their lives. They look for the image they will no longer take from their mothers.

In my generation, many of us knew that we did not want to be like our mothers, even when we loved them. We could not help but see their disappointment. Did we understand, or only resent, the sadness, the emptiness, that made them hold too fast to us, try to live our lives, run our fathers' lives, spend their days shopping or yearning for things that never seemed to satisfy them, no matter how much money they cost? Strangely, many mothers who loved their daughters—and mine was one—did not want their daughters to grow up like them either. They knew we needed something more.

But even if they urged, insisted, fought to help us educate ourselves, even if they talked with yearning of careers that were not open to them, they could not give us an image of what we could be. They could only tell us that their lives were too empty, tied to home; that children, cooking, clothes, bridge, and charities were not enough. A mother might tell her daughter, spell it out, "Don't be just a housewife like me." But that daughter, sensing that her mother was too frustrated to savor the love of her husband and children, might feel: "I will succeed where my mother failed, I will fulfill myself as a woman," and never read the lesson of her mother's life.

Recently, interviewing high-school girls who had started out full of promise and talent, but suddenly stopped their education, I began to see new dimensions to the problem of feminine conformity. These girls, it seemed at first, were merely following the typical curve of feminine adjustment. Earlier interested in geology or poetry, they now were interested only in being popular; to get boys to like them, they had concluded, it was better to be like all the other girls. On closer examination, I found that these girls were so terrified of becoming like their mothers that they could not see themselves at all. They were afraid to grow up. They had to copy in identical detail the composite image of the popular girl—denying what was best in themselves out of fear of femininity as they saw it in their mothers. One of these girls, seventeen years old, told me:

> I want so badly to feel like the other girls. I never get over this feeling of being a neophyte, not initiated. When I get up and have to cross the room, it's like I'm a beginner, or have some terrible affliction, and I'll never learn. I go to the local hangout after school and sit there for hours talking about clothes and hairdos and the twist, and I'm not that interested, so it's an effort. But I found out I could make them like me—just do what they do, dress like them, talk like them, not do things that are different. I guess I even started to make myself not different inside.
>
> I used to write poetry. The guidance office says I have this creative abil-

ity and I should be at the top of the class and have a great future. But things like that aren't what you need to be popular. The important thing for a girl is to be popular.

Now I go out with boy after boy, and it's such an effort because I'm not myself with them. It makes you feel even more alone. And besides, I'm afraid of where it's going to lead. Pretty soon, all my differences will be smoothed out, and I'll be the kind of girl that could be a housewife.

I don't want to think of growing up. If I had children, I'd want them to stay the same age. If I had to watch them grow up, I'd see myself growing older, and I wouldn't want to. My mother says she can't sleep at night, she's sick with worry over what I might do. When I was little, she wouldn't let me cross the street alone, long after the other kids did.

I can't see myself as being married and having children. It's as if I wouldn't have any personality myself. My mother's like a rock that's been smoothed by the waves, like a void. She's put so much into her family that there's nothing left, and she resents us because she doesn't get enough in return. But sometimes it seems like there's nothing there. My mother doesn't serve any purpose except cleaning the house. She isn't happy, and she doesn't make my father happy. If she didn't care about us children at all, it would have the same effect as caring too much. It makes you want to do the opposite. I don't think it's really love. When I was little and I ran in all excited to tell her I'd learned how to stand on my head, she was never listening.

Lately, I look into the mirror, and I'm so afraid I'm going to look like my mother. It frightens me, to catch myself being like her in gestures or speech or anything. I'm not like her in so many ways, but if I'm like her in this one way, perhaps I'll turn out like my mother after all. And that terrifies me.

And so the seventeen-year-old was so afraid of being a woman like her mother that she turned her back on all the things in herself and all the opportunities that would have made her a different woman, to copy from the outside the "popular" girls. And finally, in panic at losing herself, she turned her back on her own popularity and defied the conventional good behavior that would have won her a college scholarship. For lack of an image that would help her grow up as a woman true to herself, she retreated into the beatnik vacuum.

Another girl, a college junior from South Carolina told me:

I don't want to be interested in a career I'll have to give up. My mother wanted to be a newspaper reporter from the time she was twelve, and I've seen her frustration for twenty years. I don't want to be interested in world affairs. I don't want to be interested in anything beside my home and being a wonderful wife and mother. Maybe education is a liability. Even the brightest boys at home want just a sweet, pretty girl. Only sometimes I wonder how it would feel to be able to stretch and stretch and stretch, and learn all you want, and not have to hold yourself back.

Her mother, almost all our mothers, were housewives, though many had started or yearned for or regretted giving up careers. Whatever they told us, we, having eyes and ears and mind and heart, knew that their lives were somehow empty. We did not want to be like them, and yet what other model did we have?

The only other kind of women I knew, growing up, were the old-maid high-school teachers; the librarian; the one woman doctor in our town, who cut her hair like a man; and a few of my college professors. None of these women lived in the warm center of life as I had known it at home. Many had not married or had children. I dreaded being like them, even the ones who taught me truly to respect my own mind and use it, to feel that I had a part in the world. I never knew a woman, when I was growing up, who used her mind, played her own part in the world, and also loved, and had children.

I think that this has been the unknown heart of woman's problem in America for a long long time, this lack of a private image. Public images that defy reason and have very little to do with women themselves have had the power to shape too much of their lives. The images would not have such power, if women were not suffering a crisis of identity.

The strange, terrifying jumping-off point that American women reach—at eighteen, twenty-one, twenty-five, forty-one—has been noticed for many years by sociologists, psychologists, analysts, educators. But I think it has not been understood for what it is. It has been called a "discontinuity" in cultural conditioning; it has been called woman's "role crisis." It has been blamed on the education which made American girls grow up feeling free and equal to boys—playing baseball, riding bicycles, conquering geometry and college boards, going away to college, going out in the world to get a job, living alone in an apartment in New York or Chicago or San Francisco, testing and discovering their own powers in the world. All this gave girls the feeling they could be and do whatever they wanted to, with the same freedom as boys, the critics said. It did not prepare them for their role as women. The crisis comes when they are forced to adjust to this role. Today's high rate of emotional distress and breakdown among women in their twenties and thirties is usually attributed to this "role crisis." If girls were educated for their role as women, they would not suffer this crisis, the adjusters say.

But I think they have seen only half the truth.

What if the terror a girl faces at twenty-one, when she must decide who she will be, is simply the terror of growing up—growing up, as women were not permitted to grow before? What if the terror a girl faces at twenty-one is the terror of freedom to decide her own life, with no one to order which path she will take, the freedom and the necessity to take paths women before were not able to take? What if those who choose the path of "feminine adjustment"—evading this terror by marrying at eighteen, losing themselves in having babies and the details of housekeeping— are simply refusing to grow up, to face the question of their own identity?

Mine was the first college generation to run head-on into the new mystique of feminine fulfillment. Before then, while most women did indeed end up as housewives and mothers, the point of education was to discover the life of the mind, to pursue truth and to take a place in the world. There was a sense, already dulling when I went to college, that we would be New Women. Our world would be much larger than home. Forty per cent of my college class at Smith had career plans. But I remember how, even then, some of the seniors, suffering the pangs of that bleak fear of the future envied the few who escaped it by getting married right away.

The ones we envied then are suffering that terror now at forty. "Never have decided what kind of woman I am. Too much personal life in college. Wish I'd studied more science, history, government, gone deeper into philosophy," one wrote on an alumnae questionnaire, fifteen years later. "Still trying to find the rock to build on. Wish I had finished college. I got married instead." "Wish I'd developed a deeper and more creative life of my own and that I hadn't become engaged and married at nineteen. Having expected the ideal in marriage, including a hundred-per-cent devoted husband, it was a shock to find this isn't the way it is," wrote a mother of six.

Many of the younger generation of wives who marry early have never suffered this lonely terror. They thought they did not have to choose, to look into the future and plan what they wanted to do with their lives. They had only to wait to be chosen, marking time passively until the husband, the babies, the new house decided what the rest of their lives would be. They slid easily into their sexual role as women before they knew who they were themselves. It is these women who suffer most the problem that has no name.

It is my thesis that the core of the problem for women today is not sexual but a problem of identity—a stunting or evasion of growth that is perpetuated by the feminine mystique. It is my thesis that as the Victorian culture did not permit women to accept or gratify their basic sexual needs, our culture does not permit women to accept or gratify their basic need to grow and fulfill their potentialities as human beings, a need which is not solely defined by their sexual role.

Biologists have recently discovered a "youth serum" which, if fed to young caterpillars in the larva state, will keep them from ever maturing into moths; they will live out their lives as caterpillars. The expectations of feminine fulfillment that are fed to women by magazines, television, movies, and books that popularize psychological half-truths, and by parents, teachers and counselors who accept the feminine mystique, operate as a kind of youth serum, keeping most women in the state of sexual larvae, preventing them from achieving the maturity of which they are capable. And there is increasing evidence that woman's failure to grow to complete identity has hampered rather than enriched her sexual fulfillment, virtually doomed her to be castrative to her husband and sons, and caused neuroses, or problems as yet unnamed as neuroses, equal to those caused by sexual repression.

There have been identity crises for man at all the crucial turning points in human history, though those who lived through them did not give them that name. It is only in recent years that the theorists of psychology, sociology and theology have isolated this problem, and given it a name. But it is considered a man's problem. It is defined, for man, as the crisis of growing up, of choosing his identity, "the decision as to what one is and is going to be," in the words of the brilliant psycholoanalyst Erik H. Erikson:

> I have called the major crisis of adolescence the identity crisis; it occurs in that period of the life cycle when each youth must forge for himself some central perspective and direction, some working unity, out ofthe effective remnants of his childhood and the hopes of his anticipated adulthood; he must detect some meaningful resemblance between what he has come to see in himself and what his sharpened awareness tells him others judge and expect him to be. . . . In some people, in some classes, at some periods in history, the crisis will be minimal; in other people, classes and periods, the crisis will be clearly marked off as a critical period, a kind of "second birth," apt to be aggravated either by widespread neuroticisms or by pervasive ideological unrest.

In this sense, the identity crisis of one man's life may reflect, or set off, a rebirth, or new stage, in the growing up of mankind. "In some periods of his history, and in some phase of his life cycle, man needs a new ideological orientation as surely and sorely as he must have air and food," said Erikson, focusing new light on the crisis of the young Martin Luther, who left a Catholic monastery at the end of the Middle Ages to forge a new identity for himself and Western man.

The search for identity is not new, however, in American thought— though in every generation, each man who writes about it discovers it anew. In America, from the beginning, it has somehow been understood that men must thrust into the future; the pace has always been too rapid for man's identity to stand still. In every generation, many men have suffered misery, unhappiness, and uncertainty because they could not take the image of the man they wanted to be from their fathers. The search for identity of the young man who can't go home again has always been a major theme of American writers. And it has always been considered right in America, good, for men to suffer these agonies of growth, to search for and find their own identities. The farm boy went to the city, the garment-maker's son became a doctor, Abraham Lincoln taught himself to read—these were more than rags-to-riches stories. They were an integral part of the American dream. The problem for many was money, race, color, class, which barred them from choice—not what they would be if they were free to choose.

Even today a young man learns soon enough that he must decide who he wants to be. If he does not decide in junior high, in high school, in college, he must somehow come to terms with it by twenty-five or thirty, or he is lost. But this search for identity is seen as a greater problem now because more and more boys cannot find images in our culture—from their fathers or other men—to help them in their search. The old frontiers have been conquered, and the boundaries of the new are not so clearly marked. More and more young men in America today suffer an identity crisis for want of any image of man worth pursuing, for want of a purpose that truly realizes their human abilities.

But why have theorists not recognized this same identity crisis in women? In terms of the old conventions and the new feminine mystique women are not expected to grow up to find out who they are, to choose their human identity. Anatomy is woman's destiny, say the theorists of femininity; the identity of women is determined by her biology.

But is it? More and more women are asking themselves this question. As if they were waking from a coma, they ask, "Where am I . . . what am I doing here?" For the first time in their history, women are becoming aware of an identity crisis in their own lives, a crisis which began many generations ago, has grown worse with each succeeding generation, and will not end until they, or their daughters, turn an unknown corner and make of themselves and their lives the new image that so many women now so desperately need.

In a sense that goes beyond any one woman's life, I think this is the crisis of women growing up—a turning point from an immaturity that has been called femininity to full human identity. I think women had to suffer the crisis of identity, which began a hundred years ago, and have to suffer it still today, simply to become fully human.

76   *Black Jackets*

Thom Gunn

In the silence that prolongs the span
Rawly of music when the record ends,
The red-haired boy who drove a van
In weekday overalls but, like his friends,

Wore cycle boots and jacket here
To suit the Sunday hangout he was in,

Heard, as he stretched back from his beer,
Leather creak softly round his neck and chin.

Before him, on a coal-black sleeve
Remote exertion had lined, scratched, and burned
    Insignia that could not revive
The heroic fall or climb where they were earned.

On the other drinkers bent together,
Concocting selves for their impervious kit,
    He saw it as no more than leather
Which, taut across the shoulders grown to it,

Sent through the dimness of a bar
As sudden and anonymous hints of light
    As those that shipping give, that are
Now flickers in the Bay, now lost in night.

He stretched out like a cat, and rolled
The bitterish taste of beer upon his tongue,
    And listened to a joke being told:
The present was the things he stayed among.

If it was only loss he wore,
He wore it to assert, with fierce devotion,
    Complicity and nothing more.
He recollected his initiation,

And one especially of the rites.
For on his shoulders they had put tattoos:
    The group's name on the left, The Knights,
And on the right the slogan Born To Lose.

77   *I am a Rock*

Paul Simon

A winter's day in a deep and dark December:
I am alone, gazing from my window

To the streets below on a freshly fallen silent shroud of snow.
I am a rock, I am an island.

I've built walls, a fortress deep and mighty,
That none may penetrate. I have no need of friendship;
Friendship causes pain. It's laughter and it's loving I disdain.
I am a rock, I am an island.

Don't talk of love; I've heard the word before;
It's sleeping in my memory and I won't disturb the slumber
Of feelings that have died. If I never loved I never would have
   cried.
I am a rock, I am an island.

I have my books and my poetry to protect me;
I am shielded in my armour, hiding in my room,
Safe within my womb. I touch no one and no one touches me.
I am a rock, I am an island.
And a rock can feel no pain; and an island never cries.

78   No Man Is an Island

John Donne

Perchance he for whom this bell tolls may be so ill, as that he knows not it tolls for him; and perchance I may think myself so much better than I am, as that they who are about me, and see my state, may have caused it to toll for me, and I know not that. The church is Catholic, universal, so are all her actions; all that she does belongs to all. When she baptizes a child, that action concerns me; for that child is thereby connected to that body which is my head too, and ingrafted into that body whereof I am a member. And when she buries a man, that action concerns me: all mankind is of one author, and is one volume; when one man dies, one chapter is not torn out of the book, but translated into a better language; and every chapter must be so translated; God employs several translators; some pieces are translated by age, some by sickness, some by war, some by justice; but God's hand is in every translation, and his hand shall bind up all our scattered leaves again for that library where every book shall lie open to one another. As therefore the bell that rings to a sermon calls not upon the preacher only, but upon the congregation to come, so this bell calls us all; but how much more me, who am brought so near the door by this sickness. There was a contention as far as a suit (in which both poetry and dignity, religion and estimation, were mingled), which of the religious orders should ring to prayers first in the morning; and it was determined, that they should ring first that rose earliest. If we understand aright the dignity of this bell that tolls for our evening prayer, we would be glad to make it ours by rising early, in that application, that it might be ours as well as his, whose indeed it is. The bell doth toll for him that thinks it doth; and though it intermit again, yet from that minute that that occasion wrought upon him, he is united to God. Who casts not up his eye to the sun when it rises? but who takes off his eye from a comet when that breaks out? Who bends not his ear to any bell which upon any occasion rings? but who can remove it from that bell which is passing a piece of himself out of this world? No man is an island, entire of itself; every man is a piece of the continent, a part of the main. If a clod be washed away by the sea, Europe is the less, as well as if a promontory were, as well as if a manor of thy friend's or of thine own were: any man's death diminishes me, because I am involved in mankind, and therefore never send to know for whom the bell tolls; it tolls for thee. Neither can we call this a begging of misery, or a borrowing of misery, as though we were not miserable enough of ourselves, but must fetch in more from the next house, in taking upon us the misery of our neighbors. Truly it were an excusable covetousness if we did, for affliction is a treasure, and scarce any man hath enough of it. No man hath affliction enough that is not matured and ripened by it, and made fit for God by that affliction. If a man carry treasure in bullion, or in a wedge of gold, and have none coined into current money, his treasure will not defray him as he travels. Tribulation is treasure in the nature of it, but it is not current money in the use of it, except we get nearer and nearer our home, heaven, by it. Another man may be sick too, and sick to death, and this affliction may lie in his bowels, as gold in a mine, and be of no use to him; but this bell, that tells me of his affliction, digs out and applies that gold to me; if by this consideration of another's danger I take mine own into contemplation, and so secure myself, by making my recourse to my God, who is our only security.

79   *Flowers*
Anthony

80   Day after Day
Benedict J. Fernandez

Photograph by Benedict J. Fernandez. Copyright © 1968 by Benedict J. Fernandez.